Boat Navigation for the Rest of Us

Finding Your Way by Eye and Electronics

Second Edition

Captain Bill Brogdon

Illustrated by Rob Groves

International Marine / McGraw-Hill
Camden, Maine • New York • Chicago • San Francisco • Lisbon
• London • Madrid • Mexico City • Milan • New Delhi
• San Juan • Seoul • Singapore • Sydney • Toronto

To my father, Bill Sr., who taught me much about

navigating through life, as well as his excellent

methods of finding the way in the outdoors,

afloat, and on the road.

International Marine
A Division of The McGraw-Hill Companies

10 9 8 7 6

Library of Congress Cataloging-in-Publication Data

Brogdon, Bill.
   Boat navigation for the rest of us : finding your way by
eye and electronics / Bill Brodgon ; illustrated by Rob
Groves.—2nd ed.
       p.   cm.
   Includes index.
   ISBN 0-07-137226-1 (alk. paper)
     1. Navigation—United States. 2. Electronics in naviga-
tion—United States. 3. Pilots and pilotage—United States.
I. Title.
VK555.B794 2001
623.89—dc21   00-050592

Questions regarding the content of this book should be
addressed to International Marine, P.O. Box 220, Camden,
ME 04843; www.internationalmarine.com

Questions regarding the ordering of this book should be
addressed to The McGraw-Hill Companies, Customer Service
Department, P.O. Box 547, Blacklick, OH 43004
Retail customers: 1-800-262-4729
Bookstores: 1-800-722-4726

Photos by the author unless otherwise noted
Printed on 60# Finch opaque by R.R. Donnelley,
   Crawfordsville, IN
Design by Patrice M. Rossi
Production and page layout by Janet Robbins. Second
   edition by Nancy Benner
Edited by James R. Babb, Don Casey, and Alex Barnett

A special thanks to Matt Dennon for the loan of his boat,
Bandit, used in the front cover photograph.

Contents

Sidebars

Acknowledgments

It would be impossible to acknowledge all who contributed to this book, by teaching, by example, by experimenting, by inventing, by writing about navigation. Tennyson (speaking of that great navigator, Ullyses) wrote, "I am part of all that I have met, yet all experience is an arch wherethrough gleams that untravelled world, whose margin fades for ever and for ever when I move . . ." Isaac Newton said, "I have stood on the shoulders of giants." I am especially conscious of the keen minds and courage of those who have built this art and science over the centuries. Newton, for example, invented logarithms and the slide rule in addition to discovering the laws of motion. Navigation was primitive prior to his discoveries.

I now regard myself as quite fortunate to have attended an excellent public high school in an era before discipline and high academic demands began to slip. Mrs. Phyllis Peacock was most memorable, smoothing some of the rough edges from her students' grammar, demanding that we write well, yet always encouraging us. I served in the U.S. Coast Guard during a long career at sea and in the aids to navigation mission. Many officers continued to teach me, particularly Roy Hutchins, Captain of *Chilula*, my second ship. I was fortunate to have dozens of quartermasters and radarmen assigned to my ships, who were bright, professional, inventive, and eager to work out new ways of doing navigation tasks. Authors and cartographers of the past recorded excellent methods of piloting. Ship pilots unselfishly taught me valuable secrets of their profession.

Despite these advantages, I did not start writing for publication until the Lord answered a prayer for help in financial assistance with our children's early education. Within days, Jim Martenhoff, then boating editor of the *Miami Herald,* called and asked me to write an article for a tabloid boating magazine he edited. Jim got me started writing about navigation and seamanship and taught me much about the art of writing. I also owe much to the many magazine editors who bought my work, encouraged me, and taught me more about writing.

As I wrote, I gained knowledge. A pilot from Alaska taught me a simple method of detecting an electronic navigation error. I was fortunate to be deputy chief of Coast Guard R&D when we were studying Loran-C and GPS performance, differential systems, and electronic charts. The many authors of technical articles for the Institute of Navigation, the International Loran Association, and the Hydrographic Society have added greatly to my knowledge. Many manufacturers allowed me to use Loran-C and GPS receivers for tests, and I applied controlled experiments and statistical methods I had studied in graduate school to evaluate their performance. Commercial fishermen such as Julius Collins and dive charter boat operators such as Buzz Mitchell showed me practical methods of using loran for highest accuracy.

More immediately, Jim Babb of International Marine helped me develop the idea of this book from a quite different initial idea. Don Casey (author of *This Old Boat*) read the typescript, found many of the errors, and helped me make the text and sketches easier to understand. Rob Groves took my raw sketches and turned them into drawings that depict the ideas beautifully. Pamela Benner took over the editorial work after Jim left International Marine and has been most thorough and patient. Even so, I would not have completed this book without the support and encouragement of my dear wife, Joyce, who read it frequently and helped me revise obscure or difficult-to-understand passages. Despite all this help, some errors may remain; they are my responsibility.

The Second Edition

In the short space of six years, radionavigation systems have changed so rapidly that it has become necessary to publish a second edition to reflect the changes. Several manufacturers have allowed me to test their equipment or programs to ensure that the information is as up to date as possible. Alex Barnett and D. A. Oliver at International Marine have been a big help in completing this edition.

The Global Positioning System (GPS) has become extremely popular due to the decreased cost and improved capability of receivers. In addition, the Department of Defense (DOD) improved GPS accuracy dramatically on 1 May 2000 by eliminating the deliberate accuracy reduction, Selective Availability (SA). This welcome change gives civilian navigators accuracy that is about five times as good as it was prior to the change.

Improving GPS accuracy made all of the references to it in the first edition incorrect. This second edition includes the best available estimates of GPS accuracy, obtained by collecting and analyzing data. As of December 2000 DOD has not released the new GPS performance specification, but the estimates should be close.

Several older electronic aids-to-navigation-systems have been eliminated: Omega, SATNAV, and Decca. The Coast Guard has completed the coastal Differential GPS system using radiobeacons. The FAA has started broadcasting Differential GPS corrections by satellites as they develop the Wide Area Augmentation System (WAAS) for GPS. The Raytheon Corporation began selling WAAS-augmented marine GPS receivers in the summer of 2000. Several manufacturers of GPS receivers now include advanced plotters, and electronic chart packages are beginning to become popular on larger yachts. Loran-C, once the most popular system, remains in use aboard a large number of boats as the Coast Guard improves the transmitter system to provide an independent yet complementary system to GPS for navigation and timing.

Introduction

Many people buying a first boat almost immediately discover their need to navigate. They're smart, successful in demanding occupations, and more than capable of understanding navigation—they just don't know much about it.

They aren't alone. Many boats carry sophisticated navigation equipment their skippers have barely begun to learn to use. Confusing operator's manuals are intimidating. Maybe the skipper's understanding of charts or compasses is limited. Some may have taken a basic navigation course only to find classroom methods difficult to use aboard a small boat. The pedantic explanations of obscure phenomena too often featured in courses and texts can also discourage a skipper wanting simple directions for finding his way around.

A number of boatowners have learned to use a Global Positioning System (GPS) receiver or Loran-C competently but depend on it totally. When they venture offshore, everything is fine as long as the receiver is working; but when something does go wrong, their single source of information vanishes. Although the boat has the equipment to navigate without GPS or Loran-C, these skippers are unprepared to use it. They are lost.

Others have simply put off installing a key navigation instrument because they don't know what it will do for them. After all, they go out and get back home, don't they? Yes, but the trips might be more enjoyable were there less worry about getting lost and less time spent recovering from poor navigation.

Struggling with navigation, getting lost, or going aground seriously detracts from the fun of owning a boat. These problems may lead some boatowners to avoid using their boats as much as they would like to. This book is meant to help all navigators steer around the shoals and eddies of inappropriate methods and learn to navigate easily, accurately, and without fuss. Even those of you who are already competent will find new ideas for using your navigation skills or doing some things more easily. After all, navigation should be an adjunct to boating, not a full-time job.

When I first went out on boats, I learned to find my way around by seaman's eye—the relationship of the size and shape of visible objects and the angles between them, supplemented by the color of the water and the appearance of the waves. As my experience on the water progressed, skippers on larger boats taught me about compass courses and the relationship between speed and distance.

In 1948 I bought a copy of *Piloting, Seamanship, and Small Boat Handling* by C. F. Chapman and began to unfold the mysteries of chart and compass. In those days *Chapman's* was organized into a series of lessons, and I studied them intently. In 1952 I received an appointment to the U.S. Coast Guard Academy, where I learned much more about piloting, charts, celestial navigation, radar, and loran through formal courses and practical experience. When I graduated, I became navigator of a cutter and began to learn in earnest. I blush to think how immature my knowledge was then, but I served under some demanding skippers who expected me to learn more and more.

During my shipboard assignments, I served as navigator, operations officer, executive officer, and as commanding officer of three ships, with growing responsibility for safe navigation. I taught navigation: chartwork, piloting, how to use radar and loran, and how to take, reduce, and plot celestial lines of position. I studied in detail many of the things I had taken for granted about the art and science of navigation. I worked in the Coast Guard's Aids to Navigation mission, including operating, teaching, and managing the program. I was involved with new developments in research, and in evaluating the capabilities of optical, sound, and electronic navigation systems.

While I served in ships, I was never far away from boats, and I struggled to adapt my knowledge of ship navigation to boats. I fished for sport. I made trips on commercial fishing boats. I navigated in some long ocean sailing races. I began to feel that, except for the vital invention of the depthfinder, coastwise boat navigation remained in the nineteenth century. Boat compasses were seldom adjusted correctly, and it was difficult to take bearings with them. It was even more difficult to plot courses or bearings or to measure distances. Very few boats had loran or radar. Yet all of these techniques and equipment were fundamental to ship navigation, to my profession.

I began to mimic techniques I found in old sailing directions, rutters (route description books), and charts, methods of earlier navigators that were still up to date aboard boats. I learned other techniques from commercial fishermen, ship pilots, and charter-boat skippers.

Then the revolution started.

Loran-A came into common use aboard commercial fishing boats in the 1960s. In the 1970s fishing skippers began perfecting methods of navigating by Loran-C that were superior to those I had learned. The next generation of receivers could calculate the direction and distance to stored waypoints. By the 1980s, Loran-C receivers were so advanced and so inexpensive that most boats operating offshore began carrying them. I put a "water-resistant" one on a 20-foot open outboard and put it to a real test. What a revelation!

I had navigated ships by loran, satellite, radar, and gyrocompass, piloted commercial fishing boats with Loran-C and radar, and was at home finding my way around in small boats with a compass and a depthfinder, but to carry a precision navigation receiver in an open boat—that was something. Supplementing traditional small-boat navigation with modern electronics overcomes many of the problems of boat navigation that stem from limited space, small crews, and the need to do many things in addition to navigation.

By 1993, when GPS became available full-time, quality receivers had become readily available and prices were declining steadily. Despite the increasing availability of sophisticated navigation equipment for small boats, texts and courses have remained weak in teaching small-boat navigation skills. Students learning chartwork on the kitchen table find this new skill out of place aboard a small, wet, lively boat. Books on electronic navigation ignore visual navigation. Books on visual navigation ignore electronics—and fog. Classic texts like *Dutton* and *Bowditch* are excellent for ship navigation but less practical for boats.

Navigation books tend to concentrate on open waters where you can steer straight courses to the next destination, but what about people who use boats in rivers, reservoirs, and marshes? They can use modern navigation equipment, too, although there has been precious little written about how to do it.

One good guidebook dismisses the need for Loran-C in inland waters, yet makes frequent references to things difficult to find without electronics— unmarked creek entrances, aids to navigation long distances apart, poorly marked routes. Most books ignore the vital subject of using radar for collision avoidance.

Many people have asked me to combine the seven years of navigation columns I wrote for *Motor Boating & Sailing* into a book, but those were hints and ideas for experienced navigators. Instead, I've written a book for new navigators as well, one that provides simple rules of thumb along with the more complex methods of solving problems.

This is a book about the practical way to find your way around in a boat—not chart-table, gyro-repeater, radar-assisted ship navigation and neither wholly visual nor wholly electronic, but a practical blend of techniques designed to make it easy to find your way around, even aboard a small open boat.

A new navigator can learn the basics first and come back later to learn about more complex methods. The book is organized to allow the experienced skipper to skim familiar areas and concentrate on new material. Parts of this book are a smorgasbord of information that will become more interesting with increasing experience. Many problems are discussed that affect electronic navigation, some that will become of interest only as navigation skill advances. Little is lost if readers skip sections about equipment they don't use.

This book combines visual and electronic navigation, chartwork, and trip planning for boats—power or sail—taking into consideration the limitations of space and time. It includes information about navigating rivers and large reservoirs. It is specifically geared to North America. (A reader in east longitude or south latitude will have to make adjustments due to location.) It doesn't include information about compass theory, or about celestial navigation. Instead it concentrates on practical ways to make boat navigation easy, and it provides more information about the use of electronic equipment than just a list of features. It is, in short, an attempt to provide you with a no-fuss method of navigating your boat. If it does that, it will have fulfilled its purpose.

Your book will be most useful if you mark it to fit your needs as you read it. Mark important sections, underline or highlight key words, and make notes in the margins. You will be able to remember new or important facts better, and it will be easier to find them later. These are key steps in learning.

CHAPTER I

How We Navigate

Navigation is the art and science of finding where we are and of finding our way safely to our destination. We usually start at a known position, such as the seaward end of a channel, and go to another position a number of miles away—a buoy, a place where we change course, or a fishing spot. Our fundamental questions are: What is the direction to our destination? When will we arrive? Are there any hazards along the way? After we have traveled for a while, another question may arise: Where are we now? Let's preview the ways we answer these questions.

We make four essential measurements in navigation: *depth, speed, direction,* and *time.* Navigators have long relied on "lead, log, and compass" but had rather crude timepieces until about a century ago. Today we are blessed with excellent instruments for these four measurements. Along with a chart, the navigator's basic tools are a *depthfinder,* a speed or distance *log,* a *compass,* and a *watch.* We make other measurements: *radar* measures the distance and direction to an object such as a point of land. Electronic aid-to-navigation system receivers make time measurements of precise radionavigation signals, and calculate the boat's position.

Our fundamental questions are: What is the direction to our destination? When will we arrive? Are there any hazards along the way?

We use charts to identify aids to navigation and landmarks, to avoid shoals and other hazards, and to find or show the boat's position. Using a chart, we can find the direction and distance from the boat's position to a destination. We can see the depths along the way. It can help us determine where we are long after leaving the last known position. A chart is like a road map, but with a gridwork of latitude and longitude lines instead of cross streets. A navigator needs to know how to measure distances and to plot positions and courses on a chart, but this book includes methods that can substitute for some of the chartwork.

We start by finding where we are. Then we find the direction and distance from there to a destination, using either a chart or a navigation receiver. We steer the course to a distant destination by compass. We divide the distance by the boat's speed to determine the number of hours en route. None of this is complex, but peo-

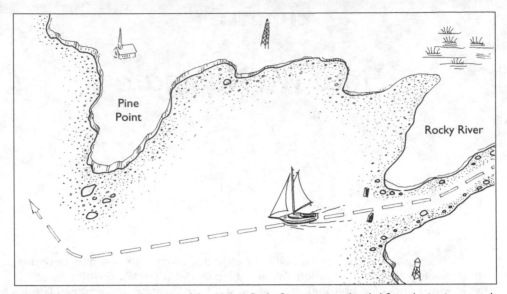

Figure 1-1. *Distance and direction. A boat leaves Rocky River entrance headed for a destination around Pine Point. Questions:*

1. *What is the direction to steer?*
2. *When will we arrive? (How far will we travel?)*
3. *Are there any hazards along the way?*

ple often skip doing it. As Thomas Edison said, "There is no expedient to which a man will not go to avoid the real labor of thinking." Navigation requires thinking.

Even running a boat in a marked channel is enhanced by thinking about it. The beginner lines up the boat by watching the buoys for guidance. So does the experienced skipper, but he also notes the compass course for that portion of the channel and remembers it. He looks for objects *in range* (in line, one in front of the other) to see if the boat is drifting left or right. If a range isn't available, he finds a *leading mark* dead ahead. If steering a different course is necessary due to the current, he remembers that course, too. He watches the depthfinder to learn the shape of the bottom, and the water surface for clues to depth and current. He knows his boat's speed at cruising rpm, and on a long channel leg may find the running time between turns. He knows the number of the buoy at the next turn and where to look for the buoys beyond. None of this requires mathematics—just being aware of surroundings and remembering or writing down information.

Experienced navigators do all this with little visible effort; a passenger can't tell that the skipper is storing up information all along the way. The beginner who only watches the buoys is bereft of guidance if for any reason he can't see them, but the experienced operator can continue to find the way along the channel safely and easily.

Going to an Object in Sight

Outside of channels, beginners tend to use the "look-go" system—they see the next destination and point the boat toward it. This requires a minimum of mental

Figure 1-2. *Navigating a channel. A beginner lines up the boat with buoys and proceeds safely. So does an experienced navigator, but the navigator also:*

1. *Notes compass course.*
2. *Notes range or leading mark ahead.*
3. *Watches water flow at buoys to estimate current.*
4. *Is alert for cross-channel set.*
5. *Notes buoy numbers as the boat passes them.*
6. *Knows the next course.*
7. *Knows where to look for buoys on the next leg.*
8. *Watches the depth to note changes.*
9. *Checks compass deviation.*

A navigator may not do all of these things every trip, but he keeps accumulating knowledge of familiar ports.

effort, but the virtue of simplicity is combined with the vice of ignoring valuable information. Beginners don't look at the compass, so they don't know what course they have steered. When will they arrive? When they get there. They don't look at the time when they leave a known position, so they don't know how long they have been en route. They don't know the boat's speed. If there is a current across their course, the boat follows a curving path, probably without the skipper even noticing. They often follow a zigzag path to keep aids to navigation in sight. They spend a lot of time looking for buoys. Most of the time they don't have a very good idea of where they are, and next week they'll know no more than today.

If they get caught in fog or a rain squall, they're like a short dog in high weeds. They have few clues as to where they are, since visible landmarks have vanished. They don't know the compass course to steer. The anxiety level aboard the boat mounts. Survival of the fittest would tend to cull such people from the gene pool; fortunately, life isn't always that harsh.

Course, Speed, and Time: The DR

Noting the time as you clear the entrance channel gives a good position. Later, you can estimate your position by a fundamental of navigation called **ded (or dead) reckoning,** or **DR**. Ded reckoning relates a boat's position to an earlier known position. Suppose you sail out of Sarasota, Florida, and travel due west from the entrance for two hours at a speed of 6 knots. It's obvious that you have gone about 2 × 6 miles, or 12 nautical miles (NM), and that you are near a line extending west (270°) from the entrance (Figure 1-3).

A DR position is an estimate, but it can be a good estimate. If you don't check the time as you leave the entrance, however, you won't be able to determine how far you've gone based on speed and time. If you don't have a log to show the boat's speed (or distance traveled), you'll have to guess. If you don't pay attention

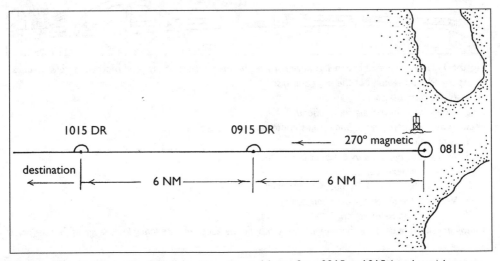

Figure 1-3. *Ded reckoning (DR). A boat traveling at 6 knots from 0815 to 1015 (two hours) has gone 12 nautical miles. The position lies close to the direction in which the boat is steered. As time passes, the accuracy of the boat's position decreases but remains sufficient to find the destination.*

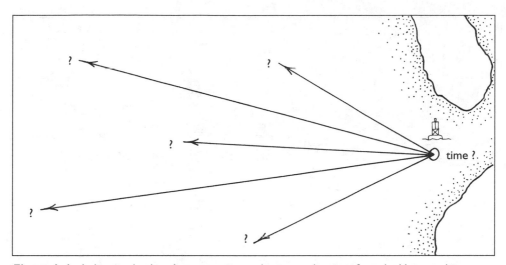

Figure 1-4. *A skipper who doesn't pay attention to the time or direction of travel adds a very large degree of uncertainty as to the boat's position.*

to the course you steer, the direction will be equally suspect. You have lost—thrown away, really—your ability to relate your position to the last known position. Instead of going from a known position to one that is known with somewhat lesser accuracy, you have gone from a known position to an unknown position.

A navigator *always* has a general idea of the boat's position, even though he may not know the position exactly. He also has a good idea of how to continue to the next destination. He may, with a little effort, know this information quite well.

> *A navigator* always *has a general idea of the boat's position, even though he may not know the position exactly.*

Finding the Boat's Position

In addition to keeping a DR, we find new positions as we go along. Positions found using fresh information are called **fixes**, and a navigator seeks them like any other addict. The longer it's been since the last fix, the more he wants a new one, but unlike drugs, navigation fixes clear your thinking rather than confuse it. Going close to a known buoy, for example, gives a useful fix. It may not be precise—the position of the buoy isn't exact, and the boat could be 30 or 80 yards from it—but this fix will be good enough for ordinary navigation.

We also find the boat's position by compass bearings to visible objects. If you sight over the compass to a water tank ashore and see that it is north of you, you know that you must be on a north–south line going through the tank. Draw such a line through the tank's symbol on the chart, label it with the time, and you have a **line of position,** or **LOP.** This is a fundamental concept of navigation. A measurement—in this case a bearing—is the same everywhere along the LOP.

Since the boat could be anywhere along an LOP, *we need two or more LOPs for a fix.* We use many types of LOPs: visual, depth, Loran-C, radio direction finder, and radar. (While GPS doesn't give LOPs, it uses them to calculate the

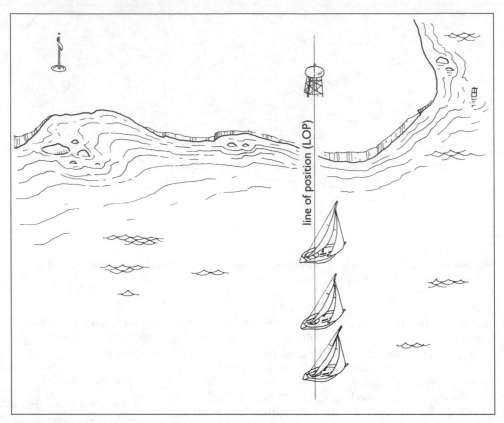

Figure 1-5. *A line of position (LOP). A navigator sights over the compass and measures the bearing to the tank: due north. The LOP is a line south from the tank, and the boat is somewhere along the LOP. A boat can be at any place on the line of position. Everywhere along the LOP, the bearing is the same— due north.*

position, as does Loran-C.) Suppose we look at the depthfinder while the boat is south of the water tank and see that we are in 60 feet of water. Looking at the chart, we see that there is a 60–foot depth-contour line. This is another LOP for our boat. There is only one place where the north-south LOP to the tank crosses the 60-foot contour line. We must be near that intersection.

A fix always includes the time. (To avoid confusion, navigators usually express time as four digits in the 24-hour clock: 8:43 A.M. is 0843, 2:00 P.M. is 1400.) You might say we have "reset" the known position to a fresh one. Our fix won't be accurate, however, if we have made a mistake in one or both readings, so we try to find an LOP to another object in a different direction. If the three LOPs form a large triangle, one of them is in error; but if the third LOP is close to the intersection of the first two, we can be reasonably sure the position is correct.

We have seen that the water tank is north of us and that we are in 60 feet of water. Even if it isn't exactly north, we can look at the chart and get a quick grasp of our approximate position along the 60-foot contour. We see a flagpole about 45° to the left of the tank, and we see that its bearing matches, roughly,

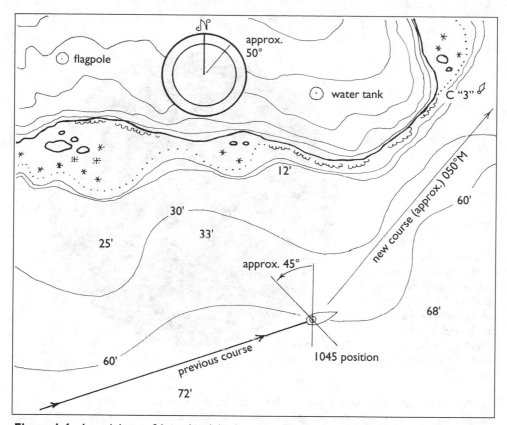

Figure 1-6. *A rough but useful visual and depth position. The water tank is approximately north of the boat at 1045. The depth is 60 feet, so the boat also lies along the 60-foot depth contour. The flagpole is about 45° to the left of the water tank, which looks about right on the chart. The position is definite, but not precise. It is accurate enough to set a new course.*

with the intersection of the other two LOPs on the chart. We note the time, and we are sure of the boat's approximate position. This rough position is good enough to let us find the appropriate course to steer.

As valuable as positions are, often we don't need a position as much as we need a way to verify that the boat stays in safe water. Ship pilots use such techniques constantly, and we use them often aboard boats, too. For example, we know that a tank ashore must be in line with a point of land when we pass a shoal. We use a simple timing method to estimate the boat's distance off a visible shore. We check the depth and the chart to be sure we are well offshore of any rocks or shoals.

We may have radar. Suppose we see pairs of buoys marking a channel entrance. They appear as a series of dots on the radar screen at distances pro-

As valuable as positions are, often we don't need a position as much as we need a way to verify that the boat stays in safe water.

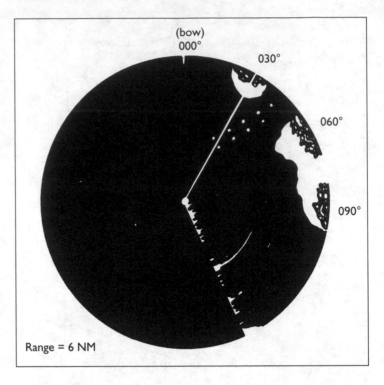

Figure 1-7. *Radar shows a boat's position. The rows of dots are channel buoys. The outer pair of buoys lie at an angle of 30° to the right of the bow. The maximum range is 6 miles, so the closest buoys are about 3 miles away.*

portional to their distance from the boat. If the radar is set to show 6 miles maximum, and the entrance buoys are halfway out from the center of the screen, they are about 3 miles away. This gives a position relative to the entrance buoys. The radar screen is aligned with the boat's bow, so if the buoys are at 030° on the screen, we look 30° to the right of the boat's bow to see them. We would change course 30° to the right to go to the entrance. As we change course, the dots move to dead ahead on the screen, or at 000°. Most of today's radars allow us to measure distance accurately, giving distance LOPs that are quite useful.

Electronic Aid-to-Navigation Systems

Modern electronic aid-to-navigation receivers give excellent information to supplement traditional navigation. The **Global Positioning System (GPS)** and **Loran-C** provide accurate positions on a nearly continuous basis. With a navigation receiver, you are at a "known position" nearly all of the time. Just as important, the receiver shows the direction and distance to any other position, also on a continuous basis. We save positions, called **waypoints**, by pressing a button or two on the receiver and the waypoint data remains in its memory even when it is turned off. The receiver can show the direction and distance to any waypoint.

Suppose we save a waypoint as we leave the channel from our home port. On the way home, we have the receiver show the direction and distance back to that waypoint. The receiver, with very little assistance from us, performs two of the basic steps of navigation. First, it finds the boat's position. We don't have to plot

LOPs; the receiver uses electronic LOPs to calculate the position. Second, it calculates the direction and distance to the waypoint at our destination. It saves us the effort of plotting the position, drawing a line to the destination, and measuring its direction and length. The receiver also gives us a way of checking our DR navigation. Is it any wonder that these electronic aids to navigation are popular?

Navigation receivers are particularly valuable when we've been sailing or fishing for several hours and don't know where we are with any degree of accuracy. Without GPS or another navigation system receiver, we head in the general direction of a landmark. When we see it, we can determine a rough position. Often we wind up off to one side or the other and have to change course to go to our destination. With a navigation receiver, we simply enter the desired waypoint as the destination, and in a few seconds the display shows the direction and distance to the waypoint from our current position.

Although today's electronic navigation systems lift boat navigation to a high level, they are not easy to learn to use. It is particularly trying when you can't stop the receiver from beeping at you instead of answering the keys, and the instruction manual jumps between normal and rare operations. This book introduces the more important features of electronic navigation systems first, saving the others for later sections.

Blending Visual, Instrument, and Electronic Information

A boatowner who learns the fundamentals of navigation can enjoy his boat free of much of the worry that accompanies uncertain positions. At first, navigation requires a lot of mental effort, but it soon becomes routine and easy. Every navigator started with a low level of knowledge. Skill in navigation isn't inherited or bought, it is learned. This book is a plan for learning, beginning with the things that are most useful.

A skipper should match the navigation method to the trip. Suppose you are heading along a relatively straight coast from one harbor entrance to the next. You could just keep the coast to starboard and find the next entrance, but if you find the course to steer, you won't zigzag as much as when steering by watching the coast. Enter a destination waypoint for the second harbor into your navigation receiver, and it will provide continuous direction and distance to the entrance. If you divide the distance by the boat speed, you can determine when you will arrive. Compare the depth with the chart, and you get a useful line of position. Note the time when you depart the first harbor, and you can keep up with the distance you have traveled. Your thought process might be: "It's been a half hour since we left, and the boat makes 20 knots, so we're about 10 miles down the coast and on the 30-foot contour."

A navigator does several of these simple things, depending on the distance, the visibility, and hazards along the route. As new conditions increase the danger or uncertainty, the navigator responds by setting intermediate waypoints, steering carefully, timing legs of the trip, finding the effect of current, and using other features of a navigation receiver.

As new conditions increase the danger or uncertainty, the navigator responds by setting intermediate waypoints, steering carefully, timing legs of the trip, finding the effect of current, and using other features of a navigation receiver.

GPS and Loran-C receivers are useful even on short, clear-weather trips. You may be a beginner, but with a navigation receiver you can navigate better than the expert who doesn't have one aboard. A navigation receiver performs many of the functions that previously required plotting on a chart, but it isn't perfect: It shows the direct course to a waypoint, ignoring intervening rocks, shoals, islands, even continents. The navigator has to use a chart to make sure the way is clear.

A receiver also can show the effect of current, the enemy of accurate DR navigation. However, these receivers are so good that it is easy to depend on them too much. A receiver sometimes gives wrong information, whether from misentered waypoints or from signal or internal problems. Can you detect these errors? When a receiver fails, a beginner's mind can be as blank as the dead screen. If you learn workable boat navigation methods while you use an electronic navigation system receiver, this won't happen to you. With this book, you'll learn how to blend electronic navigation with visual navigation, charts, and instruments. When a receiver gives false information, you'll be able to detect the problem. When it gives no information at all, you will still know where to go—just like the expert.

CHAPTER 2

Charts and Publications

*C*harts are essential to navigation. You identify landmarks, find depths, measure distances and directions, and find your way to a destination using a chart. To find the boat's position, you compare the depth, distance, and direction measured by instruments aboard the boat with the depth, distance, and direction shown on a chart. You write the time on the chart when the boat is at a known position, and you use positions from electronic navigation receivers with a chart.

The information in this chapter is elementary, but understanding charts and how to plot on them is fundamental to navigation. Later chapters give shortcuts and ways to avoid some plotting. As valuable as they are, charts don't tell everything; you will need a few other publications as well.

Charts

A chart is a map designed for navigation on the water, but it differs greatly from a road map. In a car you have little need for the map between intersections; once you're on the correct highway you stay between the lines and follow the signs. On the water there are no lines and few signs. It is essential to use the chart not only to find your way but also to avoid hazards. You use information from the chart frequently, if not continuously, when traveling along a route. No one has yet discovered how to paint white lines on the ocean, or to indicate all the underwater hazards to the boat operator.

A chart represents a portion of the earth's surface on a piece of paper. It shows symbols for land features and objects, such as aids to navigation, as they would appear from above. Of course, we see horizontally rather than from above, so we must adapt to the chart's point of view. Charts also display symbols for things that aren't visible, such as depths and lines of latitude and longitude.

The National Ocean Service (NOS), a division of the National Oceanic and Atmospheric Administration (NOAA), publishes charts for United States coastal and Great Lakes waters. NOS identifies its charts by number and publishes free catalogs showing their coverage. A number of companies reprint NOAA charts in booklets that are popular for cruising. Booklets are easier to store but are plagued by limited size and a spiral binding, which sometimes gets in the way. The Canadian Hydrographic Service also publishes excellent charts.

Latitude and Longitude

Latitude and **longitude** specify a position on a chart. You might say that each spot on earth has a unique "address," described by its latitude and longitude. Latitude is measured from the equator to the poles, and longitude is measured east or west from Greenwich, England. Latitude and longitude are angles, measured using a circle divided into 360 *degrees*. Each degree is divided into 60 *minutes* of arc. A minute of latitude is nearly the same length as a nautical mile, about 6,076 feet. At the equator, a minute of longitude is also equal to a mile, but longitude lines get closer together with increasing latitude. At the latitude of New York City, a minute of longitude is equal to about ¾ mile.

Each minute of arc is divided into 60 *seconds* of arc, as well. This sounds like time, but these minutes and seconds refer to angles. An angle of 34 degrees, 14 minutes, and 30 seconds, shown as 34° 14' 30", is also 34° 14.5' of arc. Often it is more practical to divide minutes into tenths or hundredths. Electronic navigation receivers usually use degrees, minutes, and hundredths rather than degrees, minutes, and seconds of arc.

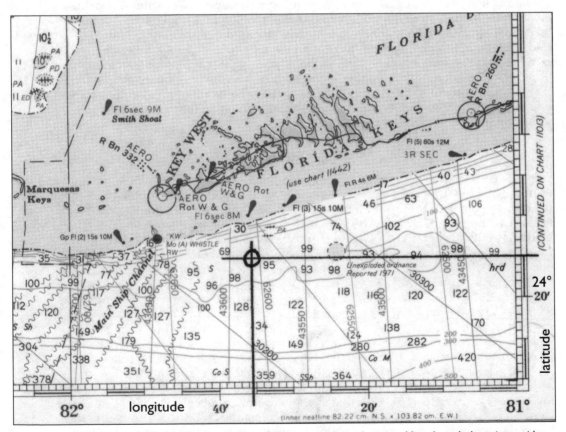

Figure 2-1. *The latitude of any point is found by extending a horizontal line through the point to either side of the chart. Longitude is determined by a vertical line to the top or bottom edge of the chart. The position marked by the circle is 24° 25' north, 81° 35.4' west.*

Latitude lines are the horizontal lines on a chart, also called *parallels of latitude*. On each *side* of a chart is a printed latitude scale. The latitude of a point on a chart is determined by a horizontal line through the point extending to the scale. To measure the latitude of a point without drawing a line, set a pair of dividers with one leg on the point and the other, aligned vertically, on a printed horizontal (latitude) line on the chart. Then move the dividers, without changing their setting, to the side of the chart. Put one leg on the same latitude line on the scale and read the latitude where the other leg touches the scale. It may be more convenient to use a strip of paper with pencil marks, called a *tick strip*. The printed scales show degrees of latitude divided into minutes. (The subdivisions of minutes are tricky because some charts have them divided into tenths while others have minutes divided into sixths, for 10 seconds.)

Longitude is measured at the *top or bottom* edge of the chart directly above or below the marked point. Set dividers to the width between a printed vertical line—called a *meridian of longitude*—and the point, and transfer this distance to the scale at the top or bottom of the chart. North America is in west longitude—the numbers increase from right to left, which can be confusing at first. *Remember to measure latitude at the sides of the chart, and longitude at the top or bottom.* On small-craft charts, the scales for latitude and longitude aren't at the edges but are printed close together in bar scales. It's easy to use the wrong one.

On small-craft charts, the scales for latitude and longitude aren't at the edges but are printed close together in bar scales. It's easy to use the wrong one.

Figure 2-2 shows the latitude and longitude bar scales from a 1:40,000-scale

(text continues on page 16)

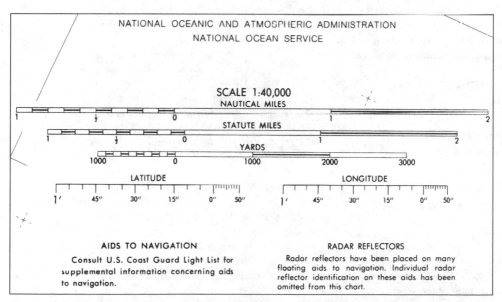

Figure 2-2. *The latitude and longitude bar scales from a 1:40,000-scale chart at 26° north latitude. A minute of latitude or longitude extends from 0" to 1' on the bar. The 50" mark shows the last 10 seconds of the minute to the right of the one on the bar, divided into 1-second intervals.*

A Better Way to Measure

There is a better way to measure latitude and longitude than the traditional method. It is particularly valuable with small-craft charts and chart booklets, and it gives a direct readout in fractions of a minute—the usual data for a navigation receiver. To use it, you need a *triangular engineer's scale*. There are two types of scales: engineer's and architect's. The *architect's scale* is marked in fractions and is not useful for this purpose. The engineer's scale, the one you want, is marked "10," "20," "30," "40," "50," and "60" on its six faces. You can get a serviceable plastic one for under $5 and a quality one with sharper lines and excellent legibility for under $10.

Let's say you're planning a trip that rounds Cape Ann, Massachusetts, and you want to set a waypoint about 300 yards offshore of lighted bell buoy "1" off the Dry Salvages. It is always a good idea to pick a waypoint about 300 to 500 yards on the "safe" side of a coastal buoy to allow for imperfections in plotting, electronic systems, and steering. It's easy to see the buoy at that distance—in fact, it looks like you're right on top of it.

Make a mark at the desired position of the waypoint, as in Figure 2-3. The chart shown is 132574, a small-craft chart at 1:40,000 scale. It has meridians of longitude and parallels of latitude marked every 2 minutes. Turn the triangular scale so the side marked "50" is visible. Put the 0 on the 42°40' latitude line and the 20 on the 42°42' line. The 10 then marks 42°41', and you can read right from the scale the latitude of any point between the two lines on the chart. Slide the scale along until the dot you have marked for the waypoint is just visible. You may have to jiggle the scale a bit to keep both the 0 and the 20 marks on the lines. In this example the waypoint dot falls

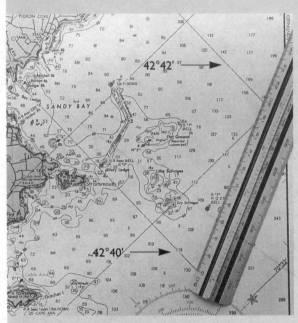

Figure 2-3. *Using the "50" side of an engineer's scale, put the 0 on the 42°40' latitude line and the 20 on the 42°42' line. You can read the latitude of the waypoint from the scale—42°40.72'.*

With the sharp divisions of a good engineer's scale, you can read positions on a 1:40,000-scale chart to about $\frac{2}{100}$ or even $\frac{1}{100}$ of a minute.

at 7.2 on the scale. The 7 line, halfway between 6 and 8, isn't numbered, but 7.2 represents 0.72 minute. The latitude of the waypoint is 42°40.72'.

Measure longitude the same way, putting the 0 to the right and the 20 to the left (Figure 2-4), but this time use the scale marked "60" to avoid too much of a slant. You'll also have to extend the 70°32' line with a sharp pencil down through the compass rose. With the 0 on 70°32' and the 20 on 70°34',

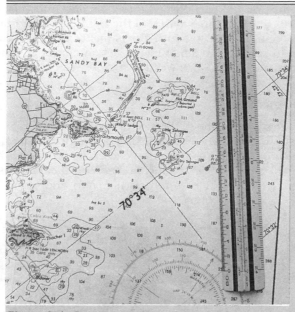

Figure 2-4. *For measuring longitude, put the 0 to the right and the 20 to the left. In this instance the "60" scale is used to reduce the slant. With the 0 on 70° 32' and the 20 on 70° 34', the waypoint dot lies at 13.8 on the scale, or 70° 33.38' west longitude.*

the waypoint dot lies at 13.8 on the scale. The 10 is at 70° 33', so the waypoint is at 70° 33.38' longitude. This is more precise than you usually need to be; anything between 70° 33.35' and 70° 33.4' would have no detectable effect on your navigation.

A nice feature of using the scale is the ability to see how slight changes in latitude or longitude affect the position on the chart. With the sharp divisions of a good engineer's scale, patience, good light, and a magnifying glass, you can read positions on a 1:40,000-scale chart to about $\frac{2}{100}$ or even $\frac{1}{100}$ of a minute. This is useful for plotting new positions of buoys but far closer than you need for practical navigation.

When using 1:80,000-scale coastal charts, use the side of the scale marked "10" to span lines of latitude or longitude 10 minutes apart. You can read to tenths of minutes easily and estimate fractions of tenths (Figure 2-5).

When I adapted this idea from a Loran-C plotting card (see Chapter 5), I thought it would be necessary to manufacture an appropriate scale, but it wasn't—the engineer's scale works beautifully. A Weems Parallel Plotter has a scale that works well for measuring latitude and longitude on 1:80,000-scale charts. This is the easiest way to read latitude and longitude from a chart.

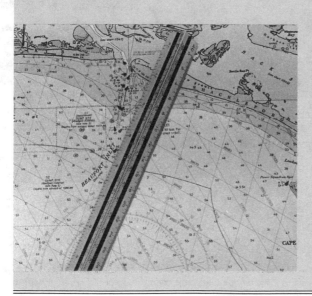

Figure 2-5. *On a 1:80,000-scale coastal chart, the side of the engineer's scale marked "10" spans lines of latitude or longitude 10 minutes apart. You can read tenths of minutes directly and estimate fractions of tenths.*

small-craft chart. A minute of latitude or longitude extends from 0" to 1' on the bar. The 50" mark might be confusing; it simply shows the last 10 seconds of the minute to the right of the one on the bar, divided into 1-second intervals. If your dividers spread from the 15" mark to three marks to the right of 0", the interval is 18 seconds. This scale is from a chart in south Texas at 26° north latitude. Its longitude scale is noticeably longer than longitude scales on charts at the higher latitudes of the Northeast or the Pacific Northwest.

Chart Scale and Projection

Charts are drawn to a *scale*, the ratio of the size of the chart to the size of the earth. A given location usually appears on several charts of different scales. *Harbor charts* often use a scale of 1:20,000—1 inch on the chart represents 20,000 inches of the earth's surface, or about 0.27 nautical mile. A nautical mile is about 3.6 inches long on the chart. This is called a *large-scale chart* and covers a rela-

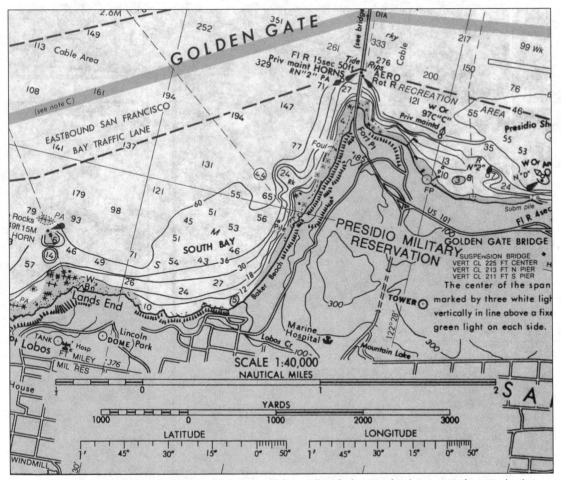

Figure 2-6. *The 1:40,000 scale is common for small-craft charts and inshore areas. A nautical mile is about 1.8 inches long on a 1:40,000-scale chart.*

tively small area, for example about 5 by 8 miles. Large-scale charts show the most detail, as if the view is zoomed in.

The 1:40,000 scale is common for *small-craft charts* (Figure 2-6) for inshore areas and the Intracoastal Waterway. A nautical mile is about 1.8 inches long on a 1:40,000-scale chart.

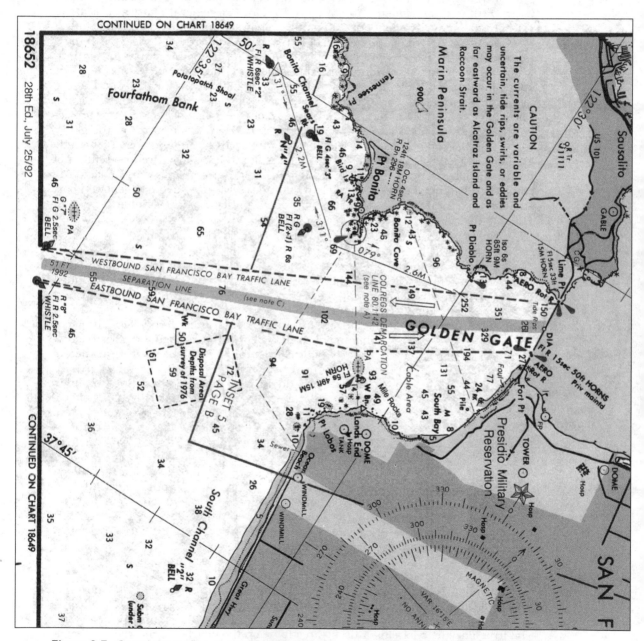

Figure 2-7. *Coastal charts often use the 1:80,000 scale and cover an area roughly 30 by 40 miles. This illustration is from a chart at 1:80,000 scale. A nautical mile is about 0.9 inch long.*

Coastal charts (Figure 2-7) often use the 1:80,000 scale and cover an area roughly 30 by 40 miles; a nautical mile is about 0.9 inch. Coastal charts show Loran-C information. They are large enough to plot courses between locations within a few hours' cruising time apart and are quite useful aboard boats.

General charts, at scales of about 1:150,000 to 1:600,000, show larger areas. *Sailing charts* show still larger areas and are seldom used aboard pleasure boats. Chart 11009, *Cape Hatteras to Straits of Florida*, is a general chart at a scale of 1:1,200,000 and extends about 600 miles. It shows a huge area but little detail.

Charts are drawn to a *projection*, which allows the nearly spherical earth to be represented on a flat piece of paper. Most charts are in the **Mercator projection**, where the vertical lines (meridians) marking longitude are the same distance apart, but the horizontal lines (parallels) marking latitude are farther apart at the top of the chart than at the bottom. (The terminology used in this book applies to North America, north of the equator and west of Greenwich.) The Mercator projection is, in a way, opposite the way latitudes and longitudes appear on the globe, where parallels of latitude are the same distance apart and meridians of longitude are closer together toward the poles. This results in a distorted representation of the earth; for example, Greenland looks too big on a Mercator world chart. The change in distance between parallels of latitude is easy to see on a general chart such as *Cape Hatteras to Charleston* but imperceptible on a harbor chart.

Chart Symbols

An understanding of the symbols and terms found on charts is essential to using charts effectively. Only the more important chart symbols are included here. For complete information, get a copy of NOS Chart No. 1: *Nautical Chart Symbols, Abbreviations, and Terms.*

Some positions on charts are accurate and others are approximate. An accurate position is shown by a dot inside a circle; an approximate position is represented by a small circle.

Depth numbers are printed vertically if the measurement is in feet or fathoms, slanted if in meters. Charts showing depths in fathoms (6 feet) or meters show tenths in superscripts. Depth contours are lines of constant depth and may be solid lines or lines made of patterns of dots. The chart title block shows the depth units (feet, fathoms, or meters) and datum, usually *mean lower low water* (MLLW). It also shows the height units and datum, usually *mean high water.*

The chart in Figure 2-8 illustrates many common symbols. Depths are in feet. Contours are solid lines at 1, 2, and 3 fathoms. The shaded water areas—tinted blue on the actual chart—show where depths are less than 6 feet. The darker-shaded marsh and sand areas are green on the actual chart. The dotted line encloses areas exposed at low tide. Towns are shown in boldface type, and some roads are shown. The railroad and its bridge are prominent. Buoys are shown by their symbols and signal abbreviations.

Two named lighthouses, Lynde Point and Saybrook Breakwater, are shown by dots and "flares"—the symbols look like exclamation marks. Saybrook Breakwater has a horn and radiobeacon, indicated by the circle and the abbreviation "R Bn." The irregular line enclosing a tinted area (blue on the chart) around the light symbol indicates riprap—boulders placed to protect the light. Riprap is deadly to boats. Note the difference between rocks that uncover at low water (chart symbol *) and

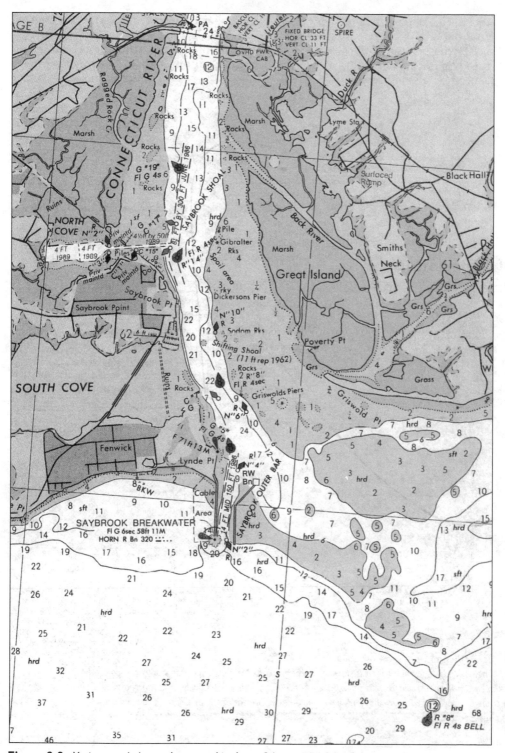

Figure 2-8. *Various symbols are shown on this chart of the mouth of the Connecticut River.*

those that don't (three or more dots). Dashed lines show the limits of the dredged channel.

Some positions on charts are accurate and others are approximate. An accurate position is shown by a dot inside a circle; an approximate position is represented by a small circle.   (text continues on page 23)

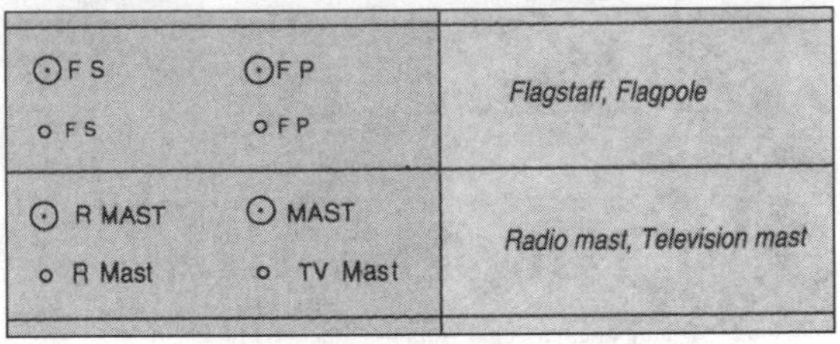

Figure 2-9. *The symbol for an object tells whether its position is accurate (dot inside circle) or approximate (small circle).*

⊙ F S ○ F S	⊙ F P ○ F P	*Flagstaff, Flagpole*
⊙ R MAST ○ R Mast	⊙ MAST ○ TV Mast	*Radio mast, Television mast*

Signal Information

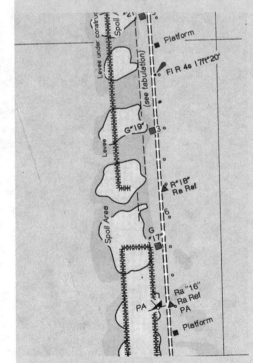

A chart provides information about lights, buoys, and sound signals both by the symbol used and with a sequence of abbreviations near the aid to navigation. The abbreviations can define shape, color, markings, light characteristics and color, height of the light, and sound signals. The abbreviations are in one or more lines of print. (See Chapter 4 for specific information about aids to navigation.)

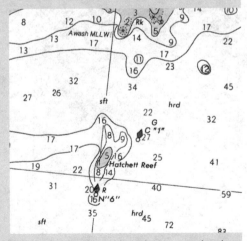

Figure 2-10. *Daybeacons are shown by squares (green) or triangles (red). The minor light is shown by a black dot and a magenta flare. This red light will have a triangular dayboard even though it isn't part of the chart symbol.*

Figure 2-11. *Nun and can buoys are colored red and green, respectively, and labeled N or C. Color abbreviations R or G aren't always shown; N implies red and C implies green.*

Figure 2-12. *This illustration shows lighted whistle buoy "KP". RG means red and green horizontal bands, red uppermost. The buoy marks a shoal that can be passed on either side; the preferred channel from seaward is found by leaving the buoy to starboard (see Chapter 4). "KP" means the buoy shows the letters KP for identification. A magenta spot indicates it is lighted. Fl (2 + 1) tells us the flashing sequence—two flashes, then one, then a longer dark period. R means the light is red, and 6s means the light sequence repeats every 6 seconds. WHISTLE means a wave-actuated whistle.*

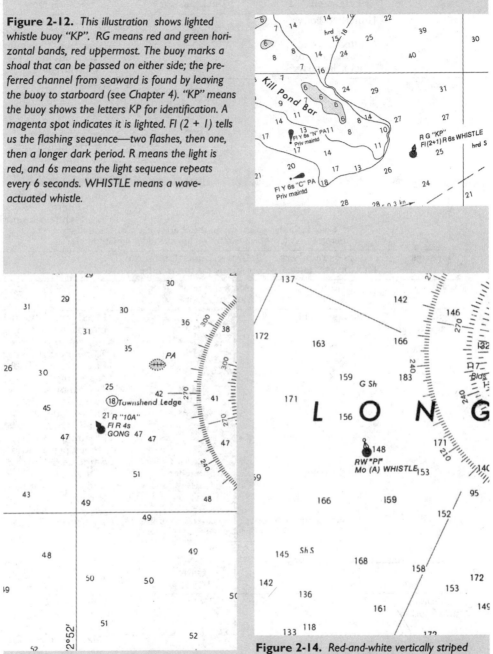

Figure 2-13. *Lighted gong buoy "10A" has a flashing red light, one flash every 4 seconds, and a wave-actuated gong.*

Figure 2-14. *Red-and-white vertically striped lighted whistle buoy "PI." The line in the diamond indicates vertical stripes, and the little circle at the top indicates a spherical topmark.*

	Navigation Aid	Chart Designation	Description
Shape	Unlighted bouys	N	Red nun (conical)
		C	Green can (cylindrical)
	Lighted buoys		Shapes not specified
	Daybeacons and	■	Green square
	light dayboards	▲	Red triangle
Color		G	Green
		R	Red
		G R	Green-over-red horizontal bands
		R G	Red-over-green horizontal bands
		RW	Red and white vertical stripes
		BRB	Black-red-black horizontal bands
		NB	Non-lateral aid, black and white diamonds

Color isn't always shown on the chart when N or C implies red or green. A few black can buoys (private aids) remain in service.

Markings	Letters or numbers	Shown in quotation marks	
	Lighthouse names	usually on the top line	
Light	Buoys	Magenta spot	
	Lights	Magenta "flare"	
Light characteristics	Flash sequence	F	Fixed (on all the time)
		ISO	Isophase (on and off for equal periods)
		E Int	Same as ISO
		Fl	Flashing, one flash at a time
		Fl (2)	Two flashes
		Fl (2 + 1)	Two flashes, then one
		Mo (A)	Morse code "A" (short flash, then long flash)
		Q	Flashing about 60 times per minute
		Qk Fl	Same as Q
	Light color	None listed	White
		R	Red
		G	Green
		Y	Yellow

Period (time between flashes or groups of flashes, given in seconds)
Height (for lights only, not listed for buoys)

Sound signal (not abbreviated)		BELL	
		GONG	
		HORN	
		WHISTLE	
Additional information		R Bn	Radiobeacon: frequency, sequence, and Morse Code identification shown. Magenta circle around light symbol.
		Racon	Radar beacon: Morse Code identification shown. Magenta circle around buoy or light symbol.
		PA	Position approximate.

Table 2-1. *Chart Symbols*

Direction and Distance

It is easy to find the direction and the distance between any two points on a chart. If you plan to go to a harbor across the bay, draw a line from the entrance buoy of your home harbor to your destination. This line is called the **intended track.** The intended track line on the chart shows the direction and distance graphically. It is at an angle with respect to north that corresponds to the direction. Its length corresponds to the distance. The graphic representation of direction and distance on a chart is fundamental to navigation.

Angles bear the correct relationship everywhere on a Mercator chart, so it's easy to measure track direction. Just transfer the track line across the chart with parallel rules to a printed compass rose. There are several types of parallel rules: hinged, roller, sliding triangles, and drafting machines. One type is about as good as another on a large chart table, but all are hard to use aboard a boat. Some parallel rules include protractors for measuring angles.

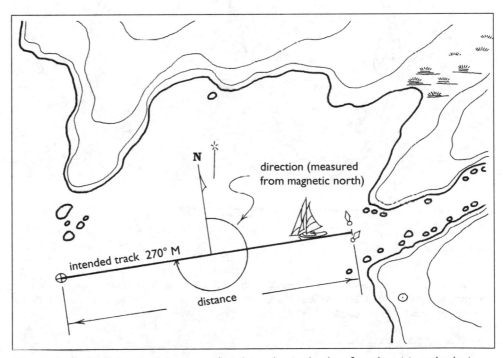

Figure 2-15. *To go from one place to another, draw a line on the chart from the origin to the destination. The arc shows the magnetic bearing, and the length of the line gives the distance.*

The Angles

Navigation is easier after you develop a grasp of the angles used to measure direction. A marine compass is divided into 360 degrees with north at 000° (and 360°). East is 090°, south is 180°, and west is 270°. Northeast, southeast, southwest, and northwest are halfway between. Three digits specify a direction in degrees.

If you're new to using a compass, it may be helpful to think in terms of a clock face until the numbers give you a mental picture of the direction. Twelve o'clock corresponds to 000°, three to 090°, six to 180°, and nine to 270°. Hour marks are 30° apart. When you can immediately visualize directions by their numerals, you are advancing from student to navigator.

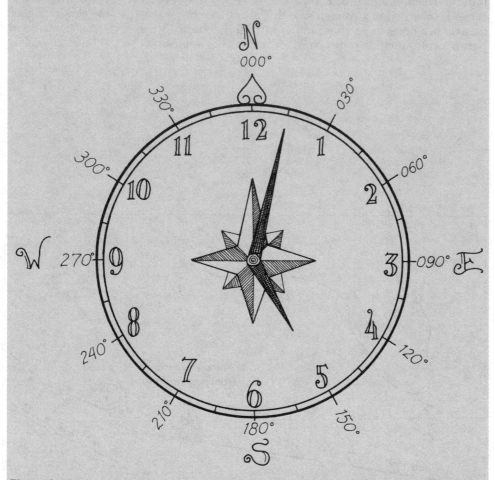

Figure 2-16. *Compass directions are measured from north around to the right through 360°. They are comparable with the face of a clock: north is 000° at "12 o'clock," east is 090° at "3 o'clock," south is 180° at "6 o'clock," and west is 270° at "9 o'clock." Hour marks are 30° apart.*

Lay the rules alongside the track line between the two points; then, maintaining this alignment, move the parallel rules across the chart to the compass rose. The compass rose's outer circle shows true direction and the inner one shows magnetic direction. The angle between true north and magnetic north is called **variation** and is discussed in the section on compasses in Chapter 3. In nearly every case you will use the inner circle to get the magnetic course since you steer using the boat's magnetic compass.

There is little difference in the actual length of a minute of latitude at different latitudes, but a Mercator chart makes minutes of latitude appear noticeably longer at higher latitudes.

Instead of using parallel rules, try a useful shortcut: Hold a straightedge along the track line and align another straightedge parallel to it at the nearest compass rose (Figure 2-19). You can align the two straightedges within a degree or two, close enough if you're only going a few miles. A strip

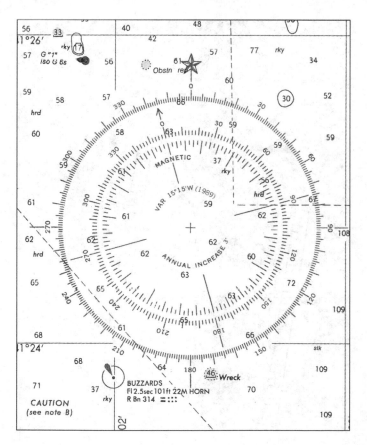

Figure 2-17. *The outer circle of a compass rose is aligned with true north. The inner circle with the arrow at 0° shows magnetic directions. Measure directions using the **inner** circle.*

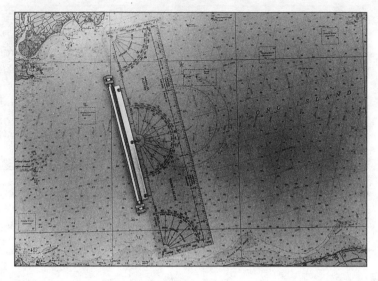

Figure 2-18. *Measure direction from one point to another by moving a parallel rule from a line between the two across the chart to the compass rose. Use the inner circle to find the magnetic course. Rolling parallel rules are a good choice for use on boats. This one also has a protractor and a distance scale.*

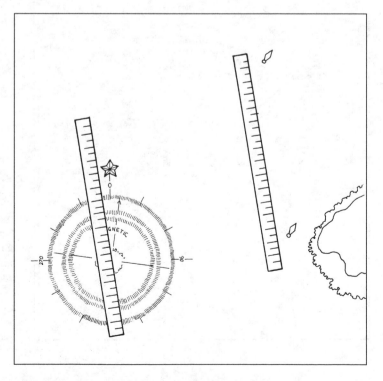

Figure 2-19. *Aboard a boat we often use this shortcut: Hold one straightedge along the course line and another parallel to it at the nearest compass rose. You can find the course within a couple of degrees—close enough if you're only going a few miles.*

of clear plastic with parallel lines (Figure 2-20) can serve the same function, allowing quick direction measurements.

For all practical purposes, a minute of latitude is the same as a nautical mile. Use the latitude scale at either *side* of the chart to measure distance. Set a pair of dividers to the length of the line, then move them to the side of the chart to find the distance. (Small-craft charts are often on a slant and have printed distance scales for measurement.)

There is little difference in the actual length of a minute of latitude at different latitudes, but a Mercator chart makes minutes of latitude *appear* noticeably longer at higher latitudes. If you measure the length of a line using the latitude scale near the top of the chart and again near the bottom, you will find different distances. To get an accurate distance, use the latitude scale near the vertical midpoint of the track line.

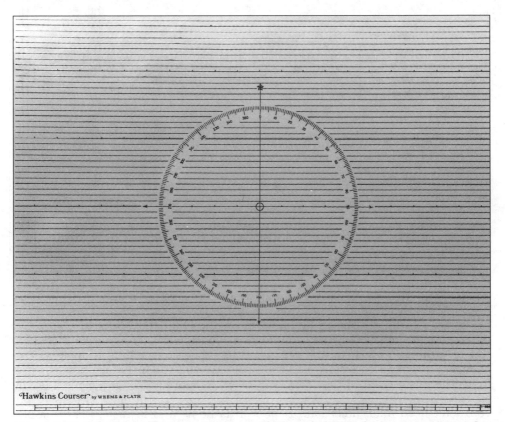

Figure 2-20. *The Hawkins Courser is often more useful than parallel rules for determining courses. Put one line at the center of the compass rose and align another line on the courser with the desired track on the chart. The Courser includes a protractor for measuring angles. (Courtesy Weems & Plath)*

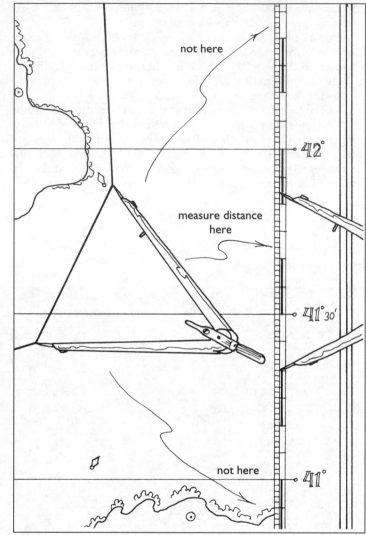

Figure 2-21. *Measure distance using the latitude scale at either side of the chart. Set a pair of dividers to the length of the track line, then move them to the side of the chart to find the distance. A minute of latitude is equivalent to a nautical mile. In order to get an accurate measurement, use the latitude scale near the vertical midpoint of the track line.*

Depths

Water depths are shown by numbers on the chart, but different charts use different depth measurements. United States charts gave depth measurements in feet or fathoms (6 feet) until 1992, when they began switching to meters. This changeover will go on for years, so you will have to watch the depth scale carefully. There is a scale on the chart for converting between feet and meters, or you can divide meters by 0.3 to get feet. (The exact conversion factor is 0.3048, but you don't need such precision.) Depths in fathoms and in meters show superscripted tenths in smaller type.

Charts show depth contour lines in addition to numerical depths. The water area inside a certain depth contour, dependent upon the scale of the chart and the prevalent depths, is tinted blue. Charts with depths in feet may have rows of dots for 1 fathom, two dots for 2 fathoms (12 feet), and on up to five dots for 5 fathoms (30 feet).

Depths refer to the **vertical datum** of the chart. Usually this is *mean lower low water (MLLW)*, the average of the lower of the two low tides per day over a 19-year period. The actual depth is usually more than the charted depth since the tide is low only a short while each day. Where the chart shows a depth of 4 feet and high tide is 5.2 feet above datum, the depth at that location is actually 9.2 feet. On a day when low tide is −1 foot, the depth is not 4 feet but 3.

It is important to check the *Tide Tables* to find the predicted height of tide to add to the charted depths when operating in shallow areas. Sensible navigators avoid areas where the depth is close to the boat's draft, usually allowing several feet of clearance. In wide, shallow areas such as Chesapeake Bay, boats often go into areas with just a couple of feet under the keel. If the chart shows a wide expanse with little depth variation or with gradual changes, and the depthfinder also shows a nearly flat bottom, it is relatively safe to venture there, but skippers who do so must take care to avoid going aground. This is especially true of twin-screw power-boats, in which the propellers and rudders extend below the keel. Going aground with one of these boats, even on sand, is an event memorable for its expense as well as its delay.

In areas that have large rocks or coral, the depths on the chart vary considerably. Look at the chart you're using; if adjacent depths differ greatly from one another, be cautious. Boulders and coral heads stick up several feet, and the depthfinder will show frequent changes. The hydrographic survey may not have found all of the rocks due to limitations of time and equipment. You certainly don't want to find one with your boat—going aground on rocks or coral is a disaster. It is particularly important to be cautious of varying soundings on a 1:80,000 chart, where the soundings may be a quarter of a mile or more apart. There's a lot of unsurveyed bottom between adjacent soundings.

Use charts with caution, keep them up to date, stay well clear of hazards, explore new areas carefully, allow extra depth as a safety factor, and you'll do fine.

In rocky or coral areas and along bold coasts, it is common practice to stay one contour line deeper than the boat's draft. Thus a sailboat drawing 6 feet would stay outside the 12-foot contour. If there is any uncertainty in the boat's position, allow additional distance from rocky areas. Professional mariners who have ignored these safeguards have made headlines. In 1992 the *Queen Elizabeth II* found a rock near Buzzards Bay that was a little shallower than the ones shown on the charted ledge. That was an expensive way to locate a rock.

Also be cautious of the depths in areas with sand or mud bottom and strong currents. The current sculpts the bottom constantly and more quickly than you might think. Inside Bogue Inlet, North Carolina, in the summer of 1992, the depth in one part of the channel changed from more than 6 feet to less than 3 feet in 10 days. Around sandy inlets the actual depths can bear little resemblance to the charted ones. Even the shape of the land changes significantly from season to season.

Does this mean the charts are bad? Of course not, but to survey thoroughly *and* frequently would cost the government huge amounts of money, and it would cost you a substantial sum to buy new charts every month or so. Use them with caution, keep them up to date, stay well clear of hazards, explore new areas carefully, allow extra depth as a safety factor, and you'll do fine.

Protecting Charts

Boat operators have little room to use a chart, seldom a place to put it, and they have to contend with lots of wind and spray. Just unrolling a chart on a boat is easier said than done. It's best to fold a chart to show the most important areas. Sometimes you can cut a small-craft chart along the margins between sections to make it easier to see two adjacent areas.

To keep the spray off, I usually slip the chart into a heavy plastic bag with a zip closure. This works fairly well with small-craft charts, which are folded to start with. The clear bag lets you flip the chart over to see the next area; you may have to make some nonstandard folds to show the right area. Slide the chart out when you need to write on it, and after the trip to let it dry. A damp chart will sweat in the bag if you leave it in direct sunlight, so keep it covered when you're not looking at it. I tend to write more in a notebook and less on the chart when it's in a bag.

A coat of clear plastic spray (clear lacquer) can waterproof a chart to some extent while still allowing you to mark it with a pencil. NOAA produces a few plastic charts that are tough, waterproof, and durable, and private companies reproduce some NOAA charts on plastic.

You can damage charts with too much writing and smudged erasures. Too many boat skippers avoid this problem by not writing on the chart at all, but that's not good either. Just use appropriate pencils and drafting erasers (see Chapter 3, "Navigator's Kit").

Chart Dates and Corrections

Chart **title blocks** or notes give the chart name and number, scale, horizontal datum, sounding datum, sounding units, and other information. A note in the lower left-hand margin gives the chart number, edition, and date.

Beginning in 1993, NOS is adding information about the hydrographic surveys on which the chart is based. The information is contained in a source diagram that gives the dates and scales of the surveys used to make the chart. This will help you evaluate the quality of the data. Surveys older than about 1960 used relatively primitive equipment and are far less reliable than more recent ones, particularly in rocky areas. Surveys at larger scale give more information; thus a survey at 1:10,000 can be expected to give more detail at higher accuracy than one at 1:40,000.

It will take several years for NOS to include source diagrams on all of its nearly 1,000 charts. In the interim, you can get source data for areas of interest by writing to: Marine Chart Division N/CG-22, Office of the Coast Survey, National Ocean Service, NOAA, 1315 East-West Highway, Silver Spring, MD 20910.

When using Loran-C or GPS, be sure to check the horizontal datum of every chart. This is the coordinate system that defines latitude and longitude. NOS is changing the datum, and this can make a significant difference in some areas, particularly Alaska and Hawaii, when entering latitude and longitude for electronic navigation (see Chapter 4). Positions measured by bearings or distances to charted objects aren't affected, nor are saved waypoints.

Use the chart edition and its date as a starting point for changes that have occurred since the chart was printed. The NOS and the Coast Guard publish corrections in the *Local Notice to Mariners* (see "Publications" later in this chapter) that must be applied to charts to keep them current. This is true of new charts as well as old; a chart you buy may be six months old and need many corrections.

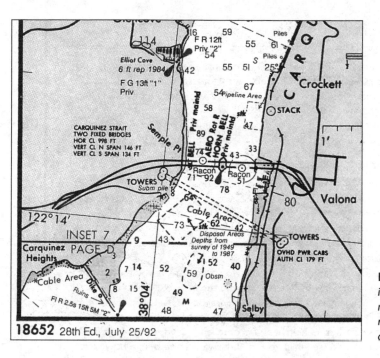

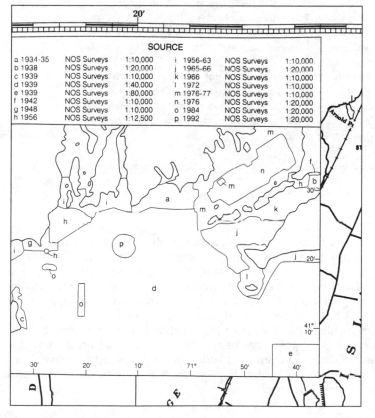

Figure 2-22. *A note in the lower left-hand margin gives the chart number, edition, and date.*

Figure 2-23. *The source diagram gives the dates and scales of the surveys used to make the chart.*

Making a Custom Chart

A new chart is like a new boat: you need to add a few things before you cast off. Even with the corrections from the *Local Notice to Mariners,* a chart isn't fully ready for use. Only when you add more information to an up-to-date chart does it live up to its promise as a navigation tool.

When you use a chart, you must draw track lines and measure courses and distances. Aboard a small boat this isn't easy, but if you're like most skippers you have a number of popular destinations in the area near your home harbor. Lay off track lines to the usual destinations in advance, and your chart becomes more usable. Find the magnetic courses and label them—034° M, for example. Put the reciprocal course (the opposite direction), 214° M, below the line. If the destination is an electronic waypoint, write its number or name on the chart.

Some small-craft charts have printed track lines. This makes your work easier, but beware: the printed courses may be true rather than magnetic. If so, write in the magnetic directions. In addition, measure the distances and write them on the chart. Write distances in nautical miles and tenths to simplify running time calculations. Be careful here, too: some small-craft charts have distance measurements in statute miles.

Sometimes you find a large expanse of water with one or two shallow spots you must avoid. It is worthwhile to highlight these humps by drawing a circle around them. You'd drive yourself nuts trying to outline every shallow spot, but used judiciously, this practice is useful.

To avoid confusion, I mark METRIC across charts with depths in meters.

Doing this work before cruising new waters helps you become familiar with an area. It's far better than trying to figure things out all at once while you're underway. Some things, however, must be done while underway; for example, there's not much information in a circled dot marked "TANK." What color is it? What shape? Tanks come in all shapes, from cylindrical to ones that look like teed-up golf balls to ones that have skeleton-tower legs. Make a small sketch of the tank near its symbol and note its color, and you will be able to identify it quickly from any direction.

The same goes for lighthouses. The black dot and exclamation-point–shaped flare tell little about a lighthouse's shape or paint scheme. When you see a lighthouse from offshore or from an odd direction, it may be confusing. So, draw and write. You don't have to be artistic to make a useful sketch showing the shape and color pattern of a lighthouse. It is helpful to draw a circle around the light symbol to make it stand out on the chart.

Great Lakes Charts

Most Great Lakes charts are on the **polyconic projection**, which represents surface areas more accurately than the Mercator projection. However, it doesn't do as well with angles. The meridians aren't vertical; they converge at the top of the chart. On a 1:80,000 chart covering about 35 miles north to south, the meridians at either side of the chart are about 500 yards closer together at the top than at the bottom. The parallels of latitude aren't straight lines, either, but arcs of circles. These effects are more visible and more important on charts that cover large areas.

Latitude is measured on a polyconic chart the same way as on a Mercator chart: Set dividers to the distance from a latitude line to the position; move them to the side of the chart, putting one divider point on the same latitude line; and read the latitude at the other divider point.

The course exhibited by the compass is often different from the magnetic course indicated by the chart—so I like to compare the actual compass courses with the magnetic ones I've written on the chart. Write the compass course on your chart—036°**C**, for example—and you can steer without having to convert magnetic to compass courses. It's just one less thing you'll have to do.

Charts don't list the timing characteristics of foghorns. Look them up in the *Light List* and write them on the chart so you can time a fog signal with a stopwatch to distinguish one horn from another on a soupy day. Since fog signals have different tones, note *high* or *low* pitch beside the chart symbol.

Write a drawbridge's operating schedule by its symbol on the chart and you won't have to search for it.

It is useful to make a mark in the approximate location of buildings and other useful landmarks that aren't shown on the chart. Use them for general information, not for exact lines of position.

I like to write in the local names of rocks, reefs, or points. Fishermen have their own names for such places, and I have been in areas where each buoy had a local name different from its official name. You can't tell what people are talking about until you know that the "*" on the chart is "East Shag Rock."

I draw a small anchor in good anchorages. It helps me remember the good spots when there is a long time between trips. A note about the bottom and a sketch of anchoring ranges are nice, too.

What about moving all this data to a new chart? You'll have to do it; charts get out of date even while you're sleeping. The new work isn't all loss, though: plotting courses, landmarks, and notes on a new chart refreshes your memory. As you compare old chart with new, you see the changes easily.

> *Even with the corrections from the* Local Notice to Mariners, *a chart isn't fully ready for use. Only when you add more information to an up-to-date chart does it live up to its promise as a navigation tool.*

Longitude is another matter. Its scale varies from top to bottom of the chart, so you can't use the printed marks at the top or the bottom. There is an **interpolator** for longitude printed on the chart. Set the dividers to match the distance between meridians at the position, and move them to the interpolator. Holding the dividers horizontally, find the location on the interpolator where the divider points touch both outside lines. Make a light line between the divider points. Then set one divider point at the position, the other at the nearest meridian. Transfer that distance to the light line on the interpolator to read the longitude of the position. (Using an engineer's scale, as described on pages 14–15, is easier.)

A straight line on a polyconic projection is very nearly a straight line in fact— a line of sight—making a slightly different angle with every meridian. The compass roses on polyconic charts are printed exactly on meridians, and apply *only at that meridian*. It is best to measure a *course* with an ordinary protractor

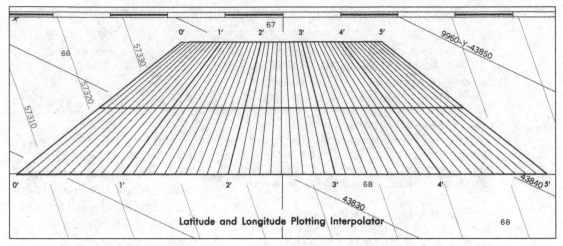

Figure 2-24. *A latitude and longitude interpolator from a polyconic chart. Since the meridians converge toward the top of the chart, you can't measure longitude accurately at the top or bottom. Use dividers (see Figure 2-25) to transfer the width between meridians at the point of interest to the interpolator, and draw a light line across it. Then measure longitude along the light line.*

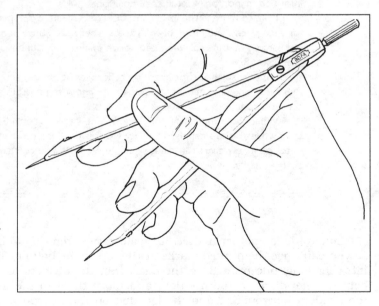

Figure 2-25. *Dividers are used to measure distance on a chart. Hold them as shown, and you can open and close them with one hand.*

aligned with a meridian near the *middle* of the track line, and remember to add or subtract the magnetic variation to the protractor (true) course. Measure a *bearing* at the meridian closest to the boat, that is, at the *near end* of the line of bearing.

Distances are easier to measure on a polyconic chart than on a Mercator chart since the distance scale is nearly the same all over the polyconic chart. The distance scale is in statute miles (5,280 feet) rather than nautical miles; use the latitude scale to measure nautical miles.

Charts for Rivers and Reservoirs

Nautical charts are not available for vast inland areas, including many fine boating locations. The U.S. Army Corps of Engineers sells maps of the rivers they maintain for navigation. These are useful even though they don't indicate latitude and longitude. If you operate your boat on a river covered by these maps, by all means get them, but keep in mind that river navigation is complicated by changing water levels and shifting shoals. The mileage on river maps is shown in statute miles.

Charts are unavailable for many other rivers and large hydroelectric reservoirs that are nevertheless excellent for boating. The U.S. Geological Survey **topographic maps** are the next best thing to charts and are available for the entire country. You can get topographic maps from: USGS Branch of Distribution, 1200 South Eads St., Arlington, VA 22202, or from map agents.

They come in two useful series, one covering 15 minutes of latitude and longitude, and a more detailed series covering 7.5 minutes of latitude and longitude at a 1:24,000 scale—about the same scale as a harbor chart.

Seven-and-a-half-minute topographic maps, as they are called, show excellent detail of land features, including buildings, power lines, roads, and bridges, all of which are good landmarks for navigation. The USGS is converting topo maps to the metric system, although they retain a printed scale of statute miles. New maps show heights in meters and have a grid with lines every kilometer, which is handy for those who think of distance in kilometers and speed in kilometers per hour. This will be great after all us old fossils who think in miles and knots die off, but for now the metric grid requires conversion.

The grid on a topographic map is not aligned with true north or with magnetic north. A small diagram at the bottom of the map shows the angles between north, grid north (GN), and magnetic north (MN). The term *declination* is used, rather than the seagoing term *variation* (Chapter 3), to mean the angle between north and magnetic north. Measuring directions is easiest using a protractor at the vertical grid lines, adding or subtracting the angle between grid north and magnetic north.

Topographic maps are excellent for navigation except that they show water depths very sparsely—as if mapmakers lose interest at the surface of the water. This is the opposite of a nautical chart, where depths are shown in great detail. Be cautious of topo map depths, especially where there is little detail. Of course it's not too difficult to put the depths in as you go along, but you can get fooled by the changing pool levels unless you pay attention to them; the water level in reservoirs changes significantly. I know a man who has an old topographic map of a river valley before the dam was built. He guards it carefully, for it shows all the contours.

The Army Corps of Engineers has maps of many of their reservoirs, but these show relatively little detail. Other reservoir maps are published by private compa-

Charts are unavailable for many rivers and large hydro-electric reservoirs that are nevertheless excellent for boating. The U.S. Geological Survey topographic maps are the next best thing to charts and are available for the entire country.

I nautical mile = 1.852 kilometers

I statute mile = 1.609 kilometers

nies. The cruder ones seem to be based on road maps, the better ones on topographic maps. Even a rough map is better than nothing. It allows you to navigate, as opposed to wandering around.

Publications

Here is a short list of navigation publications and other sources of information, most of which are mentioned in other parts of this book. You don't want to carry so many publications that they give the boat a list, but some of them are useful to you. Look them over to decide which ones you need.

Tide Tables. *Tide Tables* are essential for coastal navigation. International Marine publishes them each year for NOAA's National Ocean Service (NOS). The *Tide Tables* give time differences and height ratios for high and low water, and instructions for making the necessary corrections. Add the height from the *Tide Tables* to the charted depth to find the predicted depth at any location. If you are not operating near a *reference station*, you must correct the information to the *subordinate station* nearest your location. For example, to find the tides for Point Chehalis, Westport (Gray's Harbor), Washington, first find the tides for the reference station— Aberdeen, Washington—then apply the corrections for the subordinate station at Point Chehalis. Remember to add an hour for Daylight Savings Time in the summer. The *Tide Tables* also give the times of sun rise and set, and moon rise and set.

Wind, river run-off from rainfall, barometric pressure, and storm surges cause the tide (and current) to differ from the predicted values. At our home pier, a southwest wind lowers the water level about half a foot from the heights during a calm, and a northeast wind raises it about the same amount. NOS's internet Web site at http://www.nos.noaa.gov/ has information on charts, publications, and other NOS products. The site also provides tide and current information, some of which is available as it is measured.

Restaurants, gift shops, and other businesses give away local tide tables, but be wary of these. In the first place, they seldom give heights, only times. Heights vary significantly from day to day and from one high tide to the next. I have found numerous errors in tide tables printed in newspapers, as well. One major newspaper, for example, forgot about Daylight Savings Time until June.

Computer programs for tide predictions are available. The better ones take the excellent NOAA tide data and make it more usable. Others use their own predictions, based on heaven-knows-what. Tide clocks and watches are handy but get out of step with the tides in a few days. The interval between successive high tides varies considerably throughout the month, and a steady-running clock can't follow the variations.

Current Tables. The *Current Tables*, also published yearly by International Marine, are as important as the *Tide Tables*. Current affects boats constantly, and whether you plan to go through an inlet (roughest on the ebb) or make a trip on a bay, you should know the current. You can't determine the current from the *Tide Tables*. For example, the ebb current in many inlets changes to flood two to three hours *after* low tide. The *Current Tables*, like the *Tide Tables*, have subordinate station corrections and directions for applying them.

Coast Pilot. NOAA also publishes the *Coast Pilot*, by region. These useful volumes have a description of waterways, routes, a handy table of distances, and weather information. They include the regulations for drawbridge openings, anchorages, and restricted areas.

Ostrich Bay ★★★ [4] No Facilities

Charts: **18449**, 18474

Ostrich Bay branches south from Dyes Inlet. The east shore is crowded with waterfront homes. On the west shore is a large Navy hospital and park. Protected, warm in summer, and with no shore access, this is a fine "do-nothing" anchorage. The ambitious water-ski, or explore Oyster Bay.

Approaches. Keep in mid-channel when entering. North of Elwood Point is a flagpole and the large, monolithic structure of the Navy Hospital. Also on this west shore is Jackson Park; its fishing pier, playfields, beach, and picnic area are for use by active and retired military personnel. This area and the pier south of Elwood Point are the former site of a Naval ammunition depot. Shoals and submerged obstructions are reported along this shore.

Anchorage. There's good anchoring throughout Ostrich Bay, but the most protected and lovely is to the southwest, toward the wooded, undeveloped shore. If you set your hook south and slightly west of the abandoned ammunition pier, you'll be protected from northerlies. The major concern boaters seem to have here is calculating how far offshore to anchor in order to capture the afternoon sun.

Getting Ashore. All tidelands are private. The undeveloped woods and beach are U.S. government property, posted with NO TRESPASSING signs.

The nearest shore access is at Tracyton, at the northeast end of the Narrows, and at Chico, northwest of Erland. Both have public launching ramps. A gas station and convenience grocery are four short blocks uphill from the Tracyton launching ramp.

Oyster Bay

Charts: **18449**, 18474

As much as anything, Oyster Bay resembles a private pond. Its entrance is narrow and shallow—a fathom or less—and its basin slightly deeper. Beachfront homes and apartments completely enclose this bay; their large windows gaze, unblinking, at every boat that enters and leaves. You'll be in everyone's front yard if you anchor here. All tidelands are private.

Chico Bay ★★ [3] No Facilities

Charts: **18449**, 18474

This open bay at the southwest end of Dyes Inlet is almost entirely foul with pilings and tideflats. North of the charted pilings (a former shellfish farm) there is depth and a soft mud bottom for anchoring, and better protection from southerlies than in Silverdale. A public launching ramp at a street end on the west shore is the only place to land. There are no facilities within walking distance.

Silverdale ★★★ [3]

Charts: **18449**, 18474

As if to attract boaters to this far northern end of Dyes Inlet, the town of Silverdale has substantially renovated its waterfront. Stout wooden floats attached to steel-and-concrete

Figure 2-26. *Some cruising guides, such as the one shown here, offer detailed information about anchorages, shoreside facilities, navigation, and more. (From* A Cruising Guide to Puget Sound, *International Marine, 1995.)*

Commercial guides. Some companies publish books of tide and current information, and a number of commercial *cruising guides* are available for various areas of the country (see page 37). The best of these include detailed information about marinas, boatyards, restaurants, and other shoreside facilities, as well as helpful information about channels and anchorages.

Local Notice to Mariners. Each Coast Guard District publishes a *Local Notice to Mariners* each week. It lists aids-to-navigation discrepancies and changes, hazards to navigation, and other important information. The *Local* is the best way to learn about changes, and you can receive it free of charge from your nearest Coast Guard District. The Coast Guard also broadcasts important information on VHF-FM on a regular schedule. Consult the *Local* for broadcast times and frequencies.

> *The* Local *is the best way to learn about changes, and you can receive it free of charge from your nearest Coast Guard District.*

Notice to Mariners. The National Imagery and Mapping Agency (NIMA) issues a weekly *Notice to Mariners*, but it doesn't include all information contained in the *Local*. The NIMA *Notice to Mariners* is geared to large ships and ignores many changes in shallow areas—the very places boats frequent. NIMA also publishes the *American Practical Navigator* (Bowditch), a valuable navigation reference primarily for ships. You may purchase NIMA aeronautical charts, nautical charts, and related publications from: NOAA Distribution Division (N/ACC3), National Ocean Service, 6501 Lafayette Avenue, Riverdale, MD 20737-1199. Phone: 800-638-8972.

Light List. The Coast Guard publishes the *Light List* by region. The *Light List* contains data such as sound signal timing that isn't printed on the charts. It also has extensive information about buoys, lights, daymarks, light visibility, and all electronic aids to navigation.

The National Imagery and Mapping Agency (NIMA) operates a Web site at http://164.214.12.145/index that has extensive maritime information. The NIMA *Notice to Mariners*, their publications, and the Coast Guard *Light List* are availabale on line at this site. The Web site also has a handy *Marine Navigation Calculator*, and an excellent article, "Using Nautical Charts with Global Positioning System."

The Coast Guard Navigation Center (NAVCEN) has a Web site at http//www.navcen.uscg.mil/ with extensive information on all Federal radionavigation systems, Coast Guard maritime Aids to Navigation, Communications, and Boating information. The NAVCEN has a full-time watchstander at 703-313-5900 who can answer many questions concerning electronic aids to navigation.

The USCG *Local Notice to Mariners* is available on-line at the NAVCEN. The *Local* is valuable to boat operators since it includes changes in shallow channels, and temporary and proposed changes which aren't in the NIMA *Notice to Mariners*. It remains in a text format rather than in a searchable database, which would be far more useful.

CHAPTER 3

Navigation Instruments and Equipment

A well-found boat has good instruments for the four fundamental measurements: direction, water depth, speed (or distance traveled) through the water, and time. Trying to get by without any one of these instruments makes navigation difficult and inaccurate, even for an expert. Good instruments are particularly important aboard a sailboat, which is harder to navigate than a powerboat. Sailboats don't make steady speed or have engine rpm as a guide. Often they must tack to reach a destination, and they make significant leeway due to the wind.

Along with good measuring instruments, a navigator needs good drafting instruments for chartwork. This chapter also discusses radar, a self-contained measuring device.

The Compass

To know where you're going, you have to have a good direction reference. This is one of the more important and difficult things to achieve aboard a boat. Yes, you can install an inexpensive compass and not bother to adjust it, but it will impose navigation difficulties that you must cope with constantly. Even the best compass requires careful installation and adjustment. It is possible to adjust a compass to remove nearly all of the error, which makes navigation so much easier. Get a good compass with a large card; it will be more stable than a small card, and the numbers are easier to read. A small boat with lively motion needs a large, stable compass, not a small, nervous one.

It is easier to understand a boat's motion using a compass with a flat or dished card that displays the heading on the far side of the compass in line with a vertical **lubber's line**. The boat turns, not the compass card. A *direct-reading* compass, which displays the heading upright on the near side, seems to swing backward. It's also hard to take bearings with a direct-reading compass.

Specific compasses are designed for specific types of boats. Some are designed for the quick motion of planing boats. Others are designed for the sharp heeling

> *A well-found boat has good instruments for the four fundamental measurements: direction, water depth, speed, and time.*

Figure 3-1. *A compass with a flat or dished card (left) shows the effect of turns "naturally"—the card continues to point north as the boat turns. A direct-reading compass (right) seems to turn backward as the boat changes course and is difficult to use for taking bearings. (Courtesy E. S. Ritchie & Sons, Inc.)*

angles of sailboats. Sailboat compasses often have lines at 45° to the lubber's line.

One professional compass adjuster advises buying only a repairable compass; check the specifications to see if the one you're considering is repairable. Although you don't expect to have it in the shop very often, repairable compasses are built to a higher standard of quality than those that can't be repaired.

In recent years **flux-gate** compasses, which have a magnetic sensor unit mounted low in the hull and an indicator at the helm, have become popular. Flux-gate compasses show magnetic directions, just as conventional compasses do. They can be more stable than conventional compasses, but they require a power source and can be adversely affected by magnetic interference, such as a storm anchor or a toolbox stowed next to the sensor. Autopilots generally use flux-gate compasses. A boat with a flux-gate compass should have a backup conventional compass that needs no power or electronic gadgetry.

Direction

Navigators define compass direction in three ways: as a course, a heading, and a bearing. The **course** is the direction you intend to steer. Often it is the

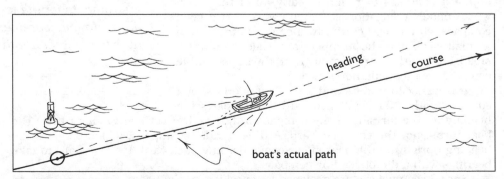

Figure 3-2. *The* course *is the direction to steer. The* heading *is the direction the boat is pointed at the moment.*

same as the direction of the track line on a chart. The **heading** is the direction the boat is pointed *at the moment*. This often differs from the course; you may be trying to steer a course of 080°, but the boat is headed 088°. A little later the heading is 074°; the course remains 080°.

No one can keep a boat precisely on course all the time. A boat swings to the left and then to the right, then left again. Even so, the boat follows the desired course more accurately than you might think. When I first went aboard ship, I thought an experienced helmsman would hold the ship closer to the desired track line than one who was learning. It wasn't so. New helmsmen did wander farther left and right than experienced ones, but at the end of an hour's trick on the wheel, both were very close to the desired track. The lesson is this: if you want to go 132°, steer 132°. If you steer 130° instead, thinking you can't keep the boat within a couple of degrees, the boat will go 130°.

A **bearing** is the direction from one object to another, for example from the compass to a lighthouse. That's a *compass bearing*. A *relative bearing* is relative to the boat: dead ahead is 000° relative, and a buoy abeam to starboard bears 090° relative.

Navigators refer to reciprocal bearings or courses. *Reciprocal bearings* are directly opposite each other. South, 180°, is the reciprocal bearing of north, 000°. They are 180° apart. If a course is 120°M (magnetic, see page 42) going out of port, the reciprocal course is 300°M coming in.

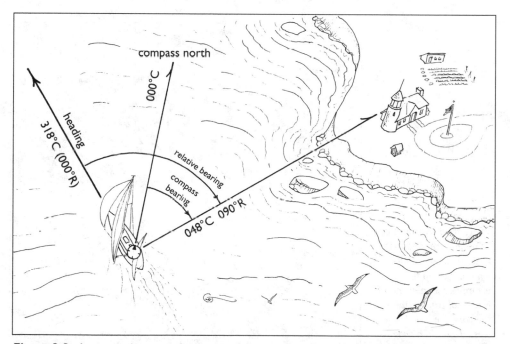

Figure 3-3. *A compass bearing is the direction from a compass to an object, such as the lighthouse, with respect to compass north. A relative bearing is the direction from the boat to an object with respect to the bow of the boat.*

HINT: To find the reciprocal, add 200, then subtract 20. If the bearing is a large number, subtract 200, then add 20.

Variation and Deviation

There is a complicating factor with compasses: magnetic north isn't identical with true north. Along the U.S. East Coast, a compass points west of true north. Near the Gulf coast of Florida, a compass points nearly true north. On the West Coast and the western part of the Gulf of Mexico, it points to the east of true north. This error is called **variation**. Variation is shown on all charts, and changes slowly over the years.

If the arrow representing magnetic north is to the left (west) of the star representing true north, variation is westerly. If magnetic north is to the right (east) of true north, variation is easterly.

Directions that refer to magnetic north are called *magnetic* courses, bearings, and headings, to distinguish them from *true* directions. Charts have a printed **compass rose** that shows both true and magnetic directions for that location. The inner circle of a compass rose is aligned with magnetic north. If the arrow representing magnetic north is to the left (west) of the star representing true north, variation is *westerly*. If magnetic north is to the right (east) of true north, variation is *easterly*. Measure directions using the inner compass rose circle to correct for variation automatically.

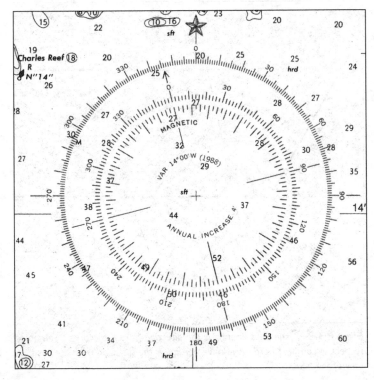

Figure 3-4. *The compass rose on a chart shows true directions on its outer circle and magnetic directions on its inner circles. In this example, magnetic north is west of true north—the variation is 14° west. To avoid having to apply variation, use the inner circle to measure magnetic directions.*

There is little reason to measure directions with respect to true north when using a magnetic or flux-gate compass. Electronic aids to navigation receivers usually show magnetic directions; don't reset them to show true directions unless your boat has a gyrocompass.

Directions measured using a compass are called, logically enough, *compass* bearings, headings, and courses. They are seldom identical with magnetic directions; the boat's own magnetism causes the compass to point slightly east or west of magnetic north. This error—the angle between magnetic north and compass north—is called **deviation**, and it changes as the boat heads in different directions.

Checking the compass. Every boat skipper can, and should, check the compass for deviation. The easiest and most accurate way to check is to use a range of two aids to navigation marking the centerline of a channel. Find the magnetic bearing of the range line, using parallel rules and the inner compass rose on the chart. Then maneuver the boat until the front and rear range dayboards are in line and the boat is pointed directly toward them. This isn't as easily done as said; it's hard to hold a boat exactly on course, and the compass swings more than the boat. Try to hold a reasonably steady heading and watch the compass for a little while to get an average reading.

Except for boats with the steering station on the centerline, it isn't easy to see exactly where the boat is pointing. If you point the bow at an object from a starboard steering position, the boat is pointed well to the right of the object. You may find it handy to put a small mark on the rail the same distance off center as the helm.

For example, you're entering Beaufort Inlet, North Carolina. The entrance range marks a line 020° magnetic (see Figure 3-6). Coming in the channel, get

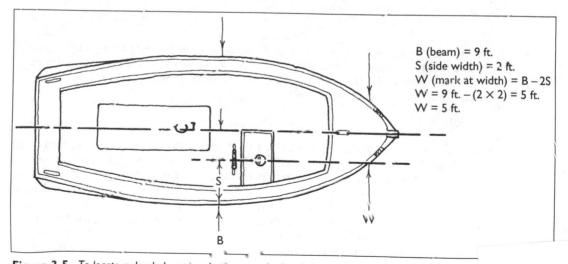

B (beam) = 9 ft.
S (side width) = 2 ft.
W (mark at width) = B – 2S
W = 9 ft. – (2 × 2) = 5 ft.
W = 5 ft.

Figure 3-5. *To locate a dead-ahead mark, measure the boat's beam at the steering station and subtract twice the distance from the wheel to the outside of the rail. Place a mark on the rail where the beam is equal to this distance.*

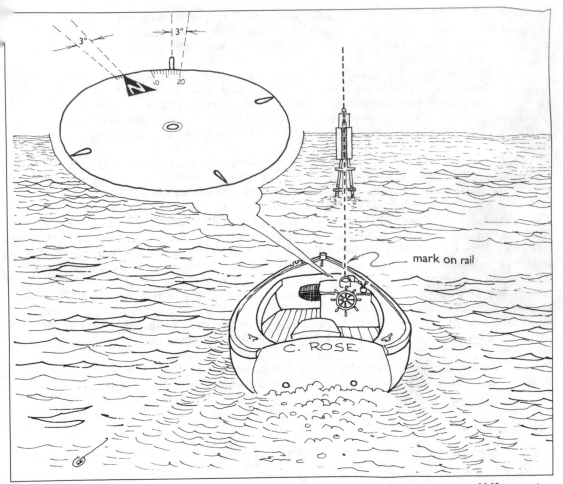

Figure 3-6. *Checking the compass on a range. The lights are in line (in range) bearing 020° magnetic. The boat is on the range line when the lights are in range and the boat is headed directly toward them. The compass heading is 017°M, which is 3° too low. The deviation on this heading is 3° easterly since compass north is to the east of magnetic north.*

right on the range line, align the boat's centerline with the range line, and read the compass. Suppose it shows 017°. That's 3° too low. In this case the boat's magnetism has caused compass north to be 3° to the right (east) of magnetic north; this is the easterly deviation. If, on the other hand, the compass had read 023° (3° too high), the deviation would have been 3° westerly.

As a boat changes heading, the deviation changes. Deviation might be zero at north, 2° easterly at 045°, and so on.

Reducing deviation. Large deviations make navigation by compass difficult; if you find your compass has large deviations, 5° or 10°, you should take steps to reduce it. Here are a few suggestions:

Where is your compass mounted? Ideally it should be on the boat's centerline.

This is commonplace on sailboats but rare on power-boats other than center-console boats. The compass must be aligned parallel to the boat's centerline and well removed from any magnetic materials.

My lobsterboat illustrates a common problem. The previous owner put a handy stowage basket high on the bulkhead of the compartment just below the compass. The basket was plastic-covered steel wire and raised hob with the compass; I had to remove it. Look underneath for wires or steel fittings. Wires shouldn't pass near the compass, but if they must, they should be twisted.

The compass must be aligned parallel to the boat's center-line and well removed from any magnetic materials.

Radio speakers and earphones, which have strong magnets, cause the most trouble. Put a Walkman by a compass, and there's no telling where it will point. Install cockpit speakers if you want to provoke huge compass errors.

After eliminating these obvious troublemakers, you should adjust the compass to remove deviation errors associated with the boat. I have found that adjusting a compass *off the boat* to remove all error is a valuable step in reducing deviation. On fiberglass boats, further adjustment often is unnecessary. When adjustment is needed, you have a good starting point.

Most compasses have adjusting screws. The one on the side is for adjustments when the boat is headed north or south (magnetic), and the one on the back is for adjustments when the boat is headed east or west. Take the compass ashore, to an area free of any iron or steel objects, and remove all the effect of the adjusting screws by turning the slots horizontal. Sight across the center pin to a distant object. If all adjustment has been removed, the bearing to the object will not change when you twist the compass in any direction.

After you re-install the compass, if you find differences of more than a few degrees between the compass and the correct magnetic courses, it needs adjustment. Do it yourself or, if the process (see page 48) seems too confusing, consider hiring a compass adjuster. It can be money well spent since the adjustment commonly makes the deviations so small they can be ignored.

After adjusting a compass, it is important to find the remaining deviations on various headings, say every 30°, and to make a **deviation table** showing their values and direction. There's no one right way to make a deviation table. A table usually lists magnetic courses and deviations east or west. However, you might find it less confusing to list the actual compass headings for various magnetic headings (along with the deviations)—like this:

M	C	DEV
000°	000°	0°
030°	032°	2°W
060°	063°	3°W
090°	090°	0°
120°	118°	2°E
150°	147°	3°E

Allowing for deviation. If the compass has more than a degree or two of deviation after adjustment, you should allow for it. This is simple in principle but confusing in practice. In our example, the compass heading was 3° too low; to correct it to the magnetic heading, we must add 3°. Because the compass north points 3° to the right (east) of magnetic north, this is easterly deviation.

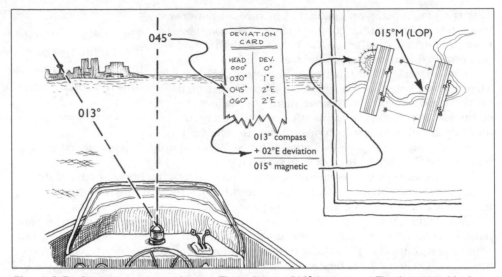

Figure 3-7. *Correcting a compass bearing. The tank bears 013° by compass. The deviation table shows that the compass has 2° easterly deviation when the boat is heading 045°. Correct the compass bearing to magnetic; remember the rule "correcting, add easterly"—013°C + 2°E = 015°M. Plot the magnetic bearing, 015°, using the inner compass rose for reference.*

We have a similar problem when we use compass bearings to plot a fix. The chart's inner compass rose shows *magnetic* bearings, but we read the bearing by *compass*. When heading 045° by compass, let's say our boat has an easterly deviation of 2°; that is, when the compass reads 045°, the boat is actually heading 047° magnetic. If we take a bearing to a tank by sighting over the compass, we must correct it to a magnetic bearing to plot it on the chart. While the boat is heading 045°, all compass bearings are 2° too low. Suppose the tank bears 013° by compass. Correct this to a magnetic bearing by adding 2°—and the bearing to the tank is 015°M. When starting with a compass direction, the rule is "**correcting, add easterly**"—correct compass headings or bearings to magnetic by adding easterly deviation.

More often you will have found a magnetic course and must apply the deviation to determine the compass course. This is the opposite of going from compass to chart. We plot a line between two points on a chart and determine its magnetic direction using the inner compass rose, or we use a navigation receiver to find the magnetic direction to a waypoint; in either case, we need the compass direction rather than the magnetic direction. It is the opposite of correcting. If we want to steer a course of 050° on our imaginary boat, we must *subtract* the 2° easterly deviation. The compass course will be 048°, which reflects the fact that it is 2° too low on northeast headings.

Since removing the deviation error from compass directions to find magnetic is called *correcting*, finding compass directions from magnetic is called *uncorrecting*. The rule "correcting, add easterly" remains true if we restate it reversing the meaning of any two words. So we can say "**uncorrecting, subtract easterly.**" Remember the word "USE" to remember this.

Easterly Deviation (compass reads too low)

How to apply deviation	Term	Operation	Mnemonic
COMPASS ———▶ MAGNETIC	Correcting	Add	CAE
COMPASS ◀——— MAGNETIC	Uncorrecting	Subtract	USE

So far we have concentrated on easterly deviations. On some headings, compass north points west of magnetic north—westerly deviation. The compass heading is higher than the magnetic heading. Suppose the boat is lined up on a range that marks a line bearing 305° magnetic, and the compass reads 307°. The deviation is 2°, and since the compass reading is too high, compass north is to the left, or west, of magnetic north, so the deviation is westerly.

When you're correcting a compass heading or bearing to magnetic, subtract westerly deviations. The little reminder still holds true with two meaning reversals—"**correcting, subtract westerly.**" If, on the other hand, you have plotted a course of 308° magnetic and need to find the course to steer, you add 2° to

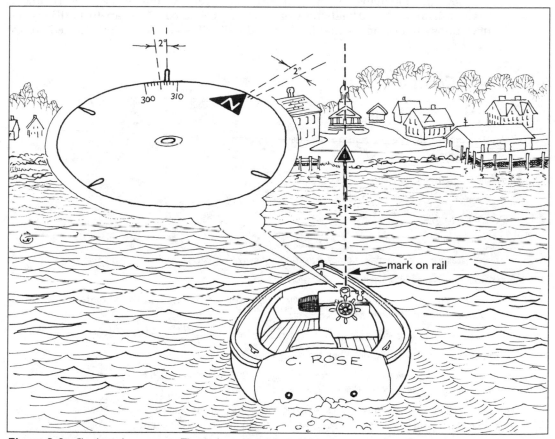

Figure 3-8. *Checking the compass. The daybeacon and the cupola are in range on a magnetic bearing of 305°. They are in range, the boat is heading directly toward them, and the compass heading is 307°— 2° too high, a westerly deviation.*

"uncorrect" the course to 310°. The reminder is now **"uncorrecting, add westerly."** Remember this by the mnemonic "United Auto Workers."

Westerly Deviation (compass reads too high)

How to apply deviation	Term	Operation	Mnemonic
COMPASS ⟶ MAGNETIC	Correcting	Subtract	CSW
COMPASS ⟵ MAGNETIC	Uncorrecting	Add	UAW

We haven't discussed true directions, since it's so easy to use magnetic directions. If you chose to measure true courses from the chart, you first must apply variation to uncorrect them to magnetic courses, then further uncorrect them to compass courses. I find it's better to skip true courses and bearings altogether and use the magnetic compass rose. Better still, adjust the compass so that it doesn't have any significant deviation, and you won't have to worry about any of this. Compass and magnetic courses will be identical. If you skip adjusting the compass and don't apply deviation, you will have a lousy direction reference; it will make all of your navigation harder.

New metallic items you bring aboard will affect the compass, and every one of them will make the deviations worse. On a recent trip I began to find varying deviations on a compass that had seemed well adjusted. The culprit turned out to

Adjusting a Compass

Basic steps:

1. Take the compass ashore and remove all deviation adjustment.

2. Reinstall the compass.

3. Head boat north magnetic:

   a) by range

   b) by distant object

   c) by sun azimuth

   Turn side adjusting screw to make compass read 000° exactly (use a non-magnetic screwdriver).

4. Head boat south magnetic. Remove half the error with side screw.

5. Head boat north magnetic again. Check for remaining error and remove half. Head south, remove half, etc., until N/S deviation is minimized.

6. Head boat east magnetic. Turn after adjusting screw to make compass indicate east exactly.

7. Head boat west magnetic. Remove half the error after adjusting screw.

8. Head boat east magnetic again. Check for remaining error and remove half. Head west, remove half, etc., until E/W deviation is minimized.

9. Head boat NE, SE, SW, or NW. Check error. Remove using quadrantal spheres (hollow iron spheres on either side of a compass, usually needed only on steel boats).

10. Find deviations on headings every 20° or 30° and make a deviation card.

be a neat little rolling parallel rule I was using to measure directions on the chart. Its roller was steel underneath the plating; when I put it near the compass, it changed the heading. While I was using it to check channel courses on the chart, it was changing the compass headings. Five minutes later the boat took a sharp roll, and the rule fell to the deck and smashed—no real loss.

Spiral-bound notepads, mechanical pencils, keys, knives, and drink cans will cause similar problems. Check your plotting instruments for magnetism by bringing them near the compass when the boat is moored. If they're magnetic, the compass will swing.

> *It's better to skip true courses and bearings altogether and use the magnetic compass rose. Better still, adjust the compass so that compass and magnetic courses will be identical.*

Make a practice of checking the compass regularly. You won't get exact readings due to imperfect steering, the swinging compass card, and the difficulty of telling when the range is precisely dead ahead, but the compass shouldn't be more than a couple of degrees off. If there isn't a range, you can do a fair job using a long, straight channel marked by lights or daybeacons. Get in the center of the channel, guided by the perspective of the lights and daybeacons, and read the compass when the boat appears to be pointing directly along the channel.

It is also handy to find a natural range such as a flagpole in the foreground and a tank beyond. For example, in Portland, Maine, the coxswains of our Coast Guard boats would bring Diamond Island Shoal Light 6 and the left edge of Little Diamond Island in range, dead ahead. In this case the compass heading should have agreed with the magnetic bearing 078°; if it didn't, they had a warning. They also used Spring Point Light in range with Portland Head Light, and knew that the bearing should be 175°M.

Bad Compass, Good Course

If a compass hasn't been adjusted, or if you're not sure of its deviation errors, you may think it's useless. That isn't necessarily true; if the compass is otherwise in good condition, it can be usable. The secret lies in compensating for deviations—even when their values are unknown.

Years ago I went salmon fishing near the Columbia River with a man who owned a 26-foot inboard cruiser. We caught a few salmon offshore, fishing most of the flood tide, then headed in. Just outside the jetties, he said, "I'm sure glad we don't have fog. I'm not too sure about this compass, and besides, I might get confused about deviation and variation."

We were headed right up the entrance channel. I said, "You know, the compass will read the same in the fog as it does right now. If you check the course with your compass, you won't get confused about the corrections."

It was as if the lightbulb lit. He grabbed his chart, checked the compass reading carefully, and wrote it beside the channel. As we headed up each leg of the channel, he wrote the compass course beside the channel. By the time we approached the boat basin, he had a complete set of compass courses for entering the river on flood tide.

Using a compass in this way may seem amateurish, but it is the most accurate way to use it. Navigation experts call this use of an instrument the **repeatable mode**, and it compensates for many ills. When you return to the same read-

A cross-channel current sets a boat to the side, and you must compensate for it. It is best to find courses on both ebb and flood currents.

ing using the same instrument, whether it is a compass or a GPS receiver, you compensate for its error. Put more simply, you're heading in the same direction when your compass reads the same course as it did before. It is only amateurish not to know the courses to steer. Following known courses is quite professional; ship pilots do it all the time.

You must be aware of the current when following compass courses. A cross-channel current sets a boat to the side, and you must compensate for it. It is best to find courses on both ebb and flood currents if there is a significant set.

Most good navigators check their compasses routinely as they run the channel, comparing the compass with courses they remember or have written on the chart. Someone unsure about a compass had better check, too. You'll be unsure of the compass on a delivery trip, a charter, or aboard a friend's boat; these are good occasions to check it.

In the early days of offshore powerboat racing—in near-stock boats—many a racer on the way to Bimini grabbed a compass check in Government Cut on the way out of Miami. The course along Dodge Island is 104°M and the direct course to Bimini is 094°M. A compass a few degrees off in the channel would have about the same deviation on the course to Bimini. They threw in a correction for current and roared on.

It is preferable to have a well-adjusted compass and a recent deviation card. But whether or not you do, check the compass by comparing it with previous readings along the channel. Any change is an alarm signal.

Depthfinders

I consider a depthfinder essential to navigation. They are so useful—and so inexpensive—that even a skiff deserves one (as well as a compass). Without a depthfinder, you can tell little about what lies beneath the water's surface. Except in shallow, clear water, you can't see the bottom, and you can't tell how deep it is without lowering a weight or, in shallow areas, using a pole. A depthfinder constantly answers the question, "How deep is it?" That continuous display of depth is extremely valuable.

First, a depthfinder alerts you to the danger of going aground—the most frequent boating mishap. Second, when you look at the chart, you often see that the boat lies along a specific depth contour. In Figure 3-9 the depthfinder indicates the boat is in 30 feet of water. The boat must be somewhere along the 30-foot depth contour. The contour is a line of position (LOP) even though it's curved. You can tell its direction and its distance offshore by looking at the chart. It is handy to find your way by depth contours, but it doesn't work everywhere. Over a rough bottom there may be dozens of humps and hollows, and you can't tell which one the boat is over.

Depthfinders are particularly useful in dredged channels such as the Intracoastal Waterway. The channel is 12 feet deep over much of the Waterway. Keeping to the right side of the channel, as you should, it is easy to edge into shallow water. When the depthfinder shows 8 feet, you know you've gone too far to the right; steer more to the left and the depth will increase. Using a depthfinder sure beats the alternate method of finding out that you're straying out of a dredged channel—bumping bottom.

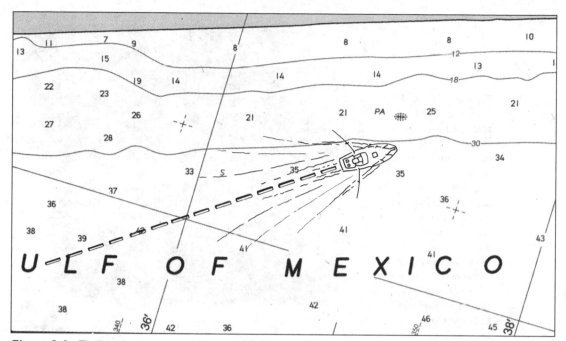

Figure 3-9. *The boat heads in toward shore until the depth is 30 feet. The boat will then be somewhere along the 30-foot depth contour, which will be a line of position (LOP).*

Types of Depthfinders

Depthfinders send pulses of high-frequency sound waves from a transducer into the water. The bottom reflects the sound pulses and the transducer receives them—the way you hear an echo. Sound waves in water travel about 4,800 feet per second, and the depthfinder measures the time interval for the round trip to determine the water depth.

The Submarine Signal Company (later Raytheon) introduced the first acoustic depthfinder, called the *Fathometer*, in the 1930s. Within a few years depthfinders were installed on most ships. This was the biggest advance in navigation equipment since the invention of the chronometer in the nineteenth century, but boatowners continued to measure depth with leadlines (see "Leadlines: Crude but Reliable" on page 55) and marked poles. In 1957 the Lowrance company produced the first practical boat depthfinders, popularly called flashers. This started a true revolution in boat navigation.

Flasher depthfinders have a rotating indicator lamp that lights to indicate the depth. The most common units rotate at 2,400 rpm and show depths to 60 feet, but there are many variations. Flasher depthfinders are easy to interpret; the brightness of the flash indicates the correct gain setting, and its width and stability give clues to the type of bottom. In addition, flashers are easy to read. If the flash is at the right side of the dial, at 3 o'clock so to speak, the depth is one-fourth of 60, or 15 feet. You seldom have to know the exact depth, so you can glance at the dial and make an estimate.

Digital depthfinders came next. Hailed as a great advance, they use electronic timing to calculate the depth, and display it as digits. More accuracy is

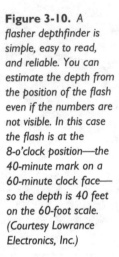

Figure 3-10. *A flasher depthfinder is simple, easy to read, and reliable. You can estimate the depth from the position of the flash even if the numbers are not visible. In this case the flash is at the 8-o'clock position—the 40-minute mark on a 60-minute clock face—so the depth is 40 feet on the 60-foot scale. (Courtesy Lowrance Electronics, Inc.)*

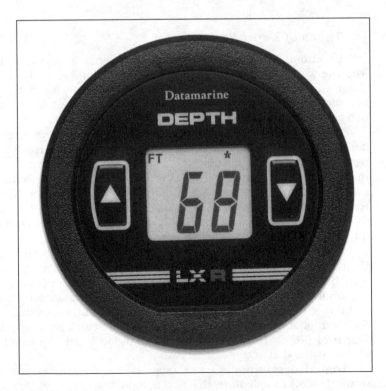

Figure 3-11. *Digital depthfinders show present depth quite accurately, but the digits change rapidly when the boat is in a seaway. They don't show depth history. (Courtesy Datamarine International, Inc.)*

always better, right? In fact, digital units have some drawbacks. The digits bounce around rapidly as the boat rises and falls with the waves, forcing you to concentrate instead of just glancing at the dial. A digital unit can't show intermediate echoes from fish, or indicate how well the gain is set. If the gain is set a bit too high, you may see shallow depths interrupted by deeper ones. Since depthfinders sometimes read a "phantom" shallow bottom, and sometimes another at twice the depth, you are left to ponder which depth is real.

I remember a sailboat race in Chesapeake Bay aboard a 40-foot yawl whose owner had just installed a digital depthfinder. Over near the eastern side of the bay, where the water is shallow, the reading jumped between 8 feet and 4 feet, and the numbers flickered rapidly. I longed for the old flasher unit, which was easy to adjust for correct gain and steady readings. Other people prefer digital depthfinders; in fairness, modern ones are quite good.

Paper-chart recorders, depthfinders that mark the depth on a roll of paper fed from one spool to another, next became popular aboard boats. Not only do they show the depth, they show the history of the depth—a big improvement over an instantaneous reading. A depth of 10 feet that is steady is a different matter from a 10-foot depth that has risen rapidly from 35 feet (see Figure 3-12). In addition, when a boat is riding up and down in a seaway, the bottom echo forms a wavy trace on a chart, or *graph*, recorder, and changes in depth are easier to see.

Paper-chart recorders show details that were never before visible. Baitfish appear as many tiny dots, larger fish as bigger "grains," and large ones as individual "boomerang" traces. You can see fish just off the bottom with the better units. But as good as they are, they have mechanical reels to move the paper and an electrical stylus that flies down the paper to mark it. The paper is expensive, subject to moisture damage, and hard to change underway. A broken stylus puts the recorder out of business and the skipper into a frantic search for a spare, or at least for leader wire of the right diameter.

Next, **liquid-crystal-chart** (or *graph*) **depthfinders** became available. These show the same type of information as paper-chart recorders, in less detail but without any moving parts—well, they do have knobs and switches. Most are easy to read in sunlight, and some units are nearly waterproof. Simple to use and

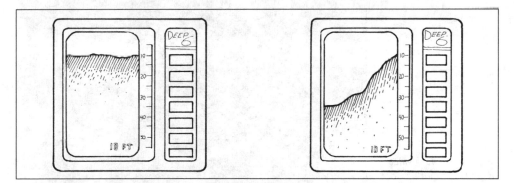

Figure 3-12. *Paper-chart, liquid-crystal, and video-graph recorders show a history of depth readings in addition to the present reading. A steady depth of 10 feet, for example, is quite different from a 10-foot depth that has risen quickly from 35 feet.*

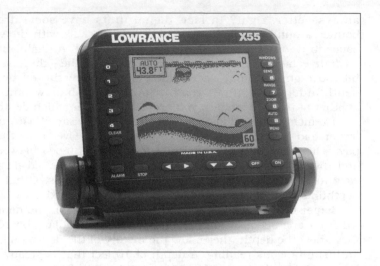

Figure 3-13. *A liquid-crystal graph depth-finder. The present depth is displayed at the right of the screen, along with a digital readout. Previous depths are also displayed as the graph moves to the left. The "boomerangs" are large fish. (Courtesy Lowrance Electronics, Inc.)*

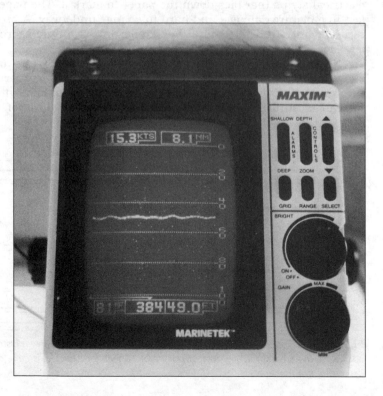

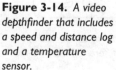

Figure 3-14. *A video depthfinder that includes a speed and distance log and a temperature sensor.*

showing an excellent history of the depth, they are perhaps the best choice for navigation. Many models offer speed and temperature sensors; the speed indicator answers the need for a log, and the temperature reading is useful to fishermen. Some also feature built-in GPS and plotter screens.

Liquid-crystal-graph depthfinders are perhaps the best choice for navigation.

During the past few years, video depthfinders have become popular. Fishermen like the excellent detail shown by monochrome or color video depthfinders and pay high prices for them. Similar in operation and features to liquid-crystal-chart depthfinders, video units are larger and use more electrical power. They are harder to read in sunlight and can interfere with other electronics, especially Loran-C receivers.

A video depthfinder is more than you need for navigation; the extra detail is unimportant. I have a video depthfinder aboard my larger boat, but I do quite a bit of fishing. The liquid-crystal unit on the 20-foot outboard boat does everything needed for navigation, and it isn't bad for fishing, either.

Depth Corrections

A depthfinder displays the depth from the transducer to the bottom, and since the transducer is usually a foot or two below the water surface, the water depth is greater than the displayed depth.

Not only do you have to add the depth of the transducer below the waterline to find the actual depth, you also have to subtract the height of the tide above the

Leadlines: Crude but Reliable

Prior to electronic depthfinders, a **leadline** was standard equipment aboard boats and ships. It is slow, intermittent, and awkward, but reliable and accurate. A leadline consists of a lead weight attached to a marked line. Ship leadlines were marked with various rags, leathers, and so on at 1-fathom intervals, although some fathoms weren't marked. The ones without marks were called *deeps*; for example, the *deep six*. A boat leadline is better marked in feet, with stripes or small whippings every foot and an additional wide stripe or whipping beginning at 5 feet and another at 10.

Leadlines are handy for scouting out anchorages in the dinghy and for finding the best way out if you go aground. A depthfinder mounted on a boat doesn't show any depth change as long as the boat stays aground. The water level does change with the tide, and it's important to have a way to measure the changes.

Some people mark the anchor line with tags or whippings at specific intervals. It's a practical way to measure the distance from the bow to the bottom as you lower the anchor, and to measure the amount of anchor line for the desired scope.

For routine operation in shallow water, a "Chincoteague Compass" is just the thing. This is a pole about 10 feet long and marked every foot. It's easier to use than a leadline, and you can push with it, too. A pole is more appropriate for a small boat while a leadline is better for a large one.

chart datum to compare the depthfinder reading with the charted depth. This is important in some parts of the country, insignificant in others.

Suppose you're off the Georgia coast, near Tybee Island. The tide has a range of about 8 feet. You note that the depth is 30 feet by your depthfinder. It is about the time of high tide. What is the charted depth?

Depthfinder reading	30 ft.
Transducer to waterline	2 ft.
Actual depth	32 ft.
Height of tide	8 ft.
Depth at chart datum	24 ft.

Your boat is not right on the 5-fathom (30-foot) curve; it is closer inshore. This could be important.

Further south, past Daytona Beach, the tidal range is less than 2 feet, and you can ignore tide corrections offshore. In shallow areas you always have to watch the tide.

There is another complication: the transducer is rarely mounted at the lowest part of the boat. The bottom of the keel or the propeller extends below the transducer. The boat may be aground when the depthfinder reads 2 feet.

Adjust the depthfinder to make the outgoing pulse start at zero on the depth scale. (*Note:* You can adjust some depthfinders to allow for the transducer or keel depth. You can make these depthfinders show (1) the depth at the transducer, or (2) the depth below the keel, or (3) the true depth from the water's surface. It's a matter of choice as to which zero you use.)

As much as we are accustomed to regarding depthfinder readings as accurate, that is a simplification. Sound travels faster in warm water than in cold, but

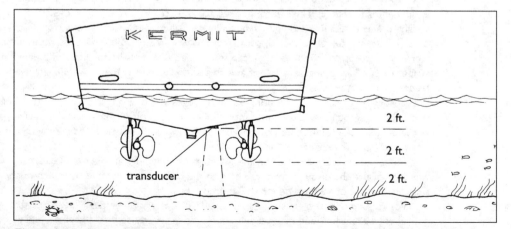

Figure 3-15. *The depthfinder reads 4 feet, but since the transducer is 2 feet below the waterline, the water depth is actually 6 feet. The wheels are 2 feet deeper than the transducer, so bottom clearance is only 2 feet.*

ordinary depthfinders have no way to compensate for sound velocity changes. Their readings assume a fixed speed of sound in water, and thus have small errors. There are several other corrections for accurate survey work, but most boatowners ignore them.

Choosing a Depthfinder

Depthfinders present a wide variety of types and features. A few people still prefer flasher units, but flasher, digital, and *analog* (showing the depth with a needle) depthfinders are limited to instantaneous readings. A depthfinder that provides a graph display is a better choice for navigation.

Most depthfinders operate at frequencies from 50 to 200 kHz, well above the range of hearing. High frequencies are best for showing detail at shallow depths, and low frequencies are best for deepwater use. The depthfinder frequency and the transducer dimensions control the beam width. A narrow beam is most effective for deep water, but a wide beam is especially good for a sailboat operating in relatively shallow water. Some depthfinders let you switch between two frequencies in the same unit.

It is an advantage to get a speed log for a depthfinder. I prefer one that logs distance as well, and most speed logs do. Get a temperature indicator as well, if you like to fish. A number of graph-type depthfinders incorporate a plotter coupled with a GPS receiver, to show a graphic presentation of the boat's path.

All except the simplest depthfinders have several depth scales. Many also have a *zoom* feature to show a portion of the depth across the full height of the display. Depthfinders suitable for deepwater operation are necessarily more powerful and use more power than those for depths up to a couple of hundred feet. Deepwater units operate at lower frequency, require larger transducers, don't show as much detail, and in some cases are unnecessary. A friend fishing with me asked how deep the LCD-graph depthfinder on my 20-foot open outboard could read. When I told him down to 120 feet, he said, "Is that all?"

"Do you have any idea," I replied, "how far offshore you have to go from Bogue Inlet to get to 100 feet of water? It's a lot farther than I'll ever go in this boat."

If you operate a boat in an area such as the eastern Gulf of Mexico, where you have to run 60 miles offshore to reach 20 fathoms, it doesn't make much sense to pop for a 100-fathom depthfinder. But if you run out of Fort Lauderdale or Miami, the 100-fathom curve is less than 5 miles offshore. When choosing a depthfinder, consider the depths in the areas where you plan to operate your boat.

Navigating in shallow bays, sounds, or channels is easiest if the depthfinder has a 0-to-15 or 0-to-20–foot scale. It's easier to see small changes on a shallow scale. Sometimes you can use the zoom feature to get an excellent scale for shallow water: 0 to 10 or 0 to 20 feet. Many depthfinders have shallow-water alarms you can set to any depth.

Many depthfinders allow you to switch the units of measurement between feet and fathoms, and some also show the depths in meters. It is an advantage to be able to show depths in the same units the local chart uses. As U.S. charts change to metric depths, depthfinders that can show depths in meters will be especially convenient for navigation.

Unless you get a very simple depthfinder, plan to spend some time learning how to use it. Check the manual to learn how to set the gain and interpret the display. As depthfinders become more complex, learning all their features takes longer. A color video depthfinder with zoom, split screen, bottom lock, a plotter, and other bells and whistles takes time to learn to use, and it will be easy to forget some features from one trip to the next. Today it's important to match the capabilities of the depthfinder to your needs. Excess capability means more time working with the depthfinder and less time simply enjoying your boat trip.

Speed and Distance Logs

A log indicates the boat's speed through the water, the distance traveled, or both. This information is important to navigation. Many planing boats have a speed log with a pressure-sensing probe at the stern; the better ones are good at high speed. Paddle-wheel logs, properly installed and calibrated, can be quite accurate at low as well as high speeds.

A log is essential for a sailboat, and a distance log, once called a "totalizer," is as important as a speed indicator. Unless your sailboat has a distance log, you have to calculate distance from speed estimates. A sailboat's speed varies, so it is difficult to make an accurate estimate of the average speed. A distance log overcomes this difficulty.

Every boat engine (except small outboards) should have a tachometer; it's impossible to set engine speed accurately without one. For that matter, a tachometer is necessary to determine if the propeller is correct for the boat and load. You should find the speed corresponding to various engine rpm, but that speed varies somewhat. Maybe your boat normally makes 18 knots at 2,200 rpm, but in a chop the log shows that the speed is only 16.2 knots. A boat kept in the water loses speed due to fouling, and owners also lug more and more gear aboard as the season goes on, slowing the boat noticeably.

In a period of four months in salt water, my lobsterboat's speed at cruising rpm dropped from 15 to 13 knots. Relying on rpm to determine speed would have been misleading, but the log showed the speed loss; so did speed calculations

Figure 3-16. *Paddle-wheel logs can give accurate information at low speed or high. This one can be switched to show speed or distance. (Courtesy Datamarine International, Inc.)*

based on time and distance. Most of the speed loss was due to barnacles on the propeller; when I went overboard and scraped them off, the speed came up to 14.5 knots at the same rpm.

Every boat engine (except small outboards) should have a tachometer; it's impossible to set engine speed accurately without one.

You may get a log as a separate instrument or as part of a depthfinder. Some logs can be calibrated to measured boat speed. Two of my boats have depth-finders with paddle-wheel logs. Neither is adjustable. One is always within ½ knot of the correct speed. The other, with a transom mount, is supposed to read MPH but is closer to the correct speed in knots. Others I've used weren't as good, so a log that can be calibrated to match the actual speed offers an advantage.

You can remove a through-hull paddle wheel for cleaning. The big holes they fit in—about 2 inches in diameter—are a potentially severe flooding hazard, but I haven't heard of a casualty with one. A blank plug is supplied; take out a pin, remove the paddle-wheel unit, and frantically shove the plug into the stream of in-rushing water. Replace the sensor unit with the blank plug when the boat is moored since barnacles will grow on the paddle wheel within a week and hurt its accuracy. I've seen barnacles grow big enough in just two weeks to keep a paddle wheel from turning.

Many speed logs have digital readings, and they work well. The digits don't jump around as fast as the ones on digital depthfinders. Distance logs are digital, like the odometer of a car. Besides being especially valuable aboard sailboats, they make navigating long legs of a route easier on any boat.

Read or zero the distance log at the beginning of the leg, and you will have a good check on the distance run. When you arrive, the log distance differs slightly from the charted distance due to inaccuracy or to current. Suppose the chart (or a navigation receiver) shows 15.4 miles between two waypoints, yet the log indicates 16.8 miles. Dividing 16.8 by 15.4 yields 1.09 miles. If the next leg is 12 miles on the chart, expect the log to show 1.09 × 12, or 13.1 miles. This simple proportion is an easy way to predict the distance shown by the log, providing the current stays the same.

Note: To check the accuracy of a log or to find the speed made good at constant rpm, refer to the section on time, speed, and distance calculations on pages 113–117 in Chapter 5.

Nearly everyone with a new GPS receiver gets the bright idea to use the *speed-made-good* function as a log. While a log shows speed through the water, a navigation receiver shows speed over the ground. Unfortunately, inaccuracies due to signal fluctuations and averaging times make the displayed speed inaccurate. There are phantom speed variations, even with the boat moored. Some receivers average the speed over a period of time to gain accuracy, but give incorrect readings after speed changes. Chapter 6 includes an excellent way to calculate *accurate* speed over the ground with a navigation receiver.

Time

You need a good timepiece, but it need not be an expensive one. I use a digital wristwatch with a stopwatch feature. Near the helm station, my boat also has a dirt-cheap digital clock that doesn't show seconds unless you push a button, but it's there and it's useful. Most of the time it's close enough to know that the time is 10:34; the fact that it's 10:34:14 makes little difference.

You need a stopwatch for timing speed over measured distances, and it will be valuable in fog, too. It's easier to reset a stopwatch to zero when you begin a leg of the trip than to keep track of the clock time. I won't presume to tell you which type of watch or stopwatch to buy; just get a good one with big, legible numerals that are easy to see in dim light. Put it near the compass to see if it is magnetic; some are.

Many navigation receivers have stopwatch functions. GPS also shows the time. If you can remember just which buttons to push at the moment you need them, a receiver can fill the stopwatch requirement.

Binoculars

Binoculars make it easier to see distant aids to navigation, landmarks, and other objects. Finding a distant object with binoculars takes a little practice, but it soon becomes easy. Binoculars need to be nearby in order to be useful, but stow them where spray won't get on the lenses.

Binoculars are designated by magnification and the size of the large *(objective)* lens. Seven-power binoculars with 35-mm objective lenses are designated 7 × 35. As power goes up, the field of view gets narrower and the image shakier. For a boat, seven power is about the practical maximum. All other things being equal, larger objective lenses are better than small ones.

But all things aren't equal. Large objective lenses mean large, heavy, expensive binoculars. While 7 × 50 binoculars are viewed as standard for marine use, they're not necessarily the best for boats. For ships operating regularly at night, 7 × 50 binoculars are the right choice. They're designed for use in inky darkness with young, night-adapted eyes. But oh, they get heavy. At the end of a watch, your neck feels permanently pulled forward.

If you divide the objective lens diameter (50 mm) by the power (7), you find the diameter of the *exit pupil*, the bundle of light rays striking your eyes. In this case, it's about 7 mm. Young people who have remained in total darkness for 15 minutes or so can have pupils as large as 7 mm, but 5 mm is more commonplace as we get longer in the tooth. For night use, be sure the objective lens diameter is at least five times the power. A pair of 7 × 35 binoculars has 5-mm exit pupils and is an excellent choice for boat use. An even better choice is 6 × 30, the lower power being more suited to a boat's motion. They are about half the weight of 7 × 50s. Although I've never seen this combination, 6 × 35 binoculars would be nearly ideal.

On land, 8 × 30 binoculars are popular, but they're not as good at sea. Compact 7 × 21 or 8 × 25 binoculars aren't good in low light. Wide-angle binoculars are larger and heavier than standard models, and the extra viewing angle isn't important at sea.

Most important, look for quality. Cheap binoculars are a poor imitation of good ones. Better ones have full-size prisms, little distortion, excellent coatings, and good alignment. It is important to choose binoculars that give a full field of view with glasses. Even though you don't need corrective lenses, you will wear sunglasses in the daytime.

Test alignment by placing the binoculars on a table or tripod, focused on a distant scene. Block first one side and then the other with a piece of cardboard, or simply close first one eye and then the other. If the image jumps significantly, the two sides of the binocular aren't aligned properly. Misalignment is a common problem in new binoculars as well as old ones. It leads to discomfort and headaches as your eyes try to compensate for the error. I once had to reject three out of a shipment of four 7×50s (costing more than $700 apiece) due to poor alignment. Whether they were damaged in shipment or poorly assembled, I don't know. The replacements were right on the button.

To focus binoculars, first adjust the distance between the two eyepieces by moving the two sides at the hinge. You want a clean, round field of view. The sideways figure-8 view appears only in movies; if you don't adjust binoculars to show a clean, round circle, they can't work correctly.

Next adjust the left eyepiece with the right eye closed. Pick a small object on the horizon and alter the focus to make it appear sharp. At night, focus on a star; a small, barely visible star is better than a bright one. In fact, a dim star is a good test for binocular quality. The star should shrink to a dot when in focus and not have a halo, points, or appear as a misshapen blob. On center-focus binoculars, a knob on the hinge focuses both sides, and the right side has a focusing ring on the eyepiece. Try closing and opening your left eye as you focus. Your eye tends to compensate for an out-of-focus situation, and when the object appears clear at once, the focus is correct.

Now focus the right eyepiece with its focusing ring. Don't alter the focus for the left eye. When you finish, note the settings. Then you can return the binoculars to the correct settings quickly.

You can buy *focus-free* binoculars that are less bother to adjust. Binoculars with an internal compass are also useful, but on 7×50s, a compass adds size and weight to an already large package. Be sure the "extras" in the field of view don't detract from the binoculars' primary purpose of seeing things clearly at a distance.

A Navigator's Kit

When I'm aboard someone else's boat, the owner often asks me to do some of the navigation. One fact is clear: The size and cost of a boat and the owner's navigational equipment doesn't indicate the quality of the small but vital navigation tools that will be aboard. A large yacht with Loran-C, GPS, radar, a plotter, weather fax, and a color sounder may well be outfitted with loose dividers with bent points, sloppy parallel rules, and not even a decent pencil.

Pretty much in self-defense, I made up a little kit with all of the small tools I use regularly for navigation. It's a natural for charters and deliveries. I can put it in my duffel and be sure of having the things I need regardless of the boat's equipment. When I bought a boat suitable for cruising, I put a similar kit aboard.

A navigator's kit starts with **pencils**, of all things. Unless you use good pencils, you can't draw neat lines on charts. The #2 pencils you used in school are only fit for writing; they make smudgy, wide lines, and their erasers leave red smears on a chart. Use #3 pencils, or better yet, F, H, or 2H drafting pencils. Drafting supply houses carry them (along with other items for the kit). You'll also need a pencil sharpener and a pointer, made with sandpaper fastened to a stick. (Grab an emery board in an emergency.) I avoid all this by using 0.5-mm pushbutton mechanical pencils with a metal sleeve around the lead. They don't need sharpening and make neat lines with leads as soft as HB or B. Be careful, though. Some mechanical pencils have magnetic clips that cause compass errors.

Unless you're perfect, you need an **eraser**. I use mine a lot. The best I have found is the Staedtler *Mars* eraser. A tubular plastic holder grips the eraser in a little collet, and this white eraser removes pencil marks from charts cleanly. Take the metal clip off and throw it away: it's magnetic. The rectangular version also is good and doesn't roll around.

> *Since discovering how to use a triangular engineer's scale to measure latitude and longitude, I consider it essential to my navigation kit.*

Include **dividers** to measure distances; one pair about 6 inches long and another about 8 inches long meet most needs. They should have replaceable points, and if the legs are beveled on the inside, they will be easy to open with one hand. You also can use a paper *tick strip* to measure distance.

A **plastic chart scale,** such as the Nautical Ruler by Nautac, is good for measuring distances on the chart. It's graduated in miles, and matches the most popular chart scales: 1:80,000, 1:40,000, and 1:20,000. It isn't quite as accurate as the one printed on the chart (since a chart stretches and shrinks with varying moisture content) but is excellent for quick measurements. If it has statute miles as well as nautical, tape over the ones you don't use.

I have added a triangular **engineer's scale** to my navigation kit. Since discovering how to use it to measure latitude and longitude (see Chapter 2, "Charts"), I consider it essential.

It's a good idea to carry a **draftsman's compass**, too. On a boat with radar, you need a compass to draw range (distance) arcs. Dividers and compasses in a

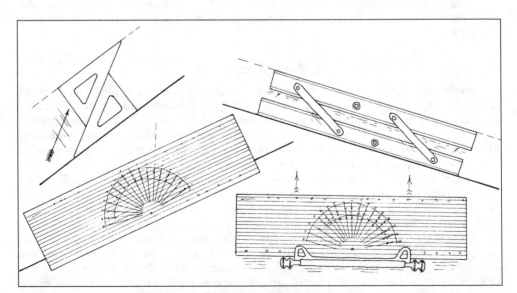

Figure 3-17. *Hinged parallel rules, the traditional tool for transferring a line across a chart while maintaining its direction, are best suited to large chart tables. So are draftsman's triangles. Roller-type rules are popular aboard boats.*

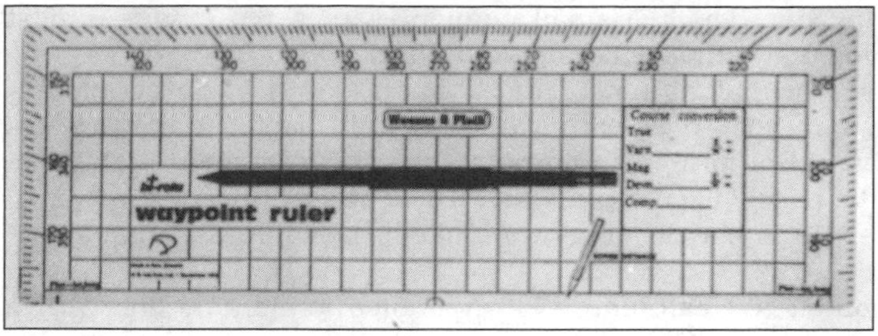

Figure 3-18. *This large protractor with parallel lines is particularly useful aboard a boat. (Courtesy Weems & Plath)*

drawer lead a rough life. If the boat has a navigation station, a little block of wood with vertical holes for pencils and dividers keeps them from harm.

You need **parallel rules** to measure courses. What kind? I usually carry a roller plotter with both a protractor and mile scales, but I have no quarrel with anyone who uses another type. It's just a matter of preference. Some people like to use two draftsman's triangles. If you use hinged parallel rules, test them for loose joints by holding them together at one end and *gently* pulling the other ends. Clear rules are preferable to opaque, regardless of type. One roller rule measures distance and angles and has a series of parallel lines. It's easy to use to find approximate courses, even in a small boat. The Weems & Plath Waypoint Ruler (Figure 3-18) has a large protractor and parallel lines; it is quite handy on a boat.

I carry a **waypoint book** of electronic navigation system waypoints. This includes GPS, DGPS, WAAS, and Loran-C waypoints, and indicates whether I measured them with a receiver or got them from some other source.

A **Loran-C plotter card** is easier to use than the Linear Interpolator printed on the chart.

I have a flat **magnifying lens** in a little case. Sometimes my reading glasses

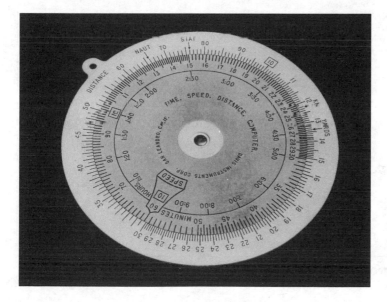

Figure 3-19. *A circular slide rule is handy for calculating time, speed, and distance problems. (Courtesy Davis Instruments)*

aren't enough for seeing fine detail. A small penlight with a red lens is almost essential; I use a surplus one with a removable red filter.

You need something for making notes, and a small loose-leaf **notebook** is a good choice. Mine is a surveyor's book with water-resistant paper. Over the years it has gained a valuable set of formulas and notes, and I can take out data from any trip by removing the pages. On a large boat with weather protection, a spiral-bound notebook works well. A plastic spiral won't affect the compass; a metal one will.

An electronic trigonometric **calculator** is my choice, preferably one with a rectangular-to-polar conversion function. I have avoided trigonometry in this book, but if you want to go further in navigation, basic trigonometry is required.

I also carry a **slide rule**, which is better than a calculator for many routine calculations. Circular slide rules are useful for time-speed-distance calculations. The Mannheim slide rule has gone the way of the dinosaur but remains more useful than a calculator for the multiplication, division, and proportion problems so common to navigation. Slide rules don't rely on batteries, and if you drench one in salt water, it isn't ruined.

A navigator needs accurate time, and I like a **stopwatch** for interval timing. A digital wrist watch with a stopwatch function works well and is always available. A **hand-bearing compass** is useful for navigation and for determining whether you're gaining or losing against another sailboat in a race.

So that's it: a simple kit of small things, most inexpensive, that make navigation easy. Of course, if I were making a long trip, I'd need a sextant, tables, a radio for time checks, and preferably a laptop computer. But for piloting, this kit works well.

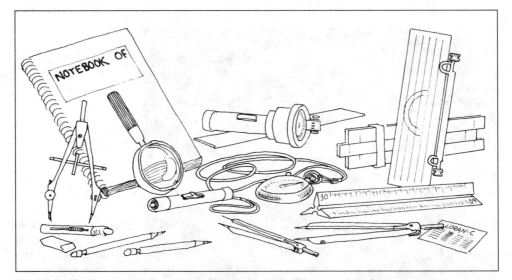

Figure 3-20. *A navigator's kit, with all of the small tools you'll use regularly for navigation, comes in handy.*

Radar

Radar, a valuable navigation device that came out of World War II, shows land, ships, and other targets in fog and clear weather alike. Radar is excellent for navigation and for collision avoidance but isn't common on small pleasure boats except in areas with lots of fog. The *Coast Pilot* has climate tables that are useful in determining how frequently fog occurs. Warm air flowing over cold water produces dense, frequent fog. Commercial boats generally have radar since they can't afford the luxury of staying in port on foggy days.

In fog, radar can mean the difference between nail-chewing anxiety and relatively easy navigation, and you will find many uses for it in clear weather as well. It has an important place on any large boat. Since the range (distance) it measures is independent of other instruments, you can get accurate lines of position from radar alone. Radar bearings depend on the compass.

Radar is an acronym for *radio detection and ranging* and, strange as it may seem, operates on the same principle as a depthfinder. A radar set has a transmitter that sends short pulses of radio waves to an antenna. The antenna focuses the radio beam somewhat like a flashlight reflector focuses a light beam, except that the radar beam is much higher than it is wide. Any object struck by the focused beam reflects the wave pulse back to the antenna, which sends the incoming signal to the set's receiver. The range to the object is determined by the time interval from transmitting to receiving the pulse of radio waves.

Radio waves travel at approximately the speed of light, or about 328 yards in a millionth of a second (microsecond). The radar set has an electronic beam that sweeps from the center of its scope to the outside edge in the time required for the pulses to travel to the maximum range and return. Return echoes appear as bright spots on the screen at distances proportional to their range from the boat. They are universally called **targets**, with no hostile implications.

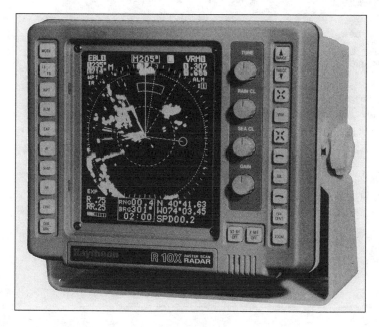

Figure 3-21. *A radar plan position indicator, or PPI scope. (Courtesy Raytheon)*

In addition to the scope beam sweeping outward 1,000 times a second or so, the beam's trace on the scope and the antenna rotate together. This makes targets appear at the correct angle and distance on the scope. The boat is at the center of the screen with the top of the scope usually representing the bow. This outward sweeping and rotation, all synchronized, paints a picture on the scope representative of the scene as viewed from above, with the boat at the center. This presentation is called the **plan position indicator** or **PPI** scope.

Few radar sets today actually sweep the beams out and around the scope; instead, they decode the information electronically and convert it to a side-to-side *raster scan* like a TV set. The appearance is essentially the same, but the method of producing it is improved. In recent years manufacturers have introduced radar units using liquid-crystal displays. While LCD screens give a coarser picture than cathode-ray tubes, they are popular. Their display units are flatter than CRTs, use less power, are easier to see in daylight, and are more water-resistant. They are particularly good aboard boats with limited mounting space near the helm.

Some radar sets can display electronic waypoints as "lollipops" on the screen, as well as present position data from a receiver and a flux-gate compass for direction sensing. When Raytheon introduced waypoint displays on the radar screen at the correct range and bearing, it was a big step in tying two systems together, making it easy to distinguish an entrance buoy from a boat, for example. Some adjustment may be needed to make the radar target and the waypoint symbol match exactly.

Radar Adjustments

Radar only performs correctly when adjusted correctly. Radar units share common control functions, but the makers give them different names. Use this as a guide, but be sure to refer to the instruction manual for your radar set.

Tuning. Every radar must be tuned for best performance. An operator can tune most radars—some are nearly automatic; others require a technician. To check tuning, choose a small target distant from the boat's usual mooring. If it doesn't appear when you turn the radar on next time, suspect trouble.

Gain. Gain adjusts the sensitivity of the radar receiver. If the gain is set too high, there will be too many false targets; too low, and the radar will miss real targets. Look at small targets at long range as you adjust the GAIN control to give frequent echoes of real targets and relatively few false (non-repetitive) echoes.

Brightness and contrast. These are practically self-explanatory, but newer radars can show targets in different intensities (or colors) depending on the strength of signal return.

Weather. The control labeled WEATHER, RAIN, CLUTTER, or FTC reduces the masking effect of squalls or rain. Ideally set, it removes most weather interference over the whole scope and leaves small targets visible.

Sea. This control is usually labeled SEA, STC, or sometimes CLUTTER. It reduces the echoes from waves, and its effect is strongest near the boat. If turned too high, it will eliminate real targets of nearby buoys or boats.

Several companies produce radar sets that can switch from PPI presentation to an electronic chart plotter. One radar/chart plotter can show the position of a selected radar target on its electronic chart. Dual presentation gets multiple use from one scope, an advantage where space is limited. The rate at which marine electronic equipment is coming to the market, it seems few boats will have enough space to mount it all.

Be careful when setting weather and clutter controls: setting them too high obscures targets.

Sea and weather conditions affect radar. Most radar units aboard boats are **X-band**. These give excellent detail on small targets and at close range but are sensitive to weather. They show squalls distinctly, which is fine if you're trying to avoid a squall but not so hot if you're trying to see a small target inside that squall. **S-band** radar sets aren't affected as much by the weather but require a longer antenna than X-band and are seldom installed aboard boats. Every radar set has controls to alleviate the noise of weather and sea conditions. Be careful when setting these controls: setting them too high obscures targets.

Installing radar aboard requires an FCC Ship Station Radio License. If your current license authorizes only a VHF-FM radio and an EPIRB, you have to get a modified license from the FCC. Some radar units can be user installed, but the FCC requires that a technician supervise the installation of many others.

Radar Measurements: Range and Bearing

Each radar has several range scales showing different maximum distances. The scale is shown at the range switch or on the screen. Short-range scales get

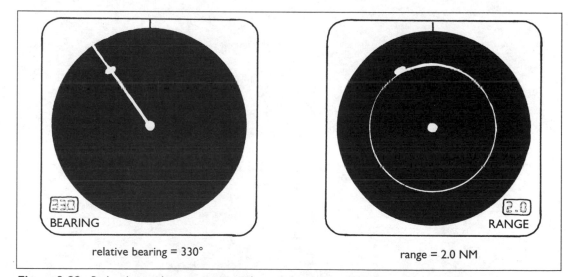

relative bearing = 330°   range = 2.0 NM

Figure 3-22. *Radars have either a cursor or an electronic bearing line (EBL) that rotates to measure bearings (left). The bow is at the top, or 000°, so the cursor measures relative bearings to targets. To measure radar range (right), adjust the VRM ring until it just touches the inner edge of a target on the scope. The digital range readout changes to match the VRM position on the scope.*

much use aboard a boat, particularly in fog. Radar functions best at moderate range on a boat due to limited antenna height. It's silly to get 48-mile radar if you operate near a low coastline that doesn't return a radar target when you're 10 miles out. On the other hand, a boat in a part of Alaska where mountains rise from the sea can use a long-range radar. To justify purchasing a long-range radar, there has to be something big enough to return an echo, and you have to be interested in it when it's far away.

Radar screens have either a **cursor** or an **electronic bearing line (EBL)** that rotates to measure bearings. Since the bow is usually at the top, or 000°, the radar measures relative bearings. You have to add the radar bearing to the boat's heading to find the compass bearing of a target. It's a good idea to compare visual and radar bearings in clear weather; radar bearings often get out of alignment with the bow.

Simple radar sets have fixed range rings on the scope—one at maximum range and usually two or three more in toward the center dot that represents your boat. Radar can measure ranges within 50 yards or so, but it's hard to accurately estimate the distance to a target using fixed range rings. To take advantage of radar's inherent distance-measuring ability, a set must have a **variable range mark**, or **VRM.** A few years ago a VRM was an expensive accessory; today it is a standard feature.

To measure range, adjust the VRM until its ring just touches the inner edge of a target. As you move the VRM to make a larger or smaller circle, the digital range read-out changes to match the ring's position on the scope. You will usually use range to plot radar fixes since radar ranges are easier to measure and more accurate than bearings.

You will find more detailed instructions for using radar for navigation and collision avoidance in Chapters 5 and 6.

CHAPTER 4

Aid-to-Navigation Systems

The Coast Guard defines an **aid to navigation** as "any device external to a vessel or aircraft intended to assist a navigator to determine position or safe course, or to warn of dangers or obstructions to navigation." Buoys, lighthouses, foghorns, and GPS are all aids to navigation. They form aid-to-navigation **systems** when combined with receivers or other aids of the same type, and with charts and plotting equipment. Onboard equipment such as compasses, depthfinders, and radar are not aids to navigation under this definition, nor are landmarks not built specifically for navigation use.

Visual Aids to Navigation

Boat operators use visual aids to navigation more frequently than other types. This section is a short description of some 40,000 U.S. Coast Guard lighthouses, minor lights, daybeacons, buoys, and sound signals (see also Chapter 2, Table 2-1). The scheme of colors and lights in coastal waters and the Great Lakes conforms to the International Association of Lighthouse Authorities *Region B* system, which is used by most nations in the Western hemisphere, and by Japan. In other areas of the world the color scheme is reversed.

We use a *lateral* system of aids to navigation, meaning aids to navigation in channels are near the *sides*. When entering a channel from seaward, leave solid red aids to navigation to starboard and green ones to port. Remember, "**red right returning**." Some channels, however, go along the coast rather than inland; for these, assume that you are "entering from seaward" when going *clockwise* around the country from Maine to Texas and from southern California north. The Coast Guard calls this the *conventional direction of buoyage*.

Visual aids to navigation show valuable, but limited, information. You must supplement this information by using charts. For example, one red buoy shows a red light flashing every 4 seconds, and another red buoy shows a red light flashing every 2.5 seconds. You can tell from the color that they should be left to starboard when entering from seaward, but to know which one is which, you have to look at the chart. Buoys can't give the depth or mark every shoal, either. You can gain additional information from a visual aid by using a compass to measure its bearing, or radar to measure its distance.

Figure 4-1. *A lighthouse has distinctive color and light characteristics. The colors usually don't indicate the side on which the lighthouse should be passed but serve to distinguish one lighthouse from another. The lights may show different colors in specific sectors. Many lighthouses have sound signals, and some include radiobeacons.*

Figure 4-2. *A minor light has specific color, shape, number, and light characteristics for identification and to indicate the side on which it should be passed.*

Figure 4-3. *A daybeacon has no light but gives the same information as a minor light. It has reflective tape and numbers for nighttime identification.*

Lighthouses are major structures that have distinctive color schemes and light-flashing sequences (*characteristics*) to avoid confusion with other lighthouses along the same stretch of coast. Many have sound signals as well. Their colors and lights don't tell you which side to pass, and they have names rather than numbers. The chart shows the name, light color and characteristic, height, and nominal range. A light must be sufficiently high to be seen above the horizon and intense enough to be seen under the prevailing conditions of visibility. The *nominal range* is the distance at which the light is readily visible in clear weather (meteorological visibility of 10 nautical miles). The Coast Guard *Light List* contains information on these subjects and on the complex flash characteristics shown by some lights.

Minor lights, or **beacons**, are smaller than lighthouses. These lighted structures have **dayboards** to make them easy to see during the day. Dayboards are usually flat plywood of significant shape and color, with numbers or letters, and retroreflective tape that reflects light from a searchlight back toward the source. Minor lights often are single-pile or multi-pile structures, but may be skeleton or masonry towers.

Daybeacons are unlighted structures with dayboards only. Daybeacons are usually single-pile structures.

Buoys may be lighted or unlighted. The shape of unlighted buoys is significant; green buoys (*cans*) are approximately cylindrical and red buoys (*nuns*) are approximately conical.

Color, Shape, Lights, and Numbers

Solid color **red** buoys and dayboards on minor lights or daybeacons are to be left to starboard when entering from seaward. The lights on red buoys and beacons are always red, usually flashing. They always have even numbers, and red dayboards are triangular, point up. Unlighted red buoys are conical; lighted red buoys are not required to be conical, and few of them are.

Solid color **green** (formerly black) buoys and dayboards on minor lights or daybeacons are to be left to port entering a channel from seaward. The lights are always green, usually flashing. They always have odd numbers and present a square outline. Unlighted green buoys are cylindrical; lighted green buoys are not required to be cylindrical, and few of them are.

The chart indicates the characteristic of flashing lights: FL G 4s means flashing green every 4 seconds. Lights designated as quick-flashing (Q on the chart)—about one flash per second—are used at sharp turns or other places where caution is required. Most lights are off in the daytime.

Some buoys and dayboards have **horizontal red and green bands.** They mark junctions or forks in channels, or wrecks or obstructions that can be passed on either side. To follow the preferred channel when entering from seaward, leave aids with a red top band to starboard and ones with a green top band to port. If lighted, the light is the same color as the top band, and they show a distinctive characteristic—two flashes, then one—shown as FL (2 + 1) on the chart. Unlighted junction buoy and dayboard shapes follow the color of the top band: if it's red, they're triangular; if it's green, they're square. They aren't numbered but usually are lettered. Horizontally banded aids to navigation can be confusing when you're heading out to sea; you can't just reverse the definitions. Check the chart carefully!

Figure 4-4. *A red nun buoy is conical and always carries an even number.*

Figure 4-5. *A green can buoy is cylindrical and always carries an odd number. Can buoys formerly were black.*

Figure 4-6. *Red-and-green horizontally banded buoys and beacons mark junctions or forks in a channel, or obstructions that may be passed on either side. This light has dayboards with a red top and a green bottom. They may have letters but not numbers.*

Figure 4-7. *Red-and-white vertically striped buoys mark safe water. They may be lettered. Lighted ones carry spherical topmarks.*

Buoys that mark **safe water**, usually the middle of a channel, are **vertically striped white and red.** Lighted ones have a red spherical topmark. The few beacons marking safe water have octagonal day-boards with red and white vertical stripes. They have letter markings and show white lights—a short flash followed by a long one. This light sequence is called Morse A and is designated Mo (A) on charts. (*CAUTION:* In the **State** (USWMS) buoyage system, red-and-white vertically striped buoys have a *completely different meaning*—it is unsafe to go between such a buoy and the nearest shore.)

Horizontally banded aids to navigation can be confusing when you're heading out to sea; you can't just reverse the definitions.

The Coast Guard has added a new class of buoys to mark "isolated dangers." There are only a handful of **isolated danger buoys,** usually to mark hazards that aren't in well-established "returning from seaward" routes. Isolated danger buoys have three bands: the top and bottom bands are black, and the middle band is red. They have two spherical black topmarks, one above the other. The lights are white and show two flashes followed by an eclipse period.

Large lighted buoys for offshore locations are built on cylindrical tanks 8 to 9 feet in diameter. Most of the tank is underwater, with a tower on the top and a long tube and counterweight on the bottom. The tower usually has a radar reflector and carries the lantern 12 to 15 feet above the water. They are large enough to be seen clearly at 2 to 3 miles in the daytime. They are visible at longer range against a sky background, but it is sometimes hard to see them at 2 miles when there is a shore behind. Their lights are usually visable at 4 to 6 miles.

The smallest lighted buoys carry their lanterns about 5 feet up and are

Figure 4-8. *This can buoy has a wider base below the cylindrical section.*

Figure 4-9. *Special marks are yellow, with yellow lights. They have letters, not numbers. Lighted buoy "C" marks a restricted area.*

harder to see, day or night. They aren't tall enough to be clear above the horizon, and where they're used, there is often a shore background. Small lighted buoys roll more than large ones, so the lantern is less likely to be vertical. Because the light is focused by a lens, you can see it at the greatest distance when the lantern is approximately vertical.

Newer green can and red nun buoys often have the cylindrical can or pointed nun sitting atop a wider "base," to provide buoyancy. The base may be the same color as the top, or it may be gray. This construction keeps the buoys from being pulled under by strong currents, and tends to keep them more nearly upright as well. Small lighted buoys, especially those used for temporary purposes, have the same wide-base construction.

Non-lateral aids to navigation, usually marking isolated islands or rocks, show four diamonds—two white and two black, green, or red—on a diamond-shaped dayboard. They indicate a place rather than the side on which you should pass. Those that are lighted have white lights.

Special marks, usually buoys, mark military exercise areas, traffic separation schemes, anchorages, and cable areas, and are used for data collection. They are yellow, carry yellow lights if lighted, and are lettered rather than numbered.

Mooring buoys are white with a blue horizontal band to distinguish them from aids to navigation.

Ranges are important aids to navigation. They are built in pairs, usually to mark the centerline of a channel. The rear range marker is higher and farther away than the front one. Range dayboards are rectangular, twice as tall as they are wide, with a central vertical stripe. Often the rear range light is *isophase*—3 seconds on and 3 seconds off—and the front range light is *quick flashing*—one flash per second. Other ranges have *fixed* (steady) lights. When range markers

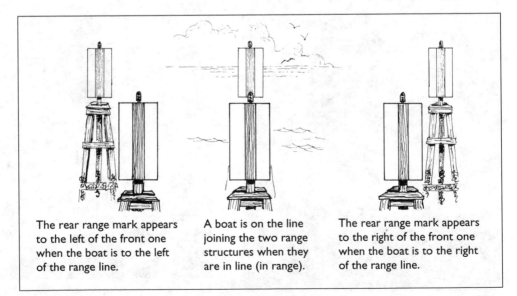

The rear range mark appears to the left of the front one when the boat is to the left of the range line.

A boat is on the line joining the two range structures when they are in line (in range).

The rear range mark appears to the right of the front one when the boat is to the right of the range line.

Figure 4-10. *Range dayboards are twice as high as they are wide, with a contrasting center stripe. The black dots are the range lanterns.*

Figure 4-11. *Range marks have rectangular dayboards with a central stripe. This one—one of a pair—is lighted.*

are lined up, or "in range," you are on the line of position they mark. If the rear range is to the right of the front range, you are to the right of the range line; if the rear range is to the left of the front range, you are to the left of the range line.

You can get an indication of how far the boat is left or right of the range line by the separation of the range dayboards or lights, but the separation angle changes as you move along the channel. At the far end the separation is small when you are at the edge of the channel, while at the near end you see a wide separation even though you are fairly close to the range line. These angles aren't consistent from one range to the next due to variations in channel and range geometry. You quickly learn how ranges you use appear at various points along a channel.

You may also see white buoys or daymarks with orange diamonds, circles, or squares. These are **information and regulatory markers**, and they indicate danger, operating restrictions, or instructions.

Offshore data collection buoys aren't aids to navigation, so they may be taken ashore for maintenance without warning. The anchored ones can be quite useful. They have red and yellow vertical stripes. Those that are free-floating have red and yellow horizontal bands.

In addition to government aids to navigation, many **private aids** are useful to the boat skipper. The most prominent of these are the flashing lights and horns on oil or gas platforms. These well-lighted platforms are shown on charts. Drilling rigs also carry prominent aids to navigation, but since they move from place to place, they aren't shown on the charts. Many small harbors have privately maintained buoys, lights, or daybeacons.

Intracoastal Waterway Aids to Navigation

The Atlantic Intracoastal Waterway begins in Norfolk, Virginia, and goes to Key West, Florida. The Gulf Intracoastal Waterway goes along portions of Florida's west coast and on to Brownsville, Texas. Intracoastal Waterway aids to navigation have **yellow markings**, and the shape of the marks on buoys and daymarks is of great importance. Since the arbitrary "entering" direction is clockwise, square yellow marks are on the ocean side and triangular yellow marks are on the land side of the waterway.

On the Intracoastal Waterway, keep yellow squares to port and yellow triangles to starboard as you go clockwise along the coast.

This is straightforward in a channel that is strictly Intracoastal Waterway: red Intracoastal Waterway aids to navigation have yellow *triangles* and are on the landward side, while green aids have yellow *squares* and are on the ocean side of the waterway.

However, where the Intracoastal Waterway coincides with another channel, a river for example, you may find yellow squares on either green or red river buoys, and yellow triangles on either color buoys as well. To follow the Intracoastal Waterway, it is vital to keep yellow squares to port and yellow triangles to starboard as you go clockwise along the coast from Norfolk to Brownsville. The little squares and triangles are hard to see until you are close aboard, so look at the chart carefully. The buoy and beacon numbers tell which system they belong to.

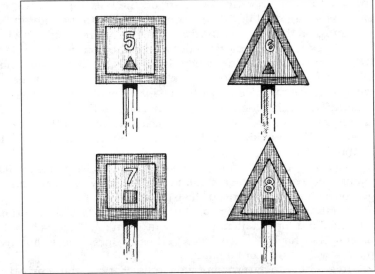

Figure 4-12. *In the Intracoastal Waterway, the shape of the small yellow mark is significant, not the shape of the buoy or daymark. Proceeding clockwise along the coast, leave yellow squares to port and yellow triangles to starboard.*

Western River and State Aids to Navigation

Western river aids. In the Mississippi–Missouri River system, the Coast Guard uses the Western River System of aids to navigation, a variation of the coastal system. The "right descending bank" has green buoys; red buoys are on the "left descending bank." In spite of the reversed terminology, you still leave red buoys to starboard and green buoys to port as you go upriver.

The buoys don't have numbers; the Coast Guard shifts them frequently to mark the changing channels, and numbers would get out of order. On shore, where the channel crosses from one side of the river to the other, there are diamond-shaped *crossing daymarks*, red or green depending on the appropriate bank. Crossing marks carry mile boards showing the number of statute miles above a reference point (such as Head of Passes on the Mississippi). Lights on green Western River aids show a single green flash. On red aids the lights are red and have a two-flash sequence—Fl (2) R on the chart.

State aids. Many states mark their internal waters using the *Uniform State Waterway Marking System (USWMS)*. State aids to navigation are similar to Coast Guard aids—red buoys are left to starboard and black or green to port going upriver. There is one important difference—a red-and-white vertically striped buoy has the opposite meaning in the two systems. The Coast Guard uses this buoy to indicate safe water, typically in mid-channel. State buoys with red and white vertical stripes indicate that it is *unsafe* to go between the buoy and the nearest shore. This can be a trap; there is a new program to change the State system.

There are two other authorized buoys in the USWMS system that have cardinal significance; that is, they indicate the compass direction for safe passage. Pass north or east of a white buoy with a black top. Pass south or west of a white buoy with a red top. The States use very few of these buoys, but you may see them.

To avoid confusion it is important to know which system is in use on the waters you use. The publication *Coast Guard Aids to Navigation* gives information on all three systems.

CR

CROSSING DAYMARK

123.5

MILE BOARD

Figure 4-13. *Western River System crossing daymark. On the Mississippi–Missouri system, places where the channel crosses from one bank to the other are marked by red or green diamond-shaped crossing daymarks and lights, and by mile boards. Distances are in statute miles above a reference point.*

Sound Signals

Most lighthouses, many large buoys, and some minor lights have sound signals. The type of sound signal is shown on the chart. The sounds of wave-actuated whistles, bells, and gongs are distinctive. Gong buoys have multiple tones, while bell buoys have one bell with several clappers. Electronic horns have replaced air horns, sirens, and diaphones—including the famous F2T two-tone (B-O) diaphones. Many horns have sensors that turn them on when it's foggy.

In my younger years I spent a fair amount of time in Long Island Sound, often out in the heavy fog so prevalent in that area. Currents are strong, hazards numerous, and sometimes the fog was so thick we could only tell we were very near one of the lights by hearing its air compressor. Near The Race, each light had a distinctive air horn. We could hear Little Gull, Race Rock, Little Dumpling, and New London Ledge, and could tell one from another by their different foghorns. It was handy, but I'd have traded that whole concert for one navigation receiver.

The audible range of a horn depends on the wind, the sea conditions, and the noise aboard your boat.

Today's electronic horns have less variety—the whole orchestra plays two or three notes. Most long-range electronic horns operate at about 300 Hz. Medium-range horns usually have 300-, 500-, or 850-Hz tones, and many small ones operate at 390 Hz. You can best learn the sound of a horn by listening to it. Although electronic horns have less variety than the old air horns, timing and tone allow you to tell one from another. The *Light List* gives the timing sequence.

The distance at which you can hear a horn varies greatly from day to day. I've heard a horn designed for a 2-mile range at more than 8 miles, and have been unable to hear the same horn at ¾ mile. The audible range depends on the wind, the sea conditions, and the noise aboard your boat. Obviously you can hear a horn from a greater distance aboard a sailboat than on a fishing boat with a turbo diesel and a dry-stack exhaust.

Wind is the critical factor. Wind is faster aloft than at the surface of the sea. Downwind of the horn, sound waves at higher altitude travel faster than those at sea level, causing them to bend downward. If the sea is flat, it reflects sound, which is again bent down. Such conditions result in sounds traveling over an extremely long range. On a day with light wind and calm seas, you may hear a sound signal two or three times as far downwind as usual.

Upwind of the horn, the upper portion of the sound wave is retarded by the wind, and the wave bends upward. Not very far upwind—maybe half the normal range or less—the sound bends so high above the sea that you can't hear it at all. A louder horn won't help; there's plenty of sound, but it's too far aloft.

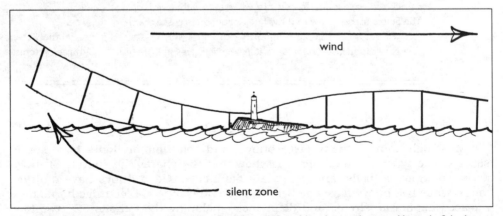

Figure 4-14. *Wind is slower at the sea surface than aloft and bends sound waves. Upwind of the horn the sound waves bend upward, making a silent zone. Downwind the sound waves bend downward; you can hear the horn at unusually long range.*

A rough sea slows the wind drastically at the surface, bending the sound waves quickly, and a rough sea doesn't reflect the sound downwind as does a calm sea. Wind and wave noises also mask the signal. The only advantage of a seaway is to make wave-actuated buoy signals louder. If the sea is flat, electronic horns can be heard at greater distances, but the wave action isn't enough to operate bell, gong, or whistle buoys.

You can't tell much from the sound intensity since it varies according to the conditions. You also can't tell the direction of the sound. A horn may be heard distinctly in one spot, while in another area closer to the horn it can't be heard at all. Beavertail Point, Rhode Island, is notorious for this effect. Wind patterns, soundwave reflections, and interference seem to be the primary causes.

Years ago radiobeacons at some light stations sent signals synchronized with the foghorn. This was called a *distance-finding station* and allowed the navigator to estimate the distance by timing the lag between hearing the radio tone and then the horn. Distance-finding stations have gone the way of the vacuum-tube portable radio.

With today's electronics it may seem strange to use sound signals, but in thick weather they remain important and welcome aids to the boat skipper. It is comforting to hear sound signals through the fog, but they are better close-range warnings than sources of position information.

The Global Positioning System and Loran-C

The **Global Positioning System (GPS)** gives a navigator information unequaled by any other system. It is the first choice in electronic aids-to-navigation systems. Yet nearly a million **Loran-C** receivers remain in use, so this book includes information on both systems. While GPS uses satellites and Loran-C uses land-based transmitters, both systems provide exactly the same information to a navigator: GPS and Loran-C receivers find a boat's position automatically and show the distance and direction to the destination. They display the information continuously, fair weather or foul, night or day, and they can perform many routine navigation calculations. You can use GPS anywhere in the world, and Loran-C throughout the United States and well out to sea. The performance of receivers continues to improve even as their cost declines. Do you need one? Which receiver is best for your boat?

Years ago I decided that even a small boat should have a depthfinder as well as a compass. Now that GPS receivers are so useful and so reasonably priced, I am equally convinced that one belongs aboard every sizable boat. Certainly every boat that ventures out of sight of land should have a navigation receiver. It changes boat navigation from rough approximation to accurate knowledge, and enhances traditional techniques. Once you have used one in fog, you never want to be without it. This book emphasizes what receivers do rather than how they work; however, a short description of these systems can be found in Appendixes A and B.

When you turn on a GPS or Loran-C receiver for the first time, you usually have to enter an approximate position—some also require the time—and then the receiver automatically selects the satellites or stations and calculates and displays the boat's position. The next time you turn on the receiver, it does everything. You don't have to reenter latitude and longitude unless you move the receiver several hundred miles while it is turned off. The receiver calculates a new

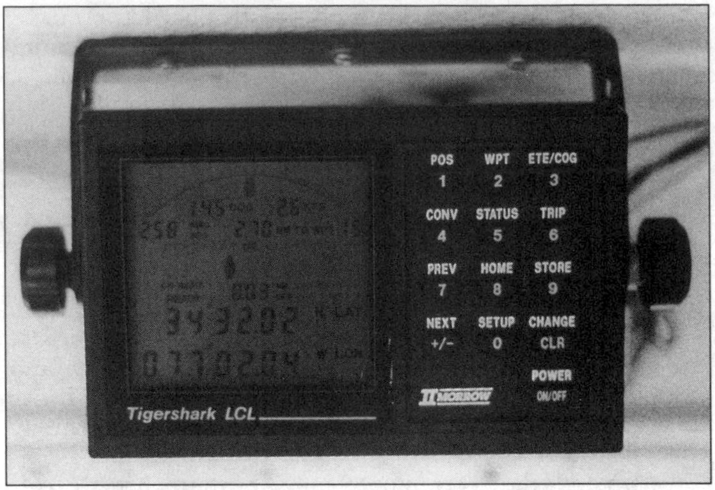

Figure 4-15. *In addition to the boat's position, a Loran-C receiver shows the distance and direction to the destination waypoint—2.70 miles at 258° magnetic to waypoint 15. It also shows course and speed over the ground—145° and 2.6 knots. This boat was fishing rather than steering for the waypoint.*

position every second. The latitude and longitude displays are useful, but, even more useful for navigation, *the distance and direction to the next destination* are also given. You merely read this information on the screen.

A navigation receiver can measure positions and store them in long-term memory. These stored positions are called **waypoints**, and receivers can store 99 to 2,500 of them. You can assign numbers, names, or both, to waypoints, depending on the receiver. You also can enter a waypoint measured by another receiver, or one taken from a chart. Suppose you want to go to the entrance of a certain channel, which you have stored as waypoint 30. You tell the receiver waypoint 30 is the destination, and in a few seconds it shows the direction and distance from your present position to the channel entrance.

Figure 4-16. *A radionavigation receiver will show the correct distance and bearing to a waypoint, but the bearing is direct, without regard to hazards along the way. The receiver does the calculation, the navigator does the thinking.*

The distance is quite accurate, usually within 20 to 50 yards. Receivers show distance in nautical miles (some can display statute miles or kilometers). A nautical mile is 6076.115 feet—about 2,000 yards—so 0.1 mile is 200 yards and 0.01 mile is 20 yards. The displayed direction is a **great circle**, which is a line of sight and the shortest route. For short distances a great circle is nearly identical to a straight line on a Mercator chart. Usually the receiver displays the *magnetic* direction for use with a boat's compass. If a receiver shows true directions, you should reset it to provide magnetic directions.

Even though you don't have to plot on the chart to find the direction and distance to your destination, it is *essential* to check that the direct course lies in safe water—the receiver doesn't know if there are shoals or islands in the way. As good as it is, it can't think. You have to provide the brains.

A boat seldom follows the desired course directly to a destination. Tidal current, leeway, inaccurate steering, and uncorrected compass errors can move the boat left or right of the desired line of travel. Without a receiver, you could estimate the speed from instruments, calculate the current, and draw a vector diagram to predict the course to steer—but few people do. Even when you do all that work, the estimated course is seldom perfect. It is common to go off to one side and follow a curving path as you make corrections.

Navigation receivers show the direction and distance to the destination waypoint all the time. If the direction varies, the boat is getting off to the side. You can correct by changing course to the new bearing. Receivers can also show *cross-track error*, the distance—to the left or right of the line—from your origin to the destination. Watch the bearing or the cross-track error to see if the boat is getting off to one side or the other. Some receivers have a display that mimics perspective, which helps visualize cross-track error. See Chapter 6 for more information.

Navigation receivers show the speed over the ground and the course made good, but these are not as accurate as the bearing to the destination point. Slight signal variations alter the displayed course and speed, as does the boat's motion in a seaway. Speed jumps up and down a knot or more. With Loran-C you can turn 90° and still see the original course and speed indicated for a minute or so. GPS receivers show speed and course changes every second, but many will be false changes due to signal variations, waves, or steering.

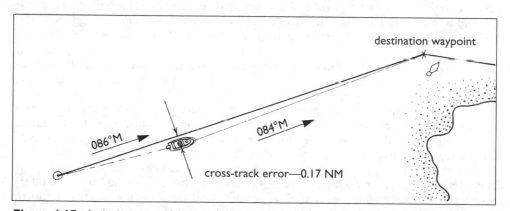

Figure 4-17. *At the beginning of the course leg, the receiver showed the destination bearing 086°M. After about 15 minutes the boat is off a bit to the right. The cross-track error is 0.17 mile, and the receiver now shows the bearing as 084°M.*

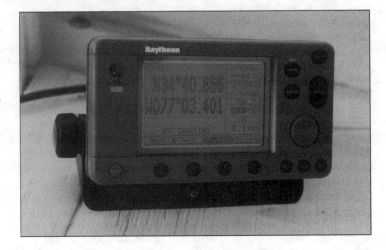

Figure 4-18. *This GPS receiver accepts differential corrections from the FAA Wide Area Augmentation System (WAAS). "SD-FIX" on the display shows that Satellite Differential corrections are being applied. WAAS corrections reduce GPS errors to about 5 yards, 95 percent of the time.*

GPS receivers calculate altitude. Loran-C can't determine altitude, but altitude is of little interest to the marine navigator. In fact, some GPS receivers are more accurate if you specify the antenna altitude. GPS receivers give the time automatically. If you enter the correct time in a Loran-C receiver, it will keep time accurately while it remains on.

Plotters

Track Plotters. In recent years navigation receivers with plotting capabilities have become popular. Many GPS receivers including handheld ones have a **track plotter**—a simple graphic screen that shows waypoints and the path that the receiver has followed. This feature lets you see the present position in relation to the waypoints, at various scales. You can zoom in and out to get a more detailed or a wider picture. These receivers also record positions automatically, usually once a minute, and plot the fixes as a series of dots on the screen. Sometimes this is called a "breadcrumb trail." A plotter is much more practical on a fixed-mount receiver than on a handheld one simply because the screen is bigger.

Now that GPS has Selective Availability set to zero (see sidebar page 89), the plotting feature is quite valuable. It is especially useful in retracing your "breadcrumb" path back into an inlet, when you didn't store a series of waypoints on your way out. It is also valuable retracing any path when the visibility has decreased. This fine feature requires no effort to store a series of fixes that appear as dots on the screen.

The paths are not stored permanently, of course. After storing the maximum number of positions, the receiver starts replacing the oldest ones with new ones. So you may find that your useful breadcrumb trail is gone, because the receiver wrote new positions in memory over the earlier ones.

So don't forget to store waypoints at key turns. I like to put in waypoints at very definite places, such as the intersection of two ranges. Using buoys as references introduces errors that are often greater than those in the electronic aid to navigation system. With a good plotter and today's accurate GPS, you can easily follow your previous track from waypoint to waypoint. The same holds true even

Figure 4-19. *This laptop computer is running The Capn electronic chart software and receiving input from a GPS receiver. This flexible and powerful combination is gaining popularity for navigation. (Courtesy SeaTech Systems)*

more so with the more accurate DGPS- and WAAS-augmented GPS receivers (see page 96). When using a plotter in a channel, you can zoom it in enough to see your side-to-side position. That usually requires a half-mile scale in narrow channels, and the next turn waypoint may be off the edge. But if you are following waypoints, you have the distance and direction to the next one displayed on the screen. This is nice in clear weather, and a huge advantage in the fog.

Electronic Charts and Displays. Electronic chart displays are a big step up in capability. They show nearly all of the features displayed on a paper chart, such as aids to navigation, shorelines, channel edges, and depth contours. You can add courses, waypoints, and other data. When a chart plotter is interfaced with the boat's GPS or Loran-C receiver, the navigator can watch the progress of the boat across an electronic representation of the chart.

With electronic charts, you can do most of the things that you can do with paper charts and plotting tools, using buttons and a keypad. It does take some time to learn how to use them, but the chartwork becomes independent of drafting skills. The size of the display prevents you from seeing more than a small part of a paper chart at the same size. As a result you will find yourself moving the displayed chart left and right and zooming in and out to see things you could take in at a glance on a paper chart. The zoom feature also has a dangerous side. It is tempting to zoom to a very large scale to see a small area in great detail. This zooming in *appears* to make the chart more accurate. It doesn't. If you have a 1:40,000-scale chart loaded into memory, zooming in to 1:10,000 to show a small area in detail does nothing to enhance the chart's accuracy. While it looks good, a zoomed-in chart has sparse soundings and inaccurate positions of landmarks and features. It *magnifies the errors* in the original paper chart, and in the survey.

Do not accept an electronic chart blindly simply because it is displayed on a plotter—it comes from paper charts, which are often woefully out of date. Leaving Bogue Inlet, North Carolina, I have to go over what appears on the plotter as dry land in order to stay in the channel. Some aids to navigation are incorrectly plotted or numbered. The same things are true of the NOAA paper chart. Sometimes chart features such as channel limits and aids to navigation are offset signifi-cantly, for readability. This isn't the fault of the plotter; it is due to the long time between chart surveys. Currently the cycle for complete chart surveys is over 50 years. A lot can happen in *one* year in a shifting inlet. It will take a long time until the aids to navigation and all other charted features are located with survey-grade GPS techniques. Until then, which probably will be after our lifetimes, navigate between waypoints measured by your receiver in restricted waters. That is the most accurate method of navigating with any electronic system.

There are a number of display options for electronic charts. Dedicated units typically display vector charts stored on data cartridges. Many integrate the GPS receiver and the chart in one monochromatic or color display unit. Combination units use a single display for charts and functions such as depthfinder or radar. Finally laptop and desktop computers can run a growing number of electronic chart programs. An electronic chart displayed on a high-resolution color monitor will deliver a close approximation of a paper chart. However, computers are the least rugged and seaworthy of the display systems.

There are two basic types of electronic charts, **raster** and **vector**. A raster chart is a graphic reproduction of the chart. A paper chart is scanned side to side and the digital image produced is then reproduced dot by dot in lines on the plotter screen. A raster chart is cheap to scan and appears as a close replica of the paper chart the navigator is already accustomed to using. You can plot or find positions on the chart electronically. When you zoom a raster chart, the lettering appears smaller or larger, and all of the depth readings and lines are preserved. This makes the chart look dense or busy with small writing when you zoom to show a large area on the screen. Raster charts require rather large amounts of data memory.

A vector chart is made by determining the positions of each significant fea-ture and storing it as a mathematical point. For instance, instead of reproducing a buoy symbol with tiny colored dots and lettering, a vector chart stores the posi-tion, an image, and the lettering. When you zoom, the buoy symbol and the let-tering can appear at a constant, readable size. It is also easy to correct individual items (such as a buoy's position) without rescanning the whole chart. The GPS receivers that show only the most important features—aids to navigation, shore-lines, depth contours, and landmarks—are actually using a highly simplified vec-tor chart. In most cases chart data are stored on little cartridges that fit into the receiver. Because data cartridges are currently sold in about ten different config-urations, few receivers can use more than one specific type.

A "real" vector chart operating on a computer will show excellent detail. National Ocean Service (NOS) is planning to produce vector charts, but as you can recognize this requires a very large number of data points. NOS's newest technology is a hybrid of the two technologies that combines the familiarity and detail of the raster chart with the flexibility of the vector chart. Electronic charts are usually stored on CDs that contain multiple charts. This makes it easy to look at several charts in one area, or to plan a long coastwise trip. They are fairly expensive, and should be updated frequently. When the vector technology is mature, it should be easier and cheaper to update the charts.

Additional Similarities and Differences

GPS and Loran-C receivers perform identical functions for a navigator. Both measure extremely small intervals of time between the arrival of electronic signals

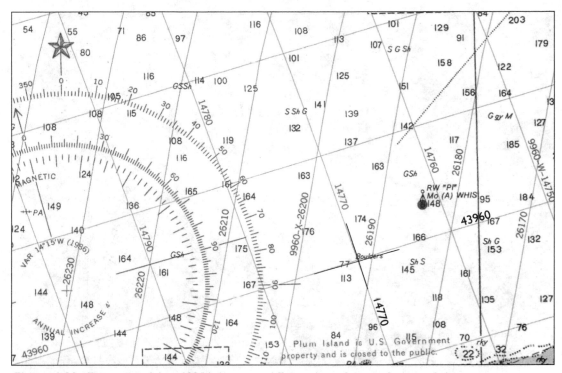

Figure 4-20. *This section of chart 12354 shows time difference lines of position for Loran-C chain 9960. If the receiver shows 14770 and 43960, we are at the intersection of "W" TD 14770 and "Y" TD 43960. In this area some receivers use X and Y.*

to calculate distances. By measuring time in *fractions of microseconds*, they can calculate distances with high accuracy. However, there are important differences between the two systems.

GPS is a satellite-based system originally called NAVSTAR. A GPS receiver calculates the range (distance) from satellites orbiting 10,900 miles above the earth to determine LOPs, which it uses to calculate the position. The satellites send up-to-date orbit information to the receiver. GPS displays positions in latitude and longitude, and altitude, and the time. It is quite easy to plot a GPS position on the chart by its latitude and longitude.

Loran-C receivers measure the time differences between signals sent from land-based transmitters that operate in groups called **chains**. Chains are identified by their **group repetition interval**, or **GRI**, such as 9940 for the U.S. West Coast Chain. The time differences, called **TDs**, are used to calculate the difference in distance from the master station and at least two secondary stations. The master station is designated M and the secondary stations are V, W, X, Y, and Z. A Loran-C receiver measures two or more TDs and displays them to 0.1 or 0.01 microsecond. The time difference (TD) lines of position are shown on charts. You can use TDs to plot a position on a chart; the receiver uses them to calculate latitude and longitude.

A navigator can designate a position by a GRI number representing a Loran-C chain and two TDs. Any Loran-C receiver can use these TDs to find the same

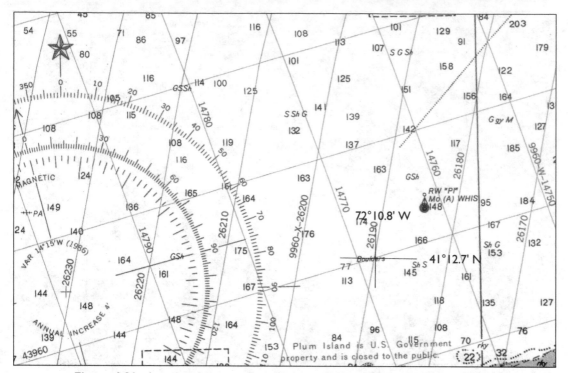

Figure 4-21. *A section of the same chart showing a GPS position plotted by its latitude and longitude.*

waypoint. It's something like describing a location in your town by saying "at the corner of Main Street and Liberty Road." The name of the town is understood.

Loran-C TD lines are somewhat like streets, except that they aren't visible and seldom cross at right angles. The TD lines on a chart represent a stable *grid* of readings. If you describe a position in Long Island Sound as 14770 and 43960, any navigator could look at the chart and find that position, north of Plum Island. The TD lines are numbered, and he merely has to find the correct ones, just as he would look for the street signs at Main Street and Liberty Road. The lines shown on the Long Island Sound chart are for the Northeast Loran-C Chain, GRI 9960, for secondary stations W, X, and Y.

Navigators often refer to TD lines for a secondary station by their first two digits rather than by letters. The "14" lines in eastern Long Island Sound run nearly north and south, magnetic; they are for the "W" secondary. The "43," or "Y," lines run very nearly east and west. (This is one area where two TD lines cross nearly at right angles.) The "26," or "X," lines run 025°/205° magnetic. Chapter 5 explains how to deal with intermediate numbers between the printed lines, such as 14773.2 or 43858.7.

Modern Loran-C receivers calculate latitude and longitude. However, Loran-C signals travel long distances near the earth's surface, which slightly alters their speed of travel. There are several correction factors, the most notable of which is the **additional secondary phase factor**, or **ASF**. ASF corrects for signal speed variations over a land path. Since the path itself varies—mountains, hills, plains—ASF corrections are imperfect, yielding slight errors in latitude and longitude. Manufacturers use slightly different ASF corrections, so different receivers get slightly different latitude and longitude from the same TD numbers. TD numbers, being the primary measurement of Loran-C, are its universal "language."

GPS receivers also use LOPs, but the LOPs move constantly as the satellites move. GPS receivers calculate and display latitude and longitude positions.

Accuracy

There is a great deal of interest in GPS and Loran-C accuracy, and a lot of misleading information has been published on this subject. Both GPS and Loran-C are more accurate than any other commonly used navigation system. Since the improvements in May of 2000, GPS is the more accurate of the two systems. Loran-C remains quite accurate in returning to measured positions. To discuss accuracy adequately, we have to describe how it is measured.

A series of fixes taken at one location fall into a pattern, the size of which indicates the system's measuring ability. (This is true of every measurement system.) Measurements may be close together, but they aren't identical. If you plot a series of positions from a receiver at a stationary location, you have an indication of the variability or **precision** of the system. A tight grouping of fixes indicates high precision; a scattered group means low precision.

Since 1 May, 2000, when the Department of Defense removed the deliberate accuracy degradation of SA, GPS receivers are giving positions that vary by about 10 to 20 meters (11 to 22 yards). Due to changing satellite geometry, GPS precision varies with time. It might be better in the morning than in the afternoon, and

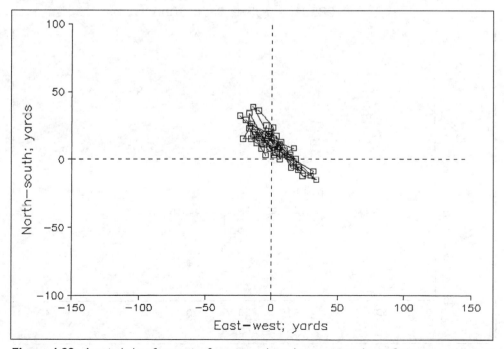

Figure 4-22. *A typical plot of successive fix positions shown by a stationary Loran-C receiver.*

worse again half an hour later. Receivers indicate GPS precision by a factor called **DOP**, **dilution of precision**, a mathematical expression of the geometry of the GPS lines of position. Lower DOP—like a lower golf score—is better. Just as shallow LOP crossing angles give a poor visual fix, when the GPS lines of position cross at shallow angles, DOP is high. For satisfactory accuracy you want a DOP of less than 6. Most of the time DOP is less than 2, which is quite good.

The Department of Defense can alter GPS precision. The most precise level is **Precise Positioning Service**, or **PPS**, in which 50 percent of the fixes fall within a 16-meter sphere. This is equivalent to 95 percent of the fixes falling within a 21-meter radius for two-dimension (latitude and longitude) positions. According to reports, PPS is now showing about ±8 meters accuracy. PPS is available *only* to military and other authorized users with dual-frequency cryptographic receivers.

The first GPS satellites broadcast at the highest precision level during the experimental phase, which made GPS more precise than Loran-C. The Air Force turned on **selective availability (SA)** from July 1991 until May 2000. Selective availability was a deliberate degradation of accuracy to deny enemies a significant targeting advantage, and was the largest factor affecting GPS precision. All ordinary marine receivers use the **Standard Positioning Service**, or **SPS**, which included the effects of SA and *anti-spoofing*, another military requirement. SA is now gone, but not lamented.

Shortly after DOD set SA to zero, there were dramatic improvements in GPS accuracy. Fixes from stationary receivers began to show errors of about ±5 to ±22 yards. Different types of receivers achieve different accuracy, but they are all good. DOD has not yet revised the specifications for the civilian signal. Their spokesmen

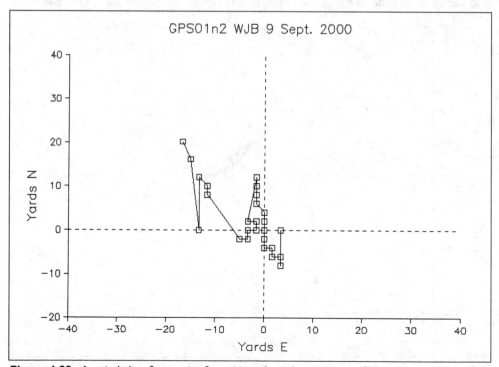

Figure 4-23. *A typical plot of successive fix positions shown by a stationary GPS receiver in September 2000.*

GPS: Selective Availability Eliminated

In the spring of 1996, a Presidential Commission announced that Selective Availability would be eliminated within ten years. On 1 May 2000 the Department of Defense announced that Selective Availability would be eliminated permanently, that evening. They also announced that accuracy would improve from within 100 meters to within 20 meters (22 yards). Since then, observations have confirmed that GPS receivers show positions that vary within 20 meters, or even 5 meters. This is a dramatic and most welcome improvement.

The government's Interagency GPS Executive Board has stated that they will present new signal specifications within a few weeks, but for now we have rather conflicting information. It appears that ordinary GPS receivers when stationary will give fixes that lie within some 10 yards of the correct position most of the time, and within 20 or 25 yards nearly all the time.

have said at various times that GPS will be accurate within 20 meters (22 yards) or within 12 meters (13 yards). Worldwide testing has shown that GPS is giving a precision of under 10 meters with high quality receivers.

In December 1993, the Department of Defense announced that GPS had achieved its Initial Operational Capability (IOC) with 24 satellites on orbit. They have added four satellites, and there are usually six to eight satellites "in view" in the United States. DOD committed to help GPS meet its SPS specifications: 100 meters (110 yards) with 95 percent probability, and 300 meters with 99.99 percent probability. The signal met these specifications from July 1991 with occasional periods of higher accuracy. On 1 May 2000, DOD reduced SA to zero, giving much improved accuracy. This change has made GPS the most accurate worldwide electronic aid to navigation.

Loran-C precision varies from place to place within its coverage area. Repetitive fixes fall in an ellipse. If the TD lines on the chart cross at nearly right angles and are close together, precision is high. When the lines cross at shallow angles or are widely spread, or both, as in the Florida Keys, precision is poor. Loran-C precision is usually about 30 to 60 yards, but is worse at the limits of coverage.

Navigators use four descriptions of accuracy for electronic navigation systems:

Predictable accuracy. Predictable accuracy, or *accuracy,* refers to how well the receiver-calculated position matches the true values. The center of the pattern of fixes may be very close to the true position, or it may be offset somewhat. This offset is called **bias** and affects every navigation system. A rifle that places all its shots in a small group exhibits high precision, but if the group is outside the bull's-eye, the rifle has an unwanted bias. If the shooter "sights in" the rifle so that the group is centered on the target, he has removed the bias. Accuracy, the ability to deliver hits at the center of the target, has improved significantly. Navigation system accuracy—predictable accuracy—includes both precision and bias. GPS has very little bias; its predictable accuracy with respect to true latitude and longitude is extremely good—usually within 10 to 22 yards.

Loran-C's bias is much larger than that of GPS. Loran-C fixes fall into a small pattern, but the center of that pattern can be a few hundred yards away from the predicted position. Loran-C's predictable accuracy is about 200 to 500 yards.

Most GPS receivers display an accuracy estimate (EPE) in feet. However, *these numbers may not be reliable.* Receivers often report better accuracy estimates than they deliver. A receiver might indicate an accuracy of 3 feet or even zero when its errors are about 50 feet.

Repeatable accuracy. Repeatable accuracy refers to how closely you can return to a position measured previously with the same system. Navigators learned early in the days of loran to remove the bias by taking TD measurements at a known position, then returning to the spot where the receiver showed identical TD readings. When you store a navigation receiver's current position as a waypoint, you can return to it with high (repeatable) accuracy. This is the most accurate and the easiest way to use GPS or Loran-C.

GPS gives excellent repeatability, now that SA is off. You can expect to be able to return to a receiver-measured position within 15 to 30 yards. At times, it is significantly better than this. This information is based on limited testing and not on a signal specification, which DOD has not released.

Loran-C typically allows you to return to a measured waypoint within 30 to 90 yards. The Coast Guard's long-term monitoring study revealed that Loran-C repeatable accuracy is better than 40 meters (44 yards) 95 percent of the time over much of the East and Gulf Coasts. On the West Coast repeatable accuracy isn't as good due to the convex coastline, but still better than 100 meters in much of the coastal zone.

These repeatable accuracies include a seasonal variation where Loran-C signals travel long distances over land that is frozen in winter. If you measure a position in July and return to the same measurements in February, you may find a shift of 30 to 40 yards. For the highest repeatable accuracy, use waypoints measured during the same season.

Relative accuracy. Relative accuracy, used infrequently by navigators, refers to the error between two receivers in the same vicinity using the same system simultaneously. For GPS, expect relative accuracy within 10 to 30 yards. For Loran-C, relative accuracy is also high—about 20 to 40 yards.

Accuracy with respect to the chart. Electronic navigation systems are used with charts, and the navigator is interested in the system's accuracy with respect to the local chart. If you plot a visual fix and simultaneously measure the position with GPS or Loran-C, the latitude and longitude of the two positions are seldom identical. This is worse than predictable accuracy, due to charting imperfections. A hydrographic survey determined the positions of the rocks and shoals shown on a chart, and may have significant position errors—up to 65 meters on an approach chart, according to NOS. A high quality chart should have 90 percent of its features within 1 mm (1/50th inch) of their correct positions. Thus a 1:40,000 chart has inherent errors of 40 meters (44 yd.), and a 1:80,000 chart has errors of 80 meters (88 yd.).

Charts are plotted on different latitude and longitude coordinate systems; they may not match the navigation receiver's coordinate system. Measuring latitude and longitude in one datum (WGS-84 for GPS) and plotting in another is sure to introduce errors. Check the chart's title block to see whether it is in the NAD-27 or NAD-83 datum. Charts using NAD-27 show significant differences from WGS-84—up to 500 yards. The C&GS is converting them to NAD-83, which is nearly identical with WGS-84. GPS receivers have built-in coordinate conversion programs. If you are using an NAD-27 chart, reset the receiver to NAD-27; for NAD-83 charts, leave it in WGS-84. The conversions (or the charts) are quite inaccurate in many parts of the world. Overseas charts often do not agree with GPS positions, and *the errors may be several miles.*

There is another factor: the accuracy of the visual or radar fix used for comparison. Errors occur in compass bearings, radar ranges, and plotting. If you go close aboard a minor light, remember that it has a tolerance in position accuracy. If you try to use a buoy to determine the errors of an electronic navigation system, you're kidding yourself. In addition to the position tolerance, the buoy's mooring chain allows it to move. The errors in taking and plotting compass bearings make it nearly impossible to plot a visual position on a chart to better than ±50 yards, and often 100 or 200 yards. This limits the accuracy with respect to the chart, even were the navigation system perfect.

In U.S. coastal waters, GPS positions usually agree with visual fixes on a chart within 50 to 150 yards. This should improve as the Coast Survey and the Coast Guard resurvey the charts and fixed aids to navigation using special GPS surveying techniques. Loran-C latitude and longitude usually match the chart within 200 to 500 yards, but there are places inland and inshore of barrier islands where Loran-C errors are much greater.

It is always important to check a navigation system with the chart to find how closely they match. You can enter correction factors into a receiver to make its output agree with the chart, *but this will shift all waypoints by the amount of the correction.* This drastic change is seldom mentioned in the receiver manuals. To avoid it, I prefer to make the corrections on paper, between chart and receiver. Remember to stick with repeatable accuracy whenever possible for the highest accuracy with any navigation system.

Accuracy Measures

There are numerous ways to describe the accuracy of a navigation receiver; unfortunately, different systems and different manufacturers use different descriptors. Here are the most popular measures:

- 2DRMS: Twice the root-mean-square (rms) value of the distances from the true location of the position fixes in a collection of measurements. 2DRMS implies a confidence level of 95 to 98 percent, depending on the pattern of the fixes. A circular pattern gives the highest confidence level.

- RMS: Half of 2DRMS. Often used in receiver specifications, probably because it is a smaller number.

- CEP: Circular Error Probable. The radius of a circle containing 50 percent of all fixes. The Federal Radionavigation Plan converts CEP to 2DRMS by multiplying by 2.5.

- SEP: Spherical Error Probable. The radius of a sphere containing 50 percent of all fixes. Used for systems giving altitude as well as latitude and longitude.

- R95: The radius containing 95 percent of all possible fixes. Technically different from 2DRMS but roughly comparable.

One navigation system's accuracy at a particular location may be described with equal validity by CEP = 20 meters, 2DRMS = 50 meters, RMS = 25 meters, or R95 = 47 meters. These measures may use any units, such as feet or yards. Most authorities consider the probable error (CEP) as inappropriate for describing navigation systems since a navigator wants a confidence level far higher than 50 percent.

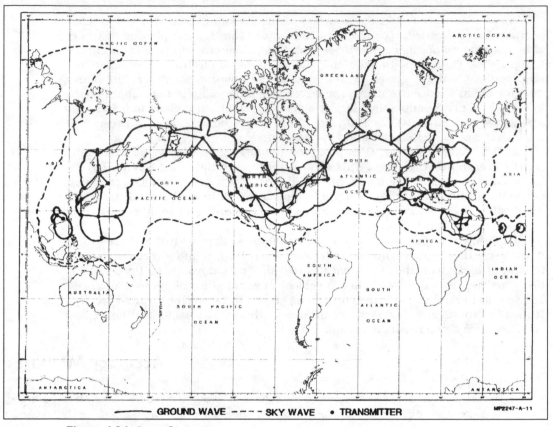

Figure 4-24. *Loran-C coverage.*

Coverage

There are two types of coverage: area and time. GPS is designed to give world-wide service. Loran-C covers the United States (including Alaska but not Hawaii), much of Canada, and many overseas areas. U.S. boat operators who go to the Virgin Islands or Mexico venture outside of good Loran-C coverage. The map shows Loran-C coverage as of 1995, but Russia, China, India, and other countries are building Loran-C systems.

Today, GPS is at Full Operating Capability, and is providing Standard Positioning Service (SPS) accuracy. The Department of Defense has reduced Selective Availability (SA) to zero, giving accuracy of approximately 20 meters, 95 percent of the time. We are waiting for an announcement of the new accuracy, velocity, and time specifications. DOD predicts that SPS is available 99.7 percent of the time averaged over the globe, or 99.16 percent of the time at any one place. Availability can fall below 95 percent at times, and fix errors can exceed 500 meters (547 yards) 36 hours per year.

DOD has announced that there will be a minimum of 48 hours notice prior to maintenance that affects accuracy or availability. Sometimes GPS shut down without warning during the experimental phase, but there have been very few outages since it became operational. DOD does, however, do interference testing that makes GPS unusable over relatively large areas.

Loran-C is designed to provide signals for fixes 99.7 percent of the time, and it has a history of doing so. For example, over the last decade, the Loran-C system has provided signals suitable for fixes for the entire eastern U.S. and parts of Canada 99.64 percent of the time. In many areas, the navigator can reduce unusable time by shifting to different TDs or different chains with overlapping coverage.

Choosing an Electronic Navigation System

Today the Global Positioning System (GPS) has major advantages over any other electronic navigation system. It is the only system giving high accuracy and near-continuous coverage worldwide. Receivers are reasonably priced and come in a wide variety of sizes, and with many variations in capabilities. GPS is more accurate than any other publicly available aid to navigation. Every navigator should carry a GPS receiver, in my opinion. The portable versions are available for less than $100, and are equally useful ashore. Fixed mount receivers are better for boats; they are more reliable, easier to read, and have more features. The big question becomes whether to get a GPS augmentation such as DGPS or WAAS. However, GPS receivers, like those for every electronic aid to navigation, occasionally give incorrect positions. They may be off by a few hundred yards or even several miles. In addition it takes the Air Force several hours to correct certain types of out-of-tolerance satellite errors.

Despite the great advantages of GPS, Loran-C still has a place, especially aboard boats that operate in coastal or Great Lakes waters. It is totally independent of GPS, and not subject to interference on the same frequencies. The navigator with both a GPS and a Loran-C receiver has an immediate indication when something goes wrong with either one. Loran-C remains inexpensive, reliable, and accurate, but there are few receivers available. It appears that Loran-C will continue to be in operation well into this century. If you fish or dive, Loran-C is almost essential; GPS doesn't give TD numbers, and the positions of many offshore wrecks and rocks are known only by their TD numbers. In time people will measure the positions by GPS, but this data is not yet widely available. (GPS receivers that calculate Loran-C TDs are subject to the same errors as Loran-C receivers that calculate latitude and longitude several hundred yards to over a mile.)

In the early 1990s, GPS receiver manufacturers introduced several multichannel modules for use by other manufacturers. New companies started production, and receiver prices have declined dramatically. The small antenna a GPS receiver uses must be mounted clear of objects that block the satellite signals. It should *not* be at the top of the mast, or the GPS will show large speed and course variations when the boat rolls. A Loran-C antenna is substantially larger and should not be mounted parallel to a nearby vertical whip antenna, mast, or metal outrigger. You can tilt it 45° without harm if it must be close to another antenna. This is unlike VHF; tilting a VHF antenna ruins its performance.

GPS is subject to interference from adjacent radio frequencies, including some TV channels. Interference affecting one system seldom affects the other since they use widely different frequencies. Phenomena associated with sunspots disrupt both systems, but not at the same time.

Loran-C is affected by thunderstorms, even storms many miles away. It also is affected by onboard interference from the alternator and other electrical and

	Loran-C	GPS
Coverage	U.S. including Alaska, Canadian coasts, Western Pacific, N. Europe, Mediterranean Sea, Saudi Arabia, Suez Canal, China, Russia	Worldwide
Frequency	100 kHz	1575.42 and 1227.6 mHz
Usable time	99.7%	99.5% to 95%
Out of tolerance notification	Under 10 sec. (blink)	Usually under 10 sec. can be 30–90 min.
Predictable accuracy	Less than 500 yd.	With SA off: 12 to 20 m 95% est. (14–22 yd.) PPS: 16 m SEP (military) now approx 8 m (9 yd.)
Repeatable accuracy	20 to 90 yd.	SA off: 17 to 28 m est. 95%
Chart	Within 0.25 mi.	U.S.: less than 100 yd. World: up to 5 mi.
Altitude	N/A	With SA off 18 to 31 m 95% est. (60–100 ft.) PPS: 28 m 95% (now about 11 m)
Velocity	N/A	PPS: 0.2 m/s (0.4 kt) 95% SA off: unspecified, reported: 0.2–0.3 kt
Time	Time interval 100 ns	Time and Time interval 40 ns
Fix accuracy	Varies with location	Varies with time
Interference	Lightning, LF transmitters, power lines, on-board electronics	Magnetic storms (sun), antenna shadowing, some radio applications
Transmitter failure mode	Lose one transmitter (lose one or more LOP). Transmitter out of tolerance (one LOP unusable).	Unhealthy satellite (lose coverage time). Satellite clock drift (inaccurate fix).

Notes:
DGPS and WAAS have about one-half to one-fifth the errors of GPS
PPS = Precise Positioning Service (Military, cryptographic)
SEP = Spherical Error Probable (50% of fixes lie within stated spherical radius)
All other accuracies: 95% of fixes within stated radius.

Table 4-1. *System Comparisons*

electronic equipment. Interference can cause a receiver to lose the signals or measure from the wrong cycle, causing errors. Many boatowners find that Loran-C will work without a ground system—when conditions are good. These are the same skippers who complain of Loran-C problems. You can eliminate most interference problems with a good installation.

In U.S. waters we have a situation that has never existed in the past: two continuous, accurate navigation systems that display distance and direction to waypoints. When the next waypoint is 13.21 miles 094°M by GPS and 13.22 miles 094°M by Loran-C, I am nearly certain that the information is correct. Were one receiver wrong, the other would reveal it. If there weren't enough satellites in view for a GPS fix, Loran-C would be working. If a Loran-C transmitter were out of tolerance and blinking, GPS would be unaffected. Many boat owners have both GPS and Loran-C; the combination is far better than either one alone.

Using two systems reveals a common error: entering a waypoint erroneously. There are plenty of ways to make errors, and I've made most of them: hit an adjacent number button, transposed numbers, copied one latitude from one waypoint on a list and the longitude from the next waypoint, looked at the wrong TD line label on the chart, and so on. Even some of the published waypoint lists have errors. On a boat that is bouncing around, it is all too easy to hit the wrong number key. Since you enter GPS waypoints in latitude and longitude and Loran-C waypoints in TDs, it is nearly impossible to make an error in one that won't show up with the other.

Today it is almost a deliberate handicap to navigate without an electronic positioning system. GPS is the obvious first choice, especially now that selective availability is reduced to zero. If you're going to Tahiti, it's silly to go without GPS in addition to a sextant. If you're buying an expensive boat, don't agonize over which navigation instrument to get. Get both, if you can—they represent a small fraction of a large boat's cost. If your boat now has Loran-C, add GPS, but don't be so foolish as to get rid of the Loran-C receiver. Although neither system is—or ever will be—perfect, they complement each other beautifully, as well as complementing traditional navigation. Just remember that these systems aren't a substitute for thinking. Errors show up, receivers fail, and it is easy to misuse their complex features.

Choosing a Receiver

When choosing a receiver for either system, you'll find so many standard features that it will be difficult to differentiate among various manufacturers. Several receivers use the same circuit designs, under license, and have nearly identical functions. Some of the more important features relate to use and some to technical design details.

Start by examining the screen display. You'll use the receiver under low light and harsh sunlight, and some screens have much larger numbers and letters than others. Is what you want to see displayed on the screen, or do you have to shift screens back and forth to see the combination of information you want? I prefer a screen that shows latitude and longitude or TDs, the name or number of the destination waypoint, its distance and bearing, the course made good and speed over the ground, and the cross-track error.

All information should be easy to identify. It's inconvenient if the screen doesn't identify the destination waypoint. One otherwise excellent receiver doesn't label the bearing and distance to the waypoint, or the course made good and speed made good. When the waypoint is about an hour away and the distance is about equal to the speed, it's easy to get confused. Screens that blink for alarms are more noticeable than ones that simply change *Ready* to *Not Ready*, or display tiny icons.

Next, look at the keyboard. Small receivers have small keyboards, making it easier to hit adjacent keys by accident, particularly underway. Portable receivers are popular, and their rechargeable batteries filter out 12-volt power interference. GPS receivers without a number keypad are now commonplace. They require you to step through the numbers or letters when entering data, which gets annoying. Some portable receivers use expensive and complex mounting kits for a boat.

It is good to be able to display signal status information easily. A receiver that can calculate the distance and bearing between any two waypoints is better for planning a trip than one that can only calculate from the present position to a waypoint.

You also must learn the receiver's functions using the manual. Is the manual clear and well organized? Does it have an index? Some manuals are significantly better than others. Some are downright terrible, omitting important instructions; unfortunately, you don't learn this until you use the receiver.

Advanced technical features add to a receiver's value. Those that acquire signals at low signal-to-noise ratios have an advantage. Quick lock-on is not a big advantage for boat use since you usually leave the receiver on, but it is an indication of the receiver's quality. Low power consumption is important for a portable receiver or on a sailboat, but not particularly so on a powerboat.

Each generation of GPS receivers is more capable than the last, so look for one with new technology. The newer receivers are multichannel and receive data from eight to twelve satellites simultaneously. This feature is more valuable around obstructions or during high-speed aircraft maneuvers than on a boat, but it does indicate new design. The number of satellites the receiver uses for position calculations is more important; in this case more is truly better. For boat use I prefer receivers that can be locked in 2-D (two dimension—latitude and longitude, but not altitude) mode, with antenna height entered. GPS receivers that show a graphic satellite display make it easy to understand which are in use. Receivers that have a track plotter, now often a standard feature, make it easy to understand the boat's path. Many GPS receivers have plotter screens, and some have a database of buoy and light waypoints. It is an advantage to purchase a GPS receiver that is ready for *differential* use, as described below.

Loran-C receivers with many notch filters or with automatic notch filters are good at reducing external interference. Loran-C receivers that can track and display more than two TDs are commonplace, as they should be. Some track two chains, another fine feature. Some have high-performance antenna couplers that give better performance when signal strength is low. Loran-C receiver technology is not a static field, despite the lack of receivers on the market today.

Differential GPS and WAAS

Although GPS gives high accuracy, there is a technique to make it even more accurate than it now is with selective availability off. If you measure a position repeatedly with GPS, its fix position will wander; typically, it will wander within about 20 yards. Signals reaching two receivers within 100 miles or so of each other have nearly identical variations at the same moment. The differential technique uses one GPS receiver to measure the changes at a precisely known position, and a transmitter to send corrections to mobile receivers.

The fixed receiver determines the errors for each satellite. A transmitter sends the data to a special receiver aboard your boat; your GPS applies a correction for each satellite to produce a highly accurate fix. The Coast Guard reports that **Differential GPS (DGPS)** gives positions accurate to within 5 to 10 meters—6 to 11 yards. DGPS reveals out-of-tolerance satellite signals more quickly than the existing monitoring network. DGPS is especially useful for returning to diving or fishing sites, for navigating in fog, and for finding course and speed over the ground quickly.

Differential GPS became fully operational in March 1996. The Coast Guard first set up an experimental DGPS station at Montauk Point on Long Island, using the existing radiobeacon there to carry additional data. They have added Differential GPS equipment to radiobeacons all around the coast and the Great Lakes, and plan to cover the interior of the country as well. In order to use DGPS, you must have a GPS receiver built for differential use, a special receiver, and an antenna for the radiobeacon signal. (An ordinary radio direction finding receiver (RDF) won't work for this purpose.) The first models designed for boat use came out in late 1992, adding about $500 to the cost of a GPS receiver. The GPS receiver must accept "Type 9" messages at 200 bits per second. The higher accuracy of DGPS also means greater cost, higher complexity, and some reduction in usable time from "straight" GPS.

There is also a system that uses satellites to provide DGPS data. The FAA is developing a **Wide Area Augmentation System** to enhance GPS accuracy and integrity. In 2000, WAAS is operating almost continually. It isn't reliable enough to be certified for navigation, but is useful aboard boats whose navigators need exceptionally high accuracy—usually under five meters. GPS receivers that apply the WAAS corrections came out in July 2000. The receiver gets the WAAS signals via its normal antenna, and shows very high accuracy over its coverage area in the western hemisphere. DGPS and WAAS enhanced GPS are so accurate that they are revealing errors in charts and the positions of aids to navigation. The chart is limited by the accuracy of the hydrographic survey, and by drafting and printing accuracies. The most accurate way to use DGPS and WAAS will be the same as the best way to use Loran-C or GPS: returning to a position measured by the same receiver.

Radiobeacons and Radio Direction Finders

The Coast Guard operates a system of about 200 radiobeacons along the coasts and on the Great Lakes. Invented in the 1920s, **radiobeacons** are the oldest and simplest radionavigation aids. They operate at frequencies from 285 kHz to 325 kHz, between Loran-C and the AM broadcast band, and transmit a radio signal with Morse code identification.

The signal radiates in all directions. The receiver indicates the direction to the transmitting antenna. A radiobeacon provides one line of position; it is simple to head toward it. If you can get LOPs from two different radiobeacons, you are *near* the position where they cross. Notice the word "near." Radiobeacon bearings depend on the receiver, the antenna, the skill of the operator, the signal strength, reflections aboard the boat, and the accuracy of the boat's compass and steering. Fifty miles offshore, a radiobeacon fix might be within 10 miles of the correct spot.

When heading directly for the transmitter—*homing* on it—the distance error

Better Than Differential?

Have you heard about GPS measurements that are accurate within inches? Surveyors collect data simultaneously with one specialized receiver at a known position and another receiver at the unknown position. Later they compare the data taken by the two receivers using a computer program, and achieve extremely high accuracy—much better than DGPS or WAAS. There are several other methods, generally known as post-processing, that give surveying accuracy using GPS. However, these methods are not useful to navigation, since the information isn't available until after the data are compared and processed.

left or right of the LOP becomes smaller as you get closer. Radiobeacons work well for homing, but for taking fixes they are something of a quaint curiosity—like a wooden-shaft golf club or a two-man crosscut saw; they still work, but not many people use them.

I have used radiobeacons a great deal and have been thankful for them. Prior to Loran-C becoming affordable, they were the only radionavigation aid aboard boats. Approaching a coast without a fix for a day or so, I welcomed even an approximate position. Now GPS and Loran-C give accurate positions with little effort, but if you have a **radio direction finder (RDF)**, at least keep fresh batteries in it for backup use. I would not buy one; an RDF is so much trouble to use and the lines of position are so inaccurate that I wouldn't use it very often.

Radiobeacons will be around for a long time. Radiobeacon receivers are required aboard many ships by international agreement, and some countries without radionavigation aids rely on them. The U.S. Coast Guard DGPS program is designed around radiobeacons, as well.

There is another radio direction finder that is useful: a portable **AM radio.** If there is a radio station antenna near the coast, you can get a reasonable idea of its bearing by turning the receiver back and forth. The signal gets loud and then faint as you turn the receiver. It is at a minimum (which is easier to detect than the maximum) when the radio antenna is pointed toward the transmitter. Try it in clear weather. This scheme has helped me to pick my way in during lousy visibility, before loran became commonplace. I could run in on an AM radio bearing toward the coast until I got to the right depth for the entrance buoy, then follow that depth contour. I might have been able to find it from a DR, but the radio was a welcome addition to the navigation equipment.

A portable AM radio is also a good squall-alert system. While you can detect squalls fairly easily if you keep your eyes (and ears) open, the lightning makes strong static on the AM band. It is especially noticeable if the radio is tuned between stations, giving only a hiss. Small AM radios are so inexpensive that you may wish to carry one along.

There are also direction finders for VHF-FM. They are useful in finding another boat but nearly useless for navigation. This is due to the Coast Guard's system of antennas; the radio operator can select one or more high-level antennas within a large geographic area. One time the signal comes from one, one time from another, and another time from all of them. The direction finder points first one way and then another. When all of them are in use, the poor direction finder can't tell which way to turn.

Racons

It is often difficult to pick out an entrance buoy from among dozens of targets on a radar screen. The Coast Guard has installed **radar beacons**, or **racons**, on some buoys to make identification easier. When a radar signal reaches a racon, it transmits a signal on the same frequency. The transmitted signal appears on the scope as a line or a specific combination of dots and dashes extending outward from the buoy.

Other Radionavigation Systems

There are several other systems of interest. **GLONASS** is a partially complete Russian satellite navigation system similar to GPS. It doesn't include deliberate accuracy degradation, so it gives high accuracy to civilian users—about 30 to 40 yards. With the breakup of the former Soviet Union, its future is uncertain, but the Russians have continued to launch satellites in groups of three. Using GLONASS and GPS simultaneously gives better coverage and error detection than either system alone. There is a proposal among foreign countries to support GLONASS in order to have an accurate navigation system free from U.S. DOD whims. If so, receivers should start to become available in the U.S.

The Navy Navigation Satellite System, called **Transit** or **SATNAV**, used satellites orbiting 600 miles up to provide highly accurate fixes worldwide every few hours. GPS has superseded Transit. The Department of Defense shut down Transit at the end of 1996.

Omega was an internationally funded and operated system that covered the earth from eight huge transmitting stations. It operated at frequencies even lower than Loran-C and gave continuous information, with fixes usually accurate within 2 to 4 miles. Weather data balloons used Omega worldwide. The Omega system was terminated prematurely at the end of September 1997.

Chayka is a navigation system in the former Soviet Union so similar to Loran-C that some receivers can use both systems. Russia and the United States have linked two Chayka and one Loran-C station to give coverage between the Aleutian Islands and Russian territory. Europe and east Asia also are building joint Loran-C/Chayka chains.

Decca was a popular radionavigation system in Europe and other parts of the world. It operated on frequencies near Loran-C, at lower power and shorter range. Within its area of coverage, it gives continuous and accurate information. While Decca is well known to European boatowners, it is unavailable here.

CHAPTER 5

Finding Where You Are

*E*ven with loran or GPS and radar, operating a ship in fog is a tense time at sea. You have to plot radar targets, keep a good lookout, keep track of the ship's position, and fit your listening and talking around the blast of the foghorn. You're always searching to the limits of visibility, vaguely shown through swirling fog.

In 1960 I was executive officer aboard a buoy tender out of Astoria, Oregon. We were picking our way slowly down the coast in dense fog. When we overheard a fishing boat call the Coos Bay Coast Guard Station, we perked up. If there were a problem, we might be close to the boat and would go to assist. The radio conversation worked along—boat name, location, situation. There didn't seem to be any life-threatening problem, yet the boat operator had called for help. Finally the Coast Guard watchstander at Coos Bay said, "Captain, what is the nature of the assistance you request?"

"Well, I'm okay for now," he said, "but I'd sure like to know where I'm at."

I chuckled in relief and in amusement. Seafarers have been trying to solve that particular problem—finding "where they're at"—for untold centuries. The fishing boat didn't have loran or radar, and a boat offshore in fog has a tough time navigating by depthfinder and compass. All contact with shore is gone, and all around, the only things visible are water and fog. After a short while a second boat in the same vicinity called, one that had radar, and the lost boat followed it in through the inlet.

Finding where the boat is *at a specific time* is the starting point of navigation. You may simply note the time when the boat passes close aboard a certain buoy in clear weather. You can use several other methods to find the boat's location, but the *where* is incomplete without the *when*; you need to note the time.

Seaman's Eye

Ship pilots, tug captains, fishermen, and most boat operators use seaman's eye navigation on every trip. It seldom yields a precise fix, but it is so quick and so useful that it is a primary piloting method in clear weather. Some people have refined seaman's eye navigation to an art, while others use only a few of its basic features.

Figure 5-1. *Look at the perspective of pairs of buoys along a straight channel to estimate the boat's side-to-side position.*

Seaman's eye navigation is the marriage of several techniques, and the first among them relies on horizontal angles between prominent objects. The simplest example is in the perspective of a line of buoys. If you're in the center of a channel, the two lines of buoys extend toward the horizon with diminishing, equal angles port and starboard. If you're to the right side of the channel, as you should be normally, the angles between successive buoys to starboard are smaller than between the ones to port.

If you were to get in line with the right edge of the channel, the buoys there would appear to be in line, while the ones to port would show greater angles. In this case you could see that you were exactly in line with the right-hand buoys. In between the center and the edge, you can get a good approximation of your distance off the channel centerline by the appearance of the buoys.

Even if you're not in a channel, you can get a good position by looking at all of the surrounding objects. The angles between them—that is, the angles formed by lines of sight from your position to the objects—have a certain relationship from one position. For example, imagine that you're standing in the center of a square room. There, the angle from each corner to the next corner is 90°; nowhere else in the room is this so. If you walk toward one side, the angle between the corners ahead of you increases. At the same time, the angle between the corners behind you decreases. At each location in the room, there is a unique set of angles between the four corners. If you were to measure the angles, leave the room, then return to a point where the angles are identical, you would have returned to the same point.

Seaman's eye uses a similar technique—looking at the angles between islands, landmarks, aids to navigation, structures, trees, and other objects. You don't measure the angles with instruments; you estimate them. Looking carefully at the angles between prominent objects yields a picture that is unique to one location. If you move to another location, the angles change, and some objects that were hidden appear, some in sight disappear.

It is remarkable how well you can judge your approximate position by carefully observing the surrounding objects and the angles between them. This is "eyeball" navigation, knowing in detail how the angles appear to change as the boat moves. Careful observation of the angular relationships from a boat is a key

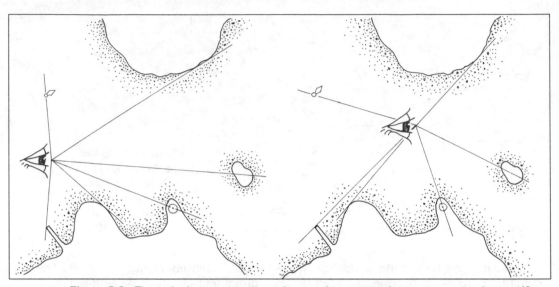

Figure 5-2. *The angles between prominent objects make a pattern that is unique to one location. If you move to another location, the angles change.*

to seaman's eye navigation. Comparing these angles with a chart is a vital part of the process of finding where you are.

Seaman's eye navigation uses **ranges** in preference to *all* other techniques. With one object farther away and higher than another, you can tell with ease when you are in line with them. You need no compass or depthfinder to verify that you are on a range line—just a glance. The range line is a line of position.

Figure 5-3. *If a lone tree on the skyline is behind a house when you are in midchannel, use that range. It will show you whether the boat is in the center of the channel or starting to move left or right.*

Everywhere along the range line, the front and rear objects appear in line; if you see them in line, you must be somewhere along the range line. Aid-to-navigation ranges are built on the centerlines of many channels, but **natural ranges** are far more common.

A pilot searches for natural ranges everywhere in a harbor. If a lone tree on the skyline is behind a house (Figure 5-3), or a rock in the water is in line with a tank when the ship is in safe water, the pilot notices it. A pilot just as often uses objects *nearly* in range, and becomes quite good at it. Using two objects nearly in range to establish a line of position is called keeping the range *open*. A range or an open range is a substitute for a fix, a way to ensure that the boat stays in safe water.

You don't need precise equipment to measure the angle between the two objects. You can get an approximation with a finger held up at arm's length: one finger is about 2° wide; hold up two fingers for 4°, or three fingers for 6°. Yes, it is a rough measurement. Different people have longer or shorter arms and thinner or thicker fingers. Yet, you can use your fingers to measure angles more accurately than you can estimate them. You also can find the angular width of your fist; for many people it's about 12°. Stick your thumb out, and it's about 15° from the tip of your thumb to the opposite side of your hand.

Suppose you come to a shoal and have to slow down and work your way around it. When you are clear of its outer edge, you see an open range ahead. One island is about *two fingers* to the right of another beyond it. Coming by again, keep the range open by at least two fingers to stay clear of the shoal. (Remember the course too, and you're ahead of the curve.) Find this clue on a good day and store it in your mind, and it will be worth rubies when it's rough and you can't see the buoys very well. You'll know the angle is the same "two fingers" you measured the first time. That's what counts—a measurement you can duplicate easily.

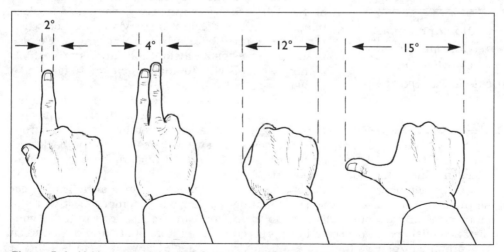

Figure 5-4. *Held up at arm's length, a finger is about 2° wide. Hold up two fingers for 4°. The average angular width of a fist is about 12°. Stick your thumb out, and it's about 15° from the tip of your thumb to the opposite side of your hand.*

Figure 5-5. *Keep a range open between one island and another beyond it to stay clear of a rock shoal between the boat and the nearest island. Remember the course, too.*

Open ranges don't form a straight line of position; they remain at the same angle along a slight curve. It is possible to plot these curves, but you seldom follow them very far. More commonly you use them to guide your boat past a danger point, then look ahead for something else. Some of these objects are charted, others aren't. Uncharted objects often form ranges that give excellent lines of position.

To know where you lie *along* any range line, you need more data. Look for another natural range or a nearby prominent object. Two ranges that cross give an excellent indication of the boat's position.

The rate of angular change between two landmarks nearly in range gives an excellent clue to sideward motion.

Aboard that CG buoy tender, we made good use of the high accuracy of ranges. We were able to place buoys within a few feet of the previous position when they were marked by nearby natural ranges. We also used the ranges as an instant indication of the ship's motion, which is vital to know when you're hoisting a buoy aboard.

Ranges that show whether the ship is drifting left or right are especially useful in seaman's eye navigation. Watch a range ahead carefully to see if the front object appears to move with respect to the back one. If it does, the boat is moving to one side. The *rate* of angular change gives an excellent clue to the sideward motion.

The angle between two landmarks about the same distance away gets larger as the boat gets closer to them. Estimating this angle and comparing it with the chart gives an idea of the distance to them. You can use this idea to judge your distance offshore. Suppose you are proceeding away from shore and are between two prominent objects that are a mile apart. The angle between them is 120°; at this point you are about ⁹⁄₁₀ mile offshore. Go farther, the angle decreases to 90°, and you are ½ mile offshore. When the angle is 60°, you are about ⁹⁄₁₀ mile

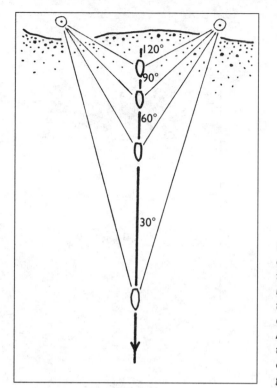

Figure 5-6. *Two objects ashore are a mile apart. At first, the angle between them is 120°; the boat is about ³/₁₀ of a mile offshore. At ¹/₂ mile offshore the angle decreases to 90°. When the angle is 60°, you are about ⁹/₁₀ of a mile offshore, and when it is 30°, about 1.9 miles. Although we calculated these distances, in practice you simply look at the objects, estimate the angle between them, then look at the chart to get a rough idea of your distance offshore.*

offshore, and when it is 30°, about 1.9 miles. In practice you don't measure the angles, and the distances are approximate (see also pages 126–127).

If you live near a rocky coast, the islands, headlands, hills, and rocks visible near shore in clear weather will allow you to easily find your way on coastwise trips by using seaman's eye navigation. Along bold coasts, it is wise to cultivate your knowledge of the appearance of your surroundings. First, learn to identify headlands and islands by their profile. Sometimes the chart shows enough height contours to indicate their shape, but often the contours aren't close enough to be useful. A little island may be steep, flat with cliffs, sloping toward one end, or some other shape. Knowing how it appears from different directions and distances helps to identify it quickly.

I find it valuable to make sketches of the island at different distances and directions. These sketches are rough, but they help me remember the island's shape. Just observing the island closely enough to draw its profile makes me remember it better. Note the time or start your stopwatch as you pass the island or rock, then find the distance by the minutes-per-mile method described later in this chapter (pages 115–116). Sight over the compass to find the direction. It is easy to determine the distance away from an island or a rock if you store a Loran-C or GPS waypoint as you pass nearby. The receiver can show the distance and direction back to the waypoint.

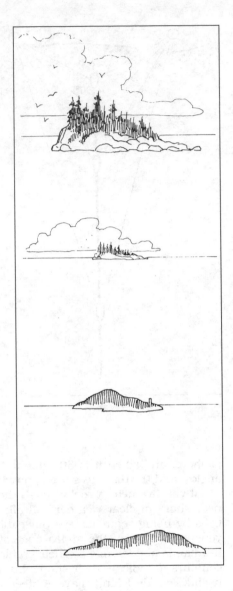

Figure 5-7. *It is valuable to make little sketches of islands at different distances and directions. The sketches are rough rather than artistic, but they help you remember the island's shape. Top: an island about a mile away. Next: the same island, about 5 miles away. The rough sketches of two other islands show their distinctive shapes.*

Identifying islands and headlands is the first step. Learning how they appear with respect to one another is the next. Look at the chart and estimate the angles between prominent objects when you are at a known point, then compare them to the angles you see. Notice particularly objects that are nearly in range. You will soon get an excellent match with the things you see and their symbols and positions on the chart. Head away from the known position and notice how the appearance changes. When I ran my boat out of Yarmouth, Maine, in Casco Bay, I seldom navigated any other way—except in fog. In clear weather, there were enough islands in view to navigate easily.

Seaman's eye navigation is useful when approaching a coast. Lighthouses, points, and buildings appear in front of specific hills and valleys on the far horizon. There is only one place where they appear the same with respect to one another. If that place is on the approach to a harbor, you can go there easily. Off-shore of the entrance, look around carefully and make a sketch of the surroundings. This was a key technique in ancient rutters (route books) and sailing directions before the days of electronics. Old charts contain sketches from various distances and directions, and the idea is just as valuable today.

People who live on flat coasts don't have the luxury of navigating by the profile of hills and islands. Few land features are distinguishable; only an occasional tank, building, or radio tower shows clearly, yet there are clues. If you are standing with your feet a foot or so above the waterline, steering a center-console boat for example, a low coast at 10 miles appears as a narrow dark line above the horizon, with an occasional tank or large building visible. At 5 miles the coast is not only higher but visible over a wider angle. Closer yet, it appears to cover nearly 180°. Spend some time identifying visible landmarks as well as looking at the angles between them, and you will have a quick indication of your approximate position just for the looking.

In addition to horizontal angles, seaman's eye navigation uses several forms of vertical angles. The first are those above the horizon. The chart provides the height of a lighthouse. By measuring its vertical angle with a sextant and using trigonometry—or a table in *Bowditch*—you can find the distance from the lighthouse that corresponds to the measured angle. Seaman's eye ignores all this math and uses simpler methods.

The apparent height of an object gives an indication of distance—an estimate, not a measurement. When the lighthouse is tiny, you are a long way away from it; the taller it seems, the closer you are. Judging apparent height is one of the skills of seaman's eye. With practice, and from known distances, you can refine that skill. I find it especially handy to use a Loran-C or GPS waypoint close aboard an object to learn to estimate its range. Seeing how it appears at 5 miles, or 2, or 1 as I approach it helps me to better estimate its distance. Radar also is a big help in learning to judge distances visually.

Using relative size as a method of judging distance is handy but not very accurate.

Everyone uses relative size as a method of judging distance. It's handy but not very accurate. However, there are some refinements that increase its accuracy. Windows are an example. At about 3 miles you can no longer see the windows of a building, just its outline. You may not know how far away that is, but you might also observe that you can't see an unlighted entrance buoy until you can see the windows of a building on the shore. It's useful to know this, but it's far from exact; windows in sunlight are visible farther than windows in shadow.

There is one version of the vertical-angle method that is quite easy: the **three-finger rule.** Holding three fingers at arm's length and using them as a height indicator covers an angle of about 6°. *An object that makes a 6° angle is ten times as far away as it is high.* So if the lighthouse is 180 feet high (60 yards), it is about 600 yards away when it is three fingers high. At twice three-fingers' height, 12°, the distance off is about five times the height—300 yards in this case. At a finger and a half (3°), the distance off is about 20 times the height—1,200 yards for a 180-foot lighthouse. These ranges are approximate, especially at long distances. Even so, the finger-height method gives you a reference that helps in judging distance.

Figure 5-8. *The three-finger rule. Three fingers at arm's length cover roughly 6°. An object such as the lighthouse that appears "three fingers" high is about 10 times as far away as its height.*

Vertical angles below the horizon also are useful. As you pass close aboard a buoy, its waterline makes an angle below the horizon. The farther you go from the buoy, the smaller the angle becomes. The angle depends on your height above the water and the distance to the buoy. Those good at seaman's eye navigation are skilled at using this vertical angle as an indication of relative distance; it provides a better clue to the distance to the buoy than size alone. Table 5-1 gives the vertical angles in degrees or minutes (1/60 of a degree) for various heights and distances.

Figure 5-9. *The vertical angle from the horizon down to the waterline of the buoy gives an indication of its distance from the boat. The angle is larger at close range.*

Height of Eye (ft.)	6	12	18	24
Distance (yd.)		Angle Below Horizon (deg. or min.)		
50	2.3°	4.5°	6.8°	9.1°
100	1.1°	2.2°	3.4°	4.5°
150	44'	1.5°	2.2°	3.0°
200	32'	1.1°	1.7°	2.2°
250	25'	52'	1.3°	1.8°
300	21'	43'	1.1°	1.5°
350	17'	36'	55'	1.2°
400	15'	31'	48'	1.1°
450	13'	27'	42'	57'
500	12'	24'	37'	50'
600	9.2'	20'	30'	41'
700	7.6'	16'	26'	35'
800	6.4'	14'	22'	30'
900	5.4'	12'	19'	26'
1,000	4.7'	11'	17'	23'
2,000	1.5'	3.9'	6.6'	9.4'
3,000	0.5'	1.8'	3.4'	5.0'
4,000	0.2'	0.9'	1.9'	2.9'

Table 5-1. *Vertical Angles for Objects Closer Than the Horizon*

The vertical angle becomes zero when the buoy is on the horizon. The higher you are, the farther away the horizon, due to the curvature of the earth. Every skipper should know the distance to the horizon at the steering station as a distance reference. Table 5-2 gives the distance to the horizon for various heights of eye above the water. It's a good idea to use the table to find the distance to the horizon for your boat. Some skippers write this distance in a convenient, visible place.

If you prefer, you can calculate the distance to the horizon, in miles, by multiplying 1.17 by the square root of the height of your eye above the water, in feet. For metric heights, find the square root of the height of your eye above the water (in meters) and multiply by 2.12 to find the distance to the horizon in miles.

Height (ft.)	Distance to Horizon (NM)
5	2.6
6	2.9
7	3.1
8	3.3
9	3.5
10	3.7
11	3.9
12	4.1
13	4.2
14	4.4
15	4.5
20	5.2
25	5.9

Table 5-2. *Determining Distance to the Horizon*

Another useful method of judging distance is by the color of objects. A tree-covered island between you and a tree-lined shore appears to be a darker and more vivid green because light is scattered by the atmosphere. This can be quite helpful in telling which island is which when looking at the chart; the closer ones are darker. This effect is most noticeable on hazy days; on a crystal-clear day it is minimal. It also varies with the angle of the sun.

Seaman's eye, used skillfully, is an instant form of navigation. With a few simple measurements, no plotting, and no delay, you can tell approximately where you are. You can find a useful "fix" as often as you look at your surroundings. This skill makes inshore piloting easy and safe. Since it is so useful, you might think that seaman's eye is all-sufficient. It isn't. Supplement it with the compass, a chart, a depthfinder, a watch, a speed log, and a navigation receiver to avoid staying in the dark ages of navigation. No matter how well you learn seaman's eye, if you don't learn the other methods, you are setting yourself up for trouble. What will you do in fog and rain—when those vital landmarks vanish?

> *Seaman's eye, used skillfully, is an instant form of navigation.*

Radar and Seaman's Eye

A radar scope gives a picture of surrounding land that is easy to relate to a chart. Although radar shows the near side of islands and not the back, and in other ways differs from the chart, you can learn rather quickly to allow for these differences. The chart and the radar give the same point of view, and you will have little trouble relating one to another. It is easiest to look at the angles between points and other prominent objects on the radar and compare that set of angles with the chart.

This is not as difficult as learning how the angles of objects around the horizon appear on a chart; the radar picture preserves the angular relationships and the relative distances. In a narrow passage, it's easy to see by looking at the radar scope that the boat is in the center or off to one side. This may be easier than comparing wide and narrow horizontal angles.

It is often difficult to see a point of land that is abeam. Radar shows the outline of the point clearly. In addition, its shape helps to distinguish it from another similar point nearby.

Precise navigation by radar involves measuring and plotting ranges to objects, but "eyeball" radar navigation is far easier and completely satisfactory for much boat navigation in confined waters. Of course, it's still important to note the times you pass key aids to navigation, and it's easier, just as in visual navigation, if you know the courses and running times along various legs of the course.

Taking Departure

An ancient and respected part of navigation is called *taking departure:* simply taking a fix when departing from land on a long ocean voyage. It is equally useful today: simply note the time the boat passes the harbor entrance buoy on the way out, and you'll have a fix that is a point of reference for the trip. Get in the habit of taking departure each time you leave a harbor entrance, and relate the rest of the trip to that initial position.

With electronic navigation, take departure by setting the destination waypoint as you pass the entrance buoy, and noting the time. That sets waypoint zero as the origin, as I explain later, and gives a fix.

Figure 5-10. *Sometimes it's difficult to distinguish headlands from one another by eye. Radar helps by showing the shapes of their near sides clearly. Areas beyond hills don't show on radar.*

Ded (Dead) Reckoning—The DR

If it has been some time since the last fix, a navigator finds an approximate position by *ded reckoning*. This is short for *deduced reckoning*; navigators aboard the old sailing ships deduced, or calculated, their new position based on compass course and the distance traveled by the log. Sometimes this is called *dead* reckoning, with the explanation that the reckoning is done for "dead" water, that is, without allowing for current. Both factions—ded and dead—hold their views with great certainty balanced by slim evidence. The truth seems buried somewhere far in the past. Take your choice; just remember that the **DR**—predicting the boat's present position based on an earlier fix—*is the very essence of navigation.*

The DR—predicting the boat's present position based on an earlier fix—is the very essence of navigation.

In an hour a boat goes a distance equal to her speed in knots, so a boat sailing for three hours at 6 knots on a southerly course can be expected to be 18 miles south of the starting point. This concept is simple to understand and to use. If a chart table is available, a navigator draws a line representing the course,

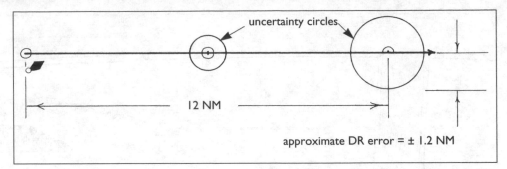

Figure 5-11. *Allowing for an error equal to 10 percent of the distance traveled, a DR after two hours' travel at 6 knots will have an uncertainty of just over a mile.*

sets a pair of dividers to the distance in miles equal to the speed in knots, and steps off the distances, beginning at the point of departure. Each step represents a DR position at hourly intervals from the departure. The standard symbol for a DR position is a dot on the course line, with a half-circle around it.

A DR position, although most useful, is not exact. At first the boat should be quite close to the DR position, but as time goes on, the boat's position becomes less certain. In planning searches, the Coast Guard estimates that the probable error in a boat's DR position is 15 percent of the distance traveled. You can do better than that: keeping errors within 10 percent is relatively easy, and 5 percent is possible with care. If you envision a DR position not so much as a pinpoint but as a circle growing larger at increasing distance from the starting point, you gain a clearer understanding of what it represents. Allowing for an error equal to 10 percent of the distance traveled, the DR after two hours' travel at 6 knots will have an uncertainty of just over a mile. That's not bad.

Once in Alaska, aboard a 110-foot king-crab boat, I woke up at midnight to take over the watch. We were heading along a bold, rocky coast. Nothing was in sight—there were no towns for over 100 miles and lights were far apart—but the radar showed an excellent picture of the shoreline. I asked where we were, checked the chart and the radar, and took over. After a while we came abeam of a point of land, and I had increasing difficulty relating the radar picture to the chart. The boat was in over 100 fathoms of water, several miles offshore, and I didn't want to wake up the man I had relieved, but something was wrong. I looked back on the chart and found he had marked the time on the chart when we passed a prominent island, two and three-quarters hours earlier.

That made it easy to reconstruct an approximate DR. In two and three-quarters hours we would have gone about 35 miles, not 40. That coast has a series of points that appear similar to each other, yet don't have any lights. The boat was approaching a point about 5 miles back from the one the previous watchstander had shown me. I was then able to get a good radar fix that agreed with the chart and the DR.

It's always a good idea to use DR, if only to avoid such embarrassment. The crab boat had a good chart table, but aboard a small boat it makes more sense to estimate the arrival time at some prominent aid to navigation or other landmark. If the boat isn't approaching the landmark at the right time, find out why.

Purists insist that the DR reflect only the course steered and the speed from rpm or the log. This enables them to compare the DR with the next fix to determine the current. If you want to be navigationally "pure," by all means plot to your heart's content: each hour you need a fix, a new DR position, and a vector plot to determine current. Aboard a boat it is more practical to use the speed and course over the ground for the last hour as a basis for the DR estimate of the boat's future position. You can use the navigation receiver to find what you really want to know: the course to steer—corrected for current—and the time when you will reach the destination.

Time, Speed, and Distance Calculations

The fundamental navigation calculations involve time, speed, and distance. Knowing any two, you can find the other one. If you don't know this cold, stop now and learn it. You can't use ded reckoning or do a competent job of navigation without knowing how to make these simple calculations.

They aren't that hard, not nearly as hard as balancing a checkbook, for example. That requires a series of arithmetic operations to get one answer—the balance. Time, speed, and distance calculations require one or two multiplications or divisions to get an answer, and become almost second nature with use.

Time

Here's a typical calculation. An offshore wreck lies 29.4 miles away from your harbor entrance buoy. Your boat cruises comfortably at 18 knots. How long will it take to get there? Divide the distance by the speed to get the time. To find time, the formula is $T = \dfrac{D}{S}$.

$$time = \frac{distance}{speed} = \frac{29.4 \text{ miles}}{18 \text{ knots}} = 1.633 \text{ hours}$$

Usually you want to know the time in hours and minutes, so multiply 0.633 hour by 60 to get 38 minutes; the estimated time en route is 1 hour and 38 minutes. You may use an electronic calculator, a time-speed-distance calculator, or a slide rule. You will do this calculation frequently.

Yes, your Loran-C or GPS receiver will give the estimated time en route, but only after you are on the way to the wreck. How do you plan before starting out? Simply divide the distance by the speed.

Speed

You might wonder how we knew the boat goes 18 knots at normal cruising rpm. Boatowners are divided into two groups: those who know how fast their boats are going and those who don't. The latter group is surprisingly large. Just last summer I was at a boatbuilder's shop, and he was finishing up a 28-foot diesel sportfishing boat. The new owner was hovering around, wondering about speed. He asked me, "Do you know anybody with a radar gun? I'd sure like to find out how fast she'll go."

I thought, *Good grief.* You don't need a radar gun to find out how fast a boat goes. In fact, it can be misleading. The numbers jump around a knot or so, and a radar gun doesn't take the current into account. You have to make two runs in opposite directions to find the boat's speed through the water.

Lots of boats have speed logs—all should have them—but they aren't perfect either. To find a boat's true speed, measure the distance between two charted objects near the channel, run between them at steady rpm, and time the run with a stop watch.

Let's say a boat runs at 2,000 rpm between two lights 2.35 miles apart in 7 minutes and 50 seconds. We use the same formula as before but solve it for speed rather than time. We know the time, but for the formula, we need it in hours. First convert 50 seconds to a fraction of a minute by dividing by 60. This gives 0.833 minute, so the run time was 7.833 minutes. Convert minutes to hours by dividing 7.833 by 60 to get 0.1306 hour. For finding speed, the formula is $S = \dfrac{D}{T}$.

$$speed = \frac{distance}{time} = \frac{2.35 \text{ miles}}{0.1306 \text{ hour}} = 18 \text{ knots}$$

Sometimes the formula is written $S = 60 \times D/T$ to calculate time in minutes. It is exactly the same calculation. Some nautical slide rules are graduated in hours and minutes, which is convenient. Again, do this calculation routinely, and you will get an excellent understanding of the speed your boat makes under normal operating conditions.

Loran-C and GPS provide an excellent way to check speed *over the ground* when heading directly toward a waypoint. At any convenient starting point, note the exact time and distance to go, and again when you're 5 miles closer. Then you can calculate the speed quite accurately. Radar is also excellent if you have it and are heading directly toward a fixed target. Using radar, it is only necessary to travel a couple of miles to get accurate speed.

In all of these methods, the time interval is critical. It's best to use a stopwatch. These calculations give the speed over the ground, but since there usually is a current, to find our speed through the water we have to make two runs in opposite directions, calculate the speeds, and find the average of the two speeds. This is also the way to check the accuracy of a speed log.

I have to caution you: *Don't average the times.* That "shortcut" doesn't work, as the following example will show. Suppose a boat takes 15 minutes to go a mile upriver and 7.5 minutes to cover the same distance going downstream.

The upstream speed is $60 \times \dfrac{1}{15} = 4$ knots.

The downstream speed is $60 \times \dfrac{1}{7.5} = 8$ knots.

The average speed is 6 knots, found by adding the speeds and dividing by 2. An accurate speed log would indicate 6 knots on both upstream and downstream runs.

If we mistakenly average the time ($15 + 7.5 \div 2 = 11.25$) and then use our formula to find "average" speed, the calculation would be $S = 60 \times 1/11.25$. That yields 5.33 knots, which is greatly in error. *Remember to solve first for speed in each direction, then find the average speed.*

Distance

In addition to calculating time and speed, we often need to find the distance run at a known speed for a certain time. Suppose a boat making 32 knots has been traveling for 47 minutes. How far has she gone? To solve for distance, we state the formula as $D = S \times T$.

Convert minutes to a fraction of an hour by dividing by 60; 47 minutes is 0.783 hour. Multiply 32 knots by 0.783 hour, and you find that you have gone 25.1 miles.

These formulas are both simple and fundamental. Distance is in miles, speed in knots, and time in hours. Take time to learn them thoroughly.

$$T = \frac{D}{S} \qquad\qquad S = \frac{D}{T} \qquad\qquad D = ST$$

To check speed through the water, solve first for speed over the ground in each direction, then find the average speed.

Remember to convert minutes to hours by dividing by 60.

Get these formulas down pat, and in the next section we will consider a handy way to do many of the calculations.

Doing the Calculations Mentally

Boat operators often skip the calculations to find the estimated time en route or the distance they have traveled, simply because the methods they have learned are poorly adapted for use aboard a boat. These calculations are fundamental to navigation, but you need a calculator or a nautical slide rule to solve the equations. Many professional mariners use a simpler way.

Several years ago, my ship, the 378-foot CG cutter *Dallas*, was standing down the channel from Guantanamo Bay on a training exercise. We had two Marine carrier pilots aboard. The executive officer asked permission to increase speed to 12 knots. Afterward, one of the pilots asked if there were some particular reason for 12 knots. "Sure," I told him. "At 12 knots, it takes exactly 5 minutes to go a mile. It's easy to calculate the distance run in your head. In a few minutes, we'll go up to 15 knots—4 minutes per mile."

They laughed, then explained that they commonly chose 360 or 420 knots for bomb runs in their A-7 aircraft. Their reasoning was the same as mine: flying at a speed giving exactly 6 (or 7) miles per minute made mental calculations easy. The pilot in a single-seat aircraft needs simplicity.

A boat skipper is often in a similar situation. He or she needs to make a quick calculation but is busy steering and watching the depthfinder, and the calculator isn't handy. If you haven't progressed from $T = D/S$ to this **minutes-per-mile** concept, your navigation calculations are too complicated.

To find the number of minutes required to travel a mile, divide 60 minutes by the boat's speed. Do this as soon as you get settled on course and come up to speed, and keep the number in mind until you change speed. For example, you're making 15 knots. Dividing 60 by 15 gives 4; it takes 4 minutes to go a mile. Suppose you want to know how long it takes to cover a distance of 3 miles. Simply multiply the distance (3) by 4 (minutes per mile); it takes 12 minutes to go 3 miles. You can do this in your head—no calculator, no batteries, no lights. The concept is so simple that experienced navigators use it all the time.

This is particularly useful when using an electronic navigation receiver to go to a waypoint. The receiver shows the bearing and distance to the waypoint, and it is easy to multiply the distance by the minutes-per-mile number to predict the time en route. This technique is just as useful with a *custom chart* that shows the bearings and distances for your most common destinations.

It happens that dividing 60 by many common speeds yields whole numbers. The ancient Babylonians used 60 as a special number since it is an even multiple of many smaller numbers. To this day, time and angle show this 60 heritage. The following table gives some speeds that require an integral number of minutes to go a mile:

Speed	Minutes per Mile
3	20
4	15
5	12
6	10
10	6
12	5
15	4
20	3
30	2

There are also speeds that contain fractions, but whose corresponding minutes-per-mile numbers are integers. Here are some of them:

Speed	Minutes per Mile
4.3	14
4.6	13
5.5	11
6.7	9
7.5	8
8.6	7

The distance often contains a fraction, but multiplying to find the estimated time en route remains easy at the "even" speeds. Suppose it's 8.22 miles to the next waypoint, and your boat is making 15 knots. It's easiest to handle the miles and the fraction separately. To go 8 miles at 4 minutes per mile will take 32 minutes (8 × 4). Then multiply 0.22 × 4 for roughly another minute. You found the estimated time en route is just under 33 minutes, without a calculator. You haven't even stirred from the helm seat.

At even speeds, it is also easy to determine how far you have gone in a certain time. Suppose you're sailing at about 6.7 knots (9 minutes per mile) and have been on that course for 42 minutes. Mentally divide 42 by 9—4 × 9 is 36, with 6 left over. You've gone 4 miles plus 6/9 of a mile, or 4⅔ miles.

When sailing, it often takes more than 10 minutes to go a mile; those of us old enough to have suffered through learning the multiplication tables above 10 finally can enjoy the benefits of that knowledge.

Usually you use mental math for short distances—which account for a high percentage of your calculations. If it takes several hours to travel a leg of the trip, you have plenty of time to get out a calculator and solve the equation.

When steering directly toward a waypoint some distance away, there is an easy and accurate way to find the number of minutes per mile. Suppose the waypoint is 23.8 miles away, and you note the time as 0810. Ten miles later, when it is 13.8 miles away, check the time: it is 0852. That's 42 minutes for 10 miles, or 4.2 minutes per mile—a bit less than 15 knots. I often think more in terms of minutes per mile than knots since the concept is so handy.

Direction and Time

There is an older and even easier method of estimating en-route times in common use aboard powerboats: simply making a note of the course and time required to run to a destination at cruising rpm. For example, it takes me about an hour and 45 minutes to run to one offshore wreck that is a good fishing spot. Remembering that saves some figuring when I'm planning a trip—usually on the phone with someone, not at a chart table.

It's a good idea to write down the course and time as you begin a leg of a trip, and the time when you reach your destination or turn on the next leg. Noting the course and time to go to popular destinations saves you a lot of measuring and calculation. Back in the days of displacement commercial fishing boats, most of which made 9 or 10 knots, skippers referred to locations by course and running time. It's a method that gives you a reasonable idea of the boat's location without a lot of work.

Here's another example. If you've run 35 minutes at cruising speed on a compass course of 285°, you can be pretty sure that running back on the reciprocal course of 105° for 35 minutes will put you close to your departure point, unless there is a current or large compass deviations.

I have found the direction and time method to be useful in large reservoirs even though the course changes to follow the curved stream bed. On a bass boat you seldom have time to do much in the way of navigation. If you know that it takes 9 minutes to reach a junction of two parts of the lake, and another 2½ minutes to get to the honey hole, both planning and going there are easier and more accurate.

In rivers, the time going to a destination is always different from the time coming back, due to the current. Time the trip in each direction. Although the current changes with the runoff and the season, this method is far better than going without any real idea how long it takes to get to a destination.

Lines of Position and Fixes

The next step beyond seaman's eye and DR navigation is finding where you are by using intersecting lines of position to form fixes. A **line of position (LOP)** is found by making a measurement from the boat, such as a compass bearing to a fixed object. An LOP is just a line that represents an unchanging measurement. A navigator sights over the compass to a landmark, such as the abandoned lighthouse in Figure 5-12, and finds its bearing. Suppose it is 045° by compass. The compass has no deviation at the present heading, so the magnetic bearing is also 045°. If you draw a line on the chart extending from out in the water to the light on a magnetic bearing of 045°, the boat is somewhere along that line. The LOP gives no clues about the distance to the lighthouse; the bearing is 045° from a boat anywhere along the line. If the boat goes a little to the northwest or to the southeast of the LOP, the bearing changes.

It is seldom practical to plot LOPs aboard a boat unless the boat is large and has space to spread out a chart. Aboard a center-console boat or a runabout,

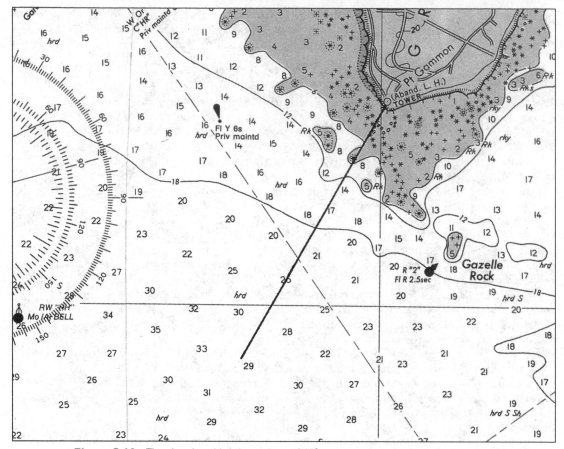

Figure 5-12. *The abandoned lighthouse bears 045° magnetic from the boat; the boat could be anywhere along the 045° line. The depth is 20 feet, corrected for transducer depth (below the waterline) and the tide, so the boat is near where the bearing line crosses the 20-foot depth contour.*

plotting is especially difficult. Methods that are easy aboard a large boat or at a drawing table can't be used. Boat navigators look at the chart for information but seldom plot LOPs.

You sighted over the compass to get an approximate bearing. That's fine; you don't need a precise position. You just need to set a safe course to your destination. You see that the old lighthouse is northeast of the boat. Look at the chart, at the *inner* compass rose, and find its 045° mark. Magnetic north of the inner compass rose is 16° west of true north on the outer circle since the variation is 16° west in this area. (The *inner-inner* rose, if we may call it that, shows the *points* of the compass. It has a line at northeast magnetic, the same as the 045°M bearing to the light.)

By eye, line up an imaginary line on the chart going northeast to the abandoned lighthouse. Aboard a boat I find this easier to do by eye than with parallel rules (see sidebar). The boat is somewhere on that line.

Parallel Lines

Ashore, or on a ship, parallel rules are essential to accurate plotting. Aboard a boat they slip and slide, and trying to use them is usually an exercise in frustration. It's more useful to learn to keep lines parallel by eye as you transfer them across the chart. Try this first when you *do* have a large table to spread out a chart.

I often use a pencil or a rule, first holding it along the inner compass rose and then moving it across the chart without changing direction. It's not precise by any means, but eyeballing a line parallel to another one is plenty close for much boat navigation. A protractor with a series of parallel lines or a plastic overlay with rows of parallel lines also is handy to transfer directions across a chart.

Eyeballing a line parallel to another one is plenty close for much boat navigation.

To know the course to steer, you often need to find the bearing of a line joining two points on the chart. Hold a pencil or a straightedge parallel to the line, then transfer it to the compass rose for the bearing. Do this several times and see how much the bearings vary, then use parallel rules to find the correct bearing. With a little practice you can eyeball the direction of a line with reasonable accuracy.

Objects for Lines of Position

You often have a choice of objects for visual bearings. The object must be visible, easy to identify, and charted. A lighthouse is ideal in this respect; it is prominent, with a distinctive color scheme and an identifiable light characteristic at night. However, there are relatively few lighthouses, so most bearings are to other objects. Minor lights are excellent for bearings. Prominent objects such as tanks, radio towers, church steeples, and cupolas are also useful. They often appear on the chart and are large enough to be seen easily; just be careful to use the correct landmark when there are several in the vicinity.

Objects located accurately on the chart are shown by a dot inside a small circle. These are excellent for visual bearings. Other objects are marked by a tiny circle without a dot, indicating that their position is approximate. They are sufficiently accurate for navigation but not for precise plotting. For boat navigation with little or no plotting, it makes little difference.

Some aids to navigation are in positions that have not been determined precisely. This is especially true of daybeacons and minor lights in remote areas. The chart gives the symbol "PA" (position approximate) by aids that aren't located accurately. The Coast Guard has a project to verify the positions of all fixed aids to navigation using DGPS. In time they will determine accurate positions and remove the PA designations.

A problem will remain with aids to navigation along narrow channels. Cartographers place them slightly outside their actual positions to keep the channel from appearing as a line. This moves them slightly from their correct positions, but it doesn't make much difference in boat navigation.

Buoys furnish useful lines of position but *not* highly accurate ones. A buoy is moored by a chain, usually two to five times as long as the maximum water depth. The buoy is free to swing, just like a boat at anchor. An entrance buoy in

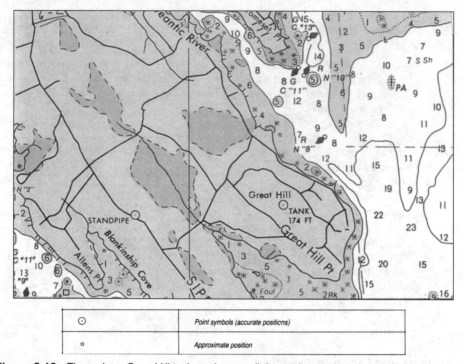

| ⊙ | Point symbols (accurate positions) |
| o | Approximate position |

Figure 5-13. *The tank on Great Hill is shown by a small dot inside a circle, indicating that its position is accurate. A small circle without a dot indicates an approximate position.*

60 feet of water can easily move 30 to 90 yards. In addition, it has a certain position tolerance since the buoy tender cannot place the sinker (anchor) in the exact same spot each time. Buoy symbols on charts include a small circle similar to the position-approximate symbol to emphasize that the buoy position is not precise. Storms, ice, strong currents, and passing vessels also move buoys from their correct positions. I don't hesitate to use buoys for bearings, but the bearings to them aren't as accurate or as reliable as bearings to lights.

Sometimes it is handy to take a bearing to the end of a point or the side of an island. Such bearings are called *tangents* since the line of bearing is tangent to the object (in the language of geometry). Tangent bearings may be good or lousy. If the side of the island is steep rock, a tangent bearing is a good one. On the other hand, avoid using tangents to any land that slopes gently into the sea; a beach extends farther out at low tide than at high tide, and shifts with storms and seasons.

Small, isolated rocks also give good bearings. Hydrographic surveyors find these positions with great accuracy, and it is easy to take a bearing to the center of the rock.

Fixes from Lines of Position

One line of position, as in our example on page 118, isn't enough to show the boat's location. Check the depthfinder. It shows 18 feet, and the transducer is

2 feet below the waterline—the boat is in 20 feet of water. It is near low tide, so the depth corrected for tide is also 20 feet. That's just outside the 3-fathom (18-foot) contour on the chart. Find the spot on the chart where the compass bearing crosses the 20-foot depth. Check the time, and you have a **fix**, found by two lines of position at a specific time.

Neither of the lines of position is precise, and one of them curves. Nevertheless they make a good, usable fix. In this area, depth is a good LOP. In others, depth varies so slowly that it is of little use. Some places have so many depth variations that the boat could be on any one of several contours marking the same depth.

The bearing and the depth give enough information to plot a fix. While fixes using two LOPs may be accurate, if there is an error in one LOP, there is no way to spot it. *To make the fix certain, you need a third line of position.* You see a large lighted buoy bearing about 120°. If the third LOP goes through the same area where the bearing to the lighthouse crosses the 20-foot depth, you are there. This is a fix that is valuable, easy to find, and verified by three lines of position at a specific time. The only thing it lacks is high accuracy. High accuracy is seldom necessary aboard a boat. That's a blessing, or we would have to spend all our time navigating (see Figure 5-12, page 118).

It's easy to make a mistake with a LOP. I speak from long experience and many errors. It's easy to use the wrong object, misread a compass bearing, make a mistake in the plot, get the time wrong, and so on. Aboard ship, errors slip in among the many good fixes taken under excellent conditions. Aboard a boat, errors are larger and more frequent. A navigator must have a somewhat suspicious mind, always alert for something that doesn't fit the other data.

The three lines of position should pass through the objects and the boat's position, but there may not be one spot that includes all three lines. Instead, they are likely to form a small triangle. Three LOPs forming a *large* triangle should always arouse suspicion; one or more of them must be wrong.

When LOPs don't agree, go back and check. You may find the error by retaking the bearings and the depth. If your measurements are correct, you may have measured a bearing to the wrong object. Scan the chart for similar objects near the objects you used.

Radar Lines of Position

Boats with radar have an excellent way to measure distances. With a good target, such as a minor light on pilings, radar range is usually accurate within 50 to 100 yards. A radar range is a circular LOP. Combine it with a second radar range or a bearing, either radar or visual, to find a fix. The depth or a third LOP may verify the fix.

A radar range is a circular LOP.

If you're plotting the LOPs on a chart, set a drafting compass to the correct range, put the point on the object, and draw a short arc with the pencil leg. On a boat it is seldom practical to draw range arcs on the chart. The navigator is more likely to get a rough fix by estimating the bearing by eye from the compass rose and measuring an approximate distance by holding a finger at the right length on a pencil.

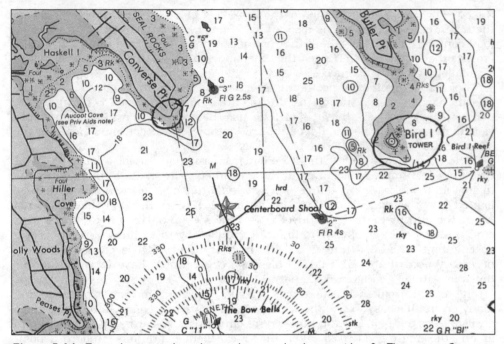

Figure 5-14. *Two radar ranges shown by arcs drawn on the chart provide a fix. The range to Converse Point is 700 yards; Bird Island is a thousand yards away. The depth helps to verify the fix.*

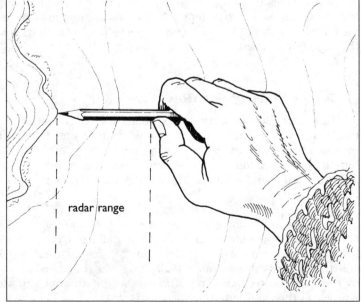

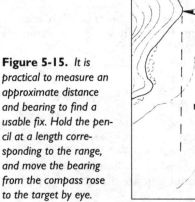

Figure 5-15. *It is practical to measure an approximate distance and bearing to find a usable fix. Hold the pencil at a length corresponding to the range, and move the bearing from the compass rose to the target by eye.*

Radar gives a useful LOP by measuring the range to a beach but is subject to inaccuracies similar to a bearing tangent to a beach. In addition, radar seldom picks up the sloping sand at water's edge. It is more likely to pick up the ridge at the storm tide line, or the dunes beyond. These errors are relatively unimportant when you're several miles offshore, but they will cause mistakes in plotting fixes.

Line-of-Position and Fix Errors

We have spoken of lines of position as though they pass exactly through an object and the boat. This is a simplification; every line of position is subject to small errors. It is better to think of a boat as being *close to* a line of position than exactly on it. The boat could be slightly to either side of the LOP and get the same bearing. Visual bearings taken from a ship are usually within 2° or 3°; bearings taken from a boat can easily be in error by 5° or 6°. Bearings are subject to compass error or swing, sighting error, and uncorrected deviations. There are also plotting errors.

If a bearing is in error by 6°, the distance error is about 1/10 the range to the object. At 1/2 mile, that's 100 yards on either side of the LOP; at 3 miles, it's 600 yards. This has a strong influence on choosing objects for fixes. *If there is a choice, take bearings to nearby objects.*

A buoy is generally a less desirable fix than a light since it moves on its mooring, but suppose you have a choice of taking a bearing to a buoy 1/4 mile from the boat, or a light 2 miles away. If you're 1/4 mile from the buoy, a 6° bearing error is about 50 yards. The total error from the bearing and the buoy motion is about 100 yards. The bearing error to the light 2 miles away is about 400 yards. In this case there is good reason to prefer the bearing to the buoy.

A depth is seldom more accurate than ±2 feet; there are depthfinder errors, chart errors, and errors in applying the tide correction. To get an idea of the width of the depth LOP, look at the chart and see the distance required to change the depth 4 feet. The line of position is actually a *band of position*, and it may be 1/2 mile wide or wider. Along the west coast of Florida, the depth increases roughly 2 feet in a mile. In contrast, just off the Florida Keys on the other coast are places where the depth drops from 10 feet to 40 feet in a couple of hundred yards. Another mile offshore, the depth is 200 feet. In an area like this, a depth LOP is quite accurate.

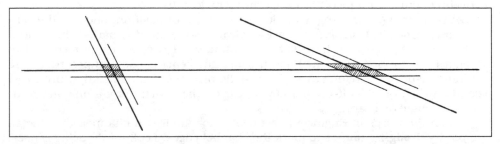

Figure 5-16. *Small errors in lines of position yield large fix errors if there are small angles where the LOPs cross.*

When the boat is underway, the LOPs mark successive positions as the boat moves, not one position. Minimize this effect by taking a bearing nearly ahead or astern first, then to the side, noting the time of the side bearing.

Two LOPs make a good fix when they cross near 90°. A small error in one LOP moves the fix a small distance along the other LOP. However, if the lines cross at a shallow angle, a small error has a large effect (Figure 5-16). When using three LOPs, it is ideal if they cross at approximately 60° to each other.

Usually three LOPs make a small triangle. There are many positions in and around the triangle where the navigator might have taken the identical bearings, given the errors that can occur. A navigator usually puts the fix symbol (⊿ or ⊙) in the center of the triangle, assuming that each bearing was in error by an equal amount. When using visual bearings, this assumption is true only when all three objects are at the same distance. If one of the three objects is much farther away than the other two, give it less weight when deciding where to place the fix inside the triangle.

In addition to measurement errors, there are plotting errors. A person can't plot better than about 1/50 of an inch consistently, nor can a cartographer draw objects on the chart much closer. The combination of these two errors gives an error of about 30 yards on a 1:40,000-scale chart, and 60 yards on a 1:80,000-scale chart. The survey on which the chart is based isn't error free either. These errors, plus bearing errors, make it nearly impossible to plot a visual fix with an accuracy better than ±50 yards, even on a 1:20,000 chart. It is more commonplace to have 100- or 200-yard errors in good visual fixes.

The principles of good fixes are universal: Use nearby objects. Use LOPs crossing at good angles. Use three LOPs to detect errors.

On a boat you'll seldom plot a three-line fix, and you needn't be as concerned about precision as with being sure that you are near a small area. However, the principles of good fixes are universal: Use nearby objects. Use LOPs crossing at good angles. Use three LOPs to detect errors.

Ranges

Ranges mark the most useful and accurate visual lines of position. A range is independent of measuring equipment aboard a boat, although binoculars can help you see the range clearly. When the objects are in line, you are on an extension of the line that joins them. No other ordinary LOPs are so accurate. Often it is useful to cross a range LOP with a bearing to get a fix.

Aids-to-navigation ranges mark a specific line of position, such as the center of a channel. The structures have vertical rectangular daymarks with central stripes, and they usually have lights. Many **natural ranges** are formed by two objects that happen to be in line on a certain bearing. Sometimes these are machine-made objects such as tanks or buildings, and sometimes they are trees, islands, rocks, or hills. If the objects appear on the chart, draw a line and measure the magnetic bearing.

When the Corps of Engineers or a contractor dredges a channel, they install temporary **dredging ranges** to mark the channel edges. Look for dredging ranges; they are quite useful. A few major channels have permanent daybeacons (shown on the chart) marking the edges of the channel in addition to the normal center-line range.

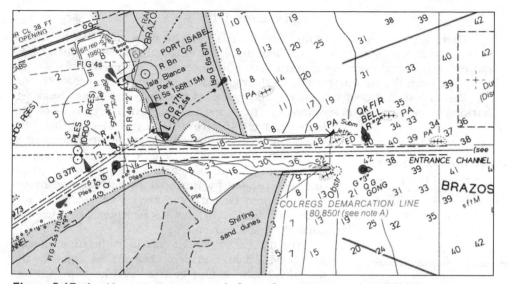

Figure 5-17. *An aid-to-navigation range marks Brazos Santiago entrance channel. Unlighted dredging ranges mark the sides of the channel as well.*

An important feature of a range is its **sensitivity**. If the range has high sensitivity, the objects appear to be in line only when you are very near the range line. The geometry of a range affects its sensitivity. Ranges marked by front and rear objects that are close together don't mark a line of position nearly as precisely as those with objects farther apart.

The distance from the boat to the range affects its sensitivity, too. The closer you are to the front object, the closer you have to be to the line between the objects for them to appear in line. Farther away, you can move more to the side and they still appear in range. *You can tell whether a range is sensitive by moving your head from side to side; if the objects appear to move with respect to one another, the range is highly sensitive.* Many good ranges, especially those used at distances of several miles, aren't as sensitive as those you use in tight quarters. You may have to get off to the side 10 or 20 yards to detect any motion.

Estimated Positions

When a navigator has more information than a DR, but not enough for a new fix, he uses an estimated position, or **EP**.

An EP is often a DR corrected for current, or a DR combined with one line of position—the only LOP that is available. This combination of a DR with a line of position is stronger than a DR alone but isn't a fix since the data aren't simultaneous. It is common practice to get a bearing to a light as you pass abeam and compare this with the DR. The DR combined with the LOP to the light makes a good EP.

Navigators usually plot a DR and the bearing LOP, and place the EP on the line of position where it is closest to the DR. The symbol for an estimated position is a dot inside a square box, with the time noted.

Distance Off

There are several ways to find how far offshore you pass an object by taking successive bearings to it. None of them are exact since they depend on the estimated boat speed over the ground. Some are complex. We prefer two simple methods, even though current affects their accuracy unless you correct for it.

The oldest and best known method is called the **bow and beam bearing**, harking back to ancient terminology. Take one bearing when a light is *on the bow*—that is, 45° from dead ahead—and another when the light is abeam. Note the time or start a stopwatch, or, better yet, check the distance log, at each bearing. You usually use approximate relative bearings judged by the boat rather than compass bearings; just be sure you are on course when you take each bearing. Compass bearings are more accurate but less convenient.

> The distance the boat travels in the time interval between the bow and beam bearings is equal to the distance offshore.

The distance the boat travels in the time interval between the *bow* and *beam* bearings is equal to the distance offshore. Our course and the two bearings form a triangle with one right angle (90°) and two 45° angles; the two legs that meet at right angles are equal in length. One leg represents the distance you have covered, or *distance run*, and the other the *distance off*, or distance from the object when it is abeam, and they are the same.

The next method is even easier, but requires a compass (a hand-bearing compass is most useful). As you pass the light, find how many minutes it takes to change the bearing to the light by a number of degrees equal to your boat's speed. Cruising at 16 knots, for example, note the time when the bearing is about

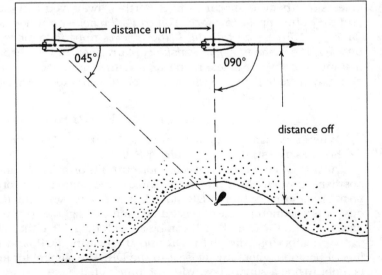

Figure 5-18. *The first bearing is 045° relative—on the bow. The second is abeam, 090°. The distance run (solid line) equals the distance off (vertical dotted line). It's easiest to calculate the distance run by the minutes-per-mile concept, pages 115–117.*

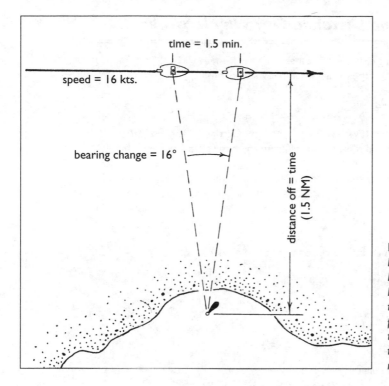

Figure 5-19. *The boat is making 16 knots. Find the time for the bearing to the landmark to change by 16° as you pass abeam of it. The time in minutes is equal to the distance off in miles.*

8° ahead of the beam. Note the time again when the bearing has changed by exactly 16°. The time in minutes is equal to the distance in miles that the boat passed offshore of the light.

This **angle = speed** method couldn't be simpler to use. If it takes a minute and a half to change the bearing by 16°, you passed 1.5 miles from the light when it was abeam. (The first bearing was 8° before the light came abeam, the second 8° afterward.) This handy approximation of distance off is accurate within a few percent. Even at 30 knots, the error is only 7 percent.

You can get a reasonably good idea of the distance off by *approximate* bearings if the distance is close and boat speed is high. Use the hand-width measurement system and glance at your watch. Errors will still be much smaller than what you can expect from distance estimates based on size alone.

Both the angle = speed method and the bow-and-beam method depend on knowing the boat's speed over the ground. Coming abeam of a light gives a time and distance that are ideal for checking speed since the last fix, so you can find the speed accurately. With accurate speed, either of these methods of finding the distance off gives a useful line of position. Combine that LOP with a bearing when the light is abeam to get an estimated position—nearly as good as a fix.

The Easiest Way to Find Distance Off: Why It Works

The **angle = speed** method of finding distance off comes from the formula to find the distance a boat will pass abeam of a light, based on the distance run between bearings.

$$D_{off} = D_{run} \sin A \sin B \div \sin A - B$$

A and B are the first and second relative bearings to the light. Certified digitheads can use this formula with their calculators to find the distance off from any two suitable bearings, but most skippers will prefer the short method.

For small bearing differences, nearly abeam, the formula can be simplified. First, the sine of an angle near 90° approaches 1. So:

$$D_{off} = \frac{D_{run}}{\sin (A - B)}$$

In addition, the sine of a small angle is very close to the angle divided by 60.

$$\sin (A - B) = \frac{A - B}{60} \text{ (approximate)}$$

The usual formula for distance run is:

$$D_{run} = \frac{S \times T}{60}$$

with speed in knots and time in minutes.

Substituting in the simplified formula gives:

$$D_{off} = \frac{\dfrac{S \times T}{60}}{\dfrac{A - B}{60}}$$

or

$$D_{off} = \frac{ST}{A - B} \quad \textit{(distance off = speed} \times \textit{time in minutes} \div \textit{angle change)}$$

To eliminate all calculations, let the difference in bearings (A − B) equal the speed (S) in knots. Then the distance off in miles equals the time between bearings in minutes:

$$D_{off} \text{ (in miles)} = T \text{ (in minutes)}$$

Electronic Navigation Systems

GPS and Loran-C have taken over much of the traditional work of finding a boat's position. Either system will indicate the position as long as it is locked on to the signals and not showing any alarms. Having nearly continuous fixes is a huge change from traditional navigation. You have to compare these electronic positions with visual and DR navigation, because any system can at times give false information. For the great majority of times, finding the position is as simple as looking at the receiver.

The receiver uses **lines of position (LOPs)** that it obtains from accurate time measurements. GPS uses LOPs that move constantly, so it isn't possible to show them on a chart. The receiver must use three satellites to calculate a two-dimension (latitude and longitude) position. The third LOP doesn't serve to verify the other two; rather, the receiver uses all three to adjust its clock to agree with the GPS system time. Loran-C uses **time-delay readings (TDs)** that are stationary LOPs. The TD readings correspond to lines of position printed on charts.

The easiest way to specify a fix with an electronic receiver is to save a waypoint, but the waypoint's latitude and longitude or TD numbers don't do much to tell you where you are without the extra work of plotting it on the chart. Then you need to plot a line from the electronic position to the destination. Fortunately, navigation receivers take over this portion of the navigator's task and calculate the direction and distance to the destination waypoint.

This is the very information you need for navigation, and it is available just by setting the destination waypoint and watching the receiver. Distance and direction to a waypoint, unlike latitude and longitude, are most useful aboard a boat. The navigator uses this receiver function more than any other.

Evaluating GPS and Loran-C Fixes

To evaluate the quality of a GPS fix, look at the **dilution of precision (DOP)** shown by the receiver. DOP is a measure of the crossing angles of the GPS lines of position (actually spheres of position); low numbers are better. (Some receivers use variations of DOP called HDOP or PDOP.) If DOP were used to evaluate a visual fix of two objects, it would be low if the visual LOPs crossed at 90°, and high if the visual LOPs crossed at 20°. Look for DOP under 2 for best accuracy, even though DOP can be up to 6 and still give useful fixes. Some GPS receivers give an **estimated position error (EPE)** in feet or yards. Don't believe these estimates; they usually indicate that the accuracy is higher than it is in fact.

TD lines for different secondaries about the same distance apart on the chart can have different intervals.

You can evaluate the quality of a Loran-C fix easily—using a chart. First determine the distance between two TD lines 10 microseconds apart for one of the TDs that the receiver is using. If the two TD lines at 10-microsecond intervals are less than a mile apart, you are in an area that gives the highest accuracy. TD lines that are 2 or 3 miles apart for each 10 microseconds give one-half or one-third the accuracy of those a mile apart. Look at the other TD, but be careful—TD lines for different secondaries may be about the same distance apart on the chart yet have different intervals.

Also look at the TD crossing angles. Acute crossing angles for any LOPs mean less precision than angles near 90°. The principles are identical regardless of the type of LOP: LOPs that cross at good angles and change rapidly with distance give good fixes.

Beginning with an Electronic Receiver

Like getting olives out of a jar, the first time you use a new electronic navigation receiver is the hardest. Use this guide to help learn to use your new receiver. Each topic (or question) requires specific steps, and they differ from one receiver to another. Look them up and make notes, or at least put markers in the manual, because these initial steps are essential. You can explore the receiver's other features later on.

1. Installation

    a. Begins with a warning not to reverse the power connections (i.e., hook – to +) to avoid damaging the receiver. This creates a state of anxiety guaranteed to make the rest of the process difficult.

    b. Fuse and circuit requirements.

    c. Location of antenna and receiver.

    d. Grounding. Loran-C will work without a ground, but not very well. Skip the ground and enjoy problems in bad weather.

    e. Interference. Wait until after the first start. A receiver may both produce and receive interference.

2. First start

    a. What does it need?—May require entry of approximate latitude and longitude. Some receivers also require date and time.

    b. How do you enter data?—A four-way button, number keys, or a repeat button for letters. Do you have to press an Enter key? How do you get to another field to enter the next group of data? How do you correct misentered data?

    c. How do you know when the receiver is locked on and ready?

    d. What button do you push to stop it from beeping when you try to enter data?

    e. How do you turn it off?

3. How do you save a receiver-measured waypoint? (Save one at the boat's home pier.)

4. How do you enter a waypoint from a chart or another source?

5. How do you make a waypoint the destination?

6. How do you make the receiver show distance and direction to the destination waypoint?

7. How do you detect and remove interference?

Learn to do these few things, and you will understand the functions that you use 90 percent of the time. There will be time later to investigate more esoteric receiver functions.

Waypoints

A *waypoint* is a position, a specific location, just like "the corner of Maple Street and Eighth Avenue." The term waypoint came into use with the first Loran-C receivers that could store positions in memory and show the distance and direction to them. Today it has the same meaning in all navigation systems. Waypoints are fundamental to electronic navigation. They are used for:

- destinations
- turn points
- origins
- temporary positions
- calculations
- trip planning

A typical leg of a trip begins at an origin waypoint and ends at a destination waypoint. You can plot waypoints on a chart, store them in a receiver, or both. Either way you can find the distance and direction between the two waypoints.

Measuring and Storing Waypoints with a Receiver

When you are at a position you wish to use for navigation in the future, save a waypoint. When a navigation receiver is "locked on" to the signals (i.e., tracking correctly), it is ready to save the location as a waypoint. Navigation receivers have a *Store*, *Save*, *Mark*, or *Event* button; push it, and the receiver stores the boat's position as a waypoint. Some receivers assign it the next unused waypoint number; others prompt you to enter a number or a name. Although there are variations, storing a receiver-measured waypoint is a simple procedure. Learn it early on; you will use it often (see sidebar page 131).

The receiver stores position data and a waypoint number or name, and GPS receivers also store the time. While the internal battery keeps waypoints stored for several years, it is a good idea to write them in a small book. List the waypoint's latitude and longitude for GPS, or the TDs for Loran-C. Loran-C can receive more than two secondary stations in many areas; it's smart to record all usable TDs.

Add a name or description of the waypoint in your book. It's easy to save several waypoints and later forget which one is which. A book allows you to look at the whole list of waypoints at once, making it easier to find the one you want. Writing down waypoints also ensures against losing them in the event of receiver problems. I use a surveyor's *Level Book* that has water-resistant paper and convenient lines. It's more durable than most little books.

Plotting GPS and Loran-C Positions on a Chart

This book emphasizes methods that don't require plotting, but there are times when you must plot the boat's position on the chart. With GPS, simply plot the displayed latitude and longitude, as discussed in Chapter 2, and note the time. With Loran-C, time-delay readings (TDs) usually give greater accuracy than receiver-calculated latitude and longitude. Coastal charts show Loran-C lines of position; you can plot positions on them using TDs from the receiver. The TD lines on a chart are labeled with the GRI number indicating the transmitter chain, a letter for the secondary station, and the TD. Your chart might show 7980 W, X, and Y, followed by the time difference numbers. The receiver shows two of those TD numbers on its display, and you can match them up with the lines on the chart.

Saving a Waypoint

Saving a waypoint is a simple procedure, yet there are many inventive ways to make mistakes. To avoid errors:

1. Check that the receiver is locked on to the signals:

    GPS: shows tracking at least three satellites.

    Loran-C: shows two TDs.

2. Check that there are no alarms:

    GPS: poor coverage, insufficient satellites, or low signal quality.

    Loran-C: blink, cycle, or low signal level.

3. Check GPS DOP, PDOP, or HDOP: should be less than 6, preferably less than 2.

4. Check GPS signal quality or Loran-C signal-to-noise ratio.

5. Check a Loran-C receiver to be sure it is using the TDs it usually uses in that area.

6. Check to see that the waypoint you plan to use is blank (latitude and longitude all zeroes).

7. Store the waypoint.

8. Copy the data into your waypoint book, along with the waypoint identification, the date, and the time.

9. For Loran-C, copy any additional usable TDs.

The technique for plotting a Loran-C line of position is similar to finding the TDs for a waypoint. Suppose there is a spot on the chart that you want to enter as a waypoint. The charted TD lines are usually 5 or 10 microseconds apart, and seldom does a position fall exactly on the lines. The easiest way to determine the correct TD is with an **interpolator card**. Choose a scale of 10 divisions slightly longer than the distance between two printed TD lines. Lay it on the chart so that each end of the 10 division scale touches a TD line, and it is easy to see

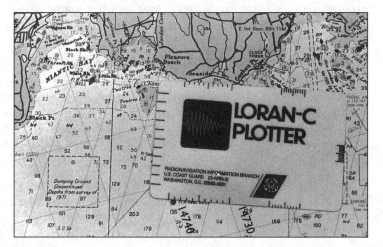

Figure 5-20. *A Loran-C plotter card. Lay it on the chart so that each end of the 10-division scale touches a TD line, and read intermediate TDs on the scale. The 10 divisions span 14730 and 14740; the buoy is at 14739.4. Check the TD difference between adjacent lines; it may be 5 to 100 microseconds.*

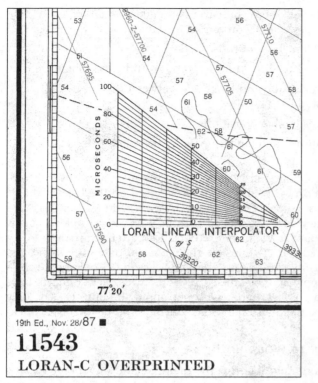

Figure 5-21. *Charts having Loran-C TDs have a linear interpolator for measuring TDs between the plotted lines. To find intermediate TD readings, transfer the intermediate distance to the interpolator with dividers, placing them where a vertical line is as long as the distance between charted TD lines.*

where the correct TD is by looking at the card. Make a mark at the correct TD reading, and draw a line parallel to the adjacent TD lines.

If you don't have an interpolator card, use the linear interpolator printed on all charts having Loran-C TDs. Set a pair of dividers to the distance between two TD lines at the point of interest. Move them to the linear interpolator and find where they fit the outside lines, being careful to hold the dividers vertical. Make a small mark at the bottom. The dividers might cover 10 microseconds; reset them to the distance from one line to the point of interest. Move them to the same place on the linear interpolator and read the distance. On the whole, an interpolator card is quicker, especially when using a folded chart.

Loran-C receivers can calculate TDs from latitude and longitude entry. For ordinary navigation in clear weather, it's fine to enter latitude and longitude. The Loran-C receiver's correction factors usually put you within ¼ mile of the waypoint. When you get there, store a receiver-measured waypoint; it's more accurate than one you pick off the chart. *Note: Some receivers don't have ASF corrections for accurate latitude and longitude calculations; always use TDs with them.*

Charts drawn at larger than 1:80,000 scale (e.g., 1:40,000) don't have Loran-C TD lines. TD lines are also omitted from the land areas and many bays and sounds shown on coastal charts, due to uncertainty in the TDs in areas where they have not been verified. Loran-C is still quite useful in these areas, using receiver-measured waypoints. The same is true of large inland bodies of water that have good Loran-C coverage but no TD lines on the map. If you want to take waypoints from a map or chart without TD lines, use this procedure:

1. Save a waypoint in a spot where you can take a good visual fix, clear of buildings, bridges, power lines, and boat antennas.

2. Find the latitude and longitude of the visual fix.

3. Set the Loran-C receiver to show the waypoint latitude and longitude.

4. Find the difference in latitude and longitude between the Loran-C waypoint and the visual fix.

5. Apply these differences to chart positions.

6. Enter waypoints in latitude and longitude using the adjusted positions.

When Loran-C became popular, the Defense Mapping Agency (DMA, the predecessor of NIMA) and NOAA drew TD lines on charts based on the best available computations. Later, the Coast Guard, DMA, and NOAA worked together to gather data to provide higher accuracy. DMA produced *Loran-C Correction Tables* to allow navigators to apply this new data to the measured TDs for better accuracy.

NOAA (NOS) also corrected the TD lines on their charts, using the same and additional data. Usually you *should not* use the DMA *Loran-C Correction Tables* with NOAA charts, to avoid applying the same corrections twice. Newer charts have a note that gives this warning. Coastal charts do not show all Loran-C TDs, only the most useful ones. If they showed all TDs, some charts would be full of TD lines.

Position with Respect to Waypoints

The most valuable position information is the distance and direction to a specific location. A canny navigator stores waypoints at key points and then uses the receiver to show the distance and direction to them—that's in addition to using a waypoint as a destination. You see on the screen that the destination waypoint is 6.75 miles, 245°M, but it's easy to designate another waypoint as a temporary destination and see that it is 3.44 miles away, 331°M. This information gives you a quick grasp of the boat's location. Many receivers allow you to scroll through the waypoints and show their distance and direction without resetting the destination. This is a handy feature.

To use this idea to best advantage, store waypoints at many prominent spots on the chart. Start with common destinations, then add other key locations that will be useful "landmarks." I have even put a waypoint near a lighthouse—where I never intend to go—but the waypoint makes it easier to find the light from a distance, and it allows me to specify distance and direction from it.

In the next chapter we will discuss placing and using waypoints, including temporary waypoints that make navigation easy on long trips.

Using Waypoints Measured by Another Receiver

Using waypoints measured by another receiver is one of the most valuable features of electronic navigation. There are many lists of waypoints for navigation, fishing spots, and diving locations. Using waypoints measured by another receiver results in a small loss in accuracy, seldom affecting navigation but enough to make finding small underwater rocks harder.

Two GPS receivers at the same spot may differ by around 20 yards. I have seen two GPS receivers display positions that differed from one another by more than 20 yards on several occasions. Which one was right? It's hard to know. The point is this: Different receivers for the same navigation system give positions that are close together *but not identical.* GPS yields smaller errors than Loran-C. Differential GPS and WAAS give accuracy within 5 to 10 yards—significantly better than straight GPS.

Loran-C receivers at the same spot usually agree within 0.1 microsecond. This is about 20 to 40 yards, depending on location. Loran-C waypoints measured in winter may not be identical with those measured in summer, so it's best to use waypoint data for the same season of the year.

Use TDs to enter waypoints in Loran-C, and any two receivers will have relatively small differences. On the other hand, different brands of Loran-C receivers calculate different latitude and longitude from identical TD inputs. I've seen receivers give differences of up to several hundred yards when waypoints were entered using latitude and longitude, so don't do it.

Converting Waypoints from Loran-C to GPS

Suppose you already have good, measured Loran-C waypoints, and you want to enter them into a GPS receiver. This is becoming more important as GPS comes into wide use. But Loran-C waypoints are best described by TD readings; using the latitude and longitude of a Loran-C waypoint as a GPS waypoint introduces errors. The most obvious alternative is actually going to each Loran-C waypoint and storing the measured position with the GPS receiver; this gives excellent results but is time-consuming.

Some GPS receivers can *calculate* Loran-C TD numbers from the GPS latitude and longitude. These receivers allow you to enter a waypoint in Loran-C TDs and let the receiver calculate a latitude and longitude. However, these TD calculations are subject to the same inaccuracies that cause the latitude and longitude calculated by a Loran-C receiver to differ from the correct values.

Don't confuse these GPS receivers with ones that *measure* Loran-C TDs with an internal loran receiver. Trimble, Raytheon, and others produced a few units that include both Loran-C and GPS receivers. They give TDs as accurate as those of a stand-alone Loran-C receiver.

If you're going to a waypoint well clear of hazards, perhaps marked by a large buoy, you can simply use the calculated latitude and longitude as the GPS waypoint. The problem occurs when it is foggy or you are heading to a waypoint marking an underwater wreck or rock. You must be as accurate as possible in these cases, or you will miss your destination entirely. I have worked out a way of converting Loran-C waypoints to GPS waypoints that has been accurate in tests.

First, stop the boat in a convenient position in open water, clear of obstructions. Large bridges can distort Loran-C signals, and big buildings can reflect GPS signals; you want your comparison free of such disturbances. Check both Loran-C and GPS receivers to be sure the numbers aren't jumping around. Check that the Loran-C is locked on the usual TDs, that the SNR is high, and that the GPS has low DOP and high signal quality. Save a Loran-C and a GPS waypoint at the same time. Shift the Loran-C receiver to indicate latitude and longitude, and compare these readings with the GPS position. This is sample data from my GPS and Loran-C receivers:

GPS	N 34° 42.040'	W 76° 59.172'
Loran-C	N 34° 41.970'	W 76° 59.130'
difference	0.070'	0.042'

With these two receivers in this area, adding these differences to the latitude and longitude of Loran-C waypoints gives the latitude and longitude to be entered as a GPS waypoint. This method has proven quite accurate.

There are some precautions, however. First, use your own receivers—two other receivers at this same spot gave corrections of +0.23 minute of latitude and +0.16 minute of longitude. Second, the corrections are valid over relatively short distances. Due to the way most Loran-C receivers calculate latitude and longitude, these corrections will be most accurate within the 1° square containing the waypoint. The corrections in the example are most accurate from 34°N to 35°N, and from 76°W to 77°W. Only a few hundred yards to the west, beyond 77°W, new corrections are necessary for the highest accuracy. Third, when you go to each waypoint, save it in the GPS receiver. That is the most accurate GPS data.

With some GPS receivers, you can enter a waypoint as a range and bearing from a known position. You also could use the Loran-C receiver to find range and bearing from the common waypoint to other waypoints, for entry as GPS waypoints. This isn't a good idea for long distances; the bearings are only accurate to 1°. At 10 miles, there will be an error of up to 350 yards; at 20 miles, 700 yards. It's more accurate to use corrections to Loran-C latitude and longitude to establish GPS waypoints.

You also can use computer programs plus position observations to convert Loran-C TDs to latitude and longitude for GPS. Andren Software Co., 906 S. Ramona Ave., Indialantic, FL 32903-3435, http://www.andren.com has an excellent Windows-based program that stores, converts, and maps GPS and loran waypoints.

Corrections to Waypoint Positions

Loran-C receivers calculate latitude and longitude from the measured time-delay (TD) readings. Since Loran-C signals travel long distances over land and sea, the measured TDs don't agree exactly with the predicted ones. Receivers use three correction factors to make them agree as well as possible, and the last factor, **additional secondary phase factor (ASF)**, differs from one receiver to another. Each receiver designer uses proprietary methods of calculating latitude and longitude, and different receivers give somewhat different latitude and longitude at identical TD readings.

Most Loran-C and some GPS receivers have methods for correcting latitude and longitude to agree with a position taken from the chart. They are usually called *home-port*, *local*, or *ASF* corrections. You can enter a correction either to the latitude and longitude or to the TDs to make the calculated latitude and longitude agree with the chart, but this has two undesirable consequences.

First, *the receiver shifts all waypoints in memory* by the amount of the correction. This isn't the displayed latitude and longitude but the physical location of the waypoints. I have yet to find a manual that mentions this, or a receiver that doesn't do it. If you plan to enter a home-port correction, do it before you start to enter waypoints. Otherwise, you will have to reenter each one using the correct TDs.

Second, *the Loran-C receiver will no longer adjust ASF corrections* as you move to different locations. You could go several hundred miles, yet the receiver will be using corrections that are valid only within 30 to 50 miles of your home port.

For these reasons I prefer not to enter home-port corrections in navigation receivers. I find the differences and make the corrections by adding and subtracting when converting from chart to receiver or the other way around. That has no effect on other waypoints.

Avoiding GPS and Loran-C Errors

Check before Getting Underway

It is best to check a navigation receiver each time you get underway. Save a waypoint at the home slip or at the usual launching ramp. I use waypoint 01 for this purpose. *After starting the engine(s),* turn on the receiver and the rest of the electronics. Starting an engine causes the voltage to drop drastically and creates spikes of higher voltage. If the receiver is on when you start an engine, the power variations can alter its memory or destroy internal components.

When the receiver is operating correctly and ready for use, set waypoint 01 as the destination. The distance to it should be 0.0 to 0.01 mile (0 to 20 yd.) for GPS and 0.0 to 0.03 mile for Loran-C (0 to 60 yd.). A hundredth of a mile is about 20 yards. GPS receivers occasionally show unusual errors when they start up, showing the home slip to be several hundred yards away. Usually this error decreases quickly to 20 yards (0.01 mi.) or less.

Receivers for either system display alarms for most other types of errors. Be sure that the alarms are off and that the receiver is ready.

Loran-C provides usable TDs from more than two secondary stations of a chain in many places. When you turn on a receiver, it can lock on to a secondary that it doesn't use normally. This causes an error of a few hundred yards to over a mile. If your Loran-C shows a large distance to the home slip waypoint, check the displayed TDs. In Long Island Sound, for example, a receiver might normally display TDs in the 14000 and 44000 range. If the receiver is showing TDs near 26000 and 44000, it has shifted from the W to the X secondary station for chain 9960.

Usually a receiver showing an error has simply used the first pair of secondaries it has been able to track reliably; in a minute or two it will begin tracking the other secondary and switch to the pair it usually uses. Then the position will jump to the home slip.

Electronic Position Jumps

GPS receivers show a jump when switching satellites. These jumps are small now that selective availability is off. DGPS receivers often show a small position jump when switching from one differential beacon transmitter to another.

Most Loran-C receivers show a jump in position when shifting to another secondary. Normally they change secondaries when moving into an area where another pair of secondaries gives better accuracy, but the jump can be disconcerting.

Loran-C receivers also show a position jump when shifting to another chain. If you cross into an area where an adjacent chain gives better accuracy, the receiver will shift to that chain. These jumps are a problem if your receiver is programmed to switch secondaries or chains within a few miles of your harbor. It will shift back and forth every time you cross the line, which is annoying. In this case, get out the manual and learn to lock the receiver on to a specific chain (GRI) and pair of secondaries. It will then work fine in your area since it won't switch. Remember to set it back to automatic chain selection if you travel out of the area.

Out of Tolerance Signals

When a GPS satellite gets out of tolerance, or requires maintenance, the Air Force sets it unusable. The satellite broadcasts this information within a few seconds, and receivers don't use it for fixes. It takes a relatively long time for the ground control segment of GPS to detect and correct certain types of satellite errors—90 minutes to four hours. During that time, GPS will give incorrect information. Sometimes a satellite nearing the end of its service life has frequent problems that lead to position errors. You can make the receiver ignore that satellite.

If a GPS receiver is not giving positions, check that it is tracking at least three satellites. Look at the signal quality, often shown as a vertical bar. It should be within the normal range. Sometimes the receiver is tracking three satellites, but the geometry is poor—like visual bearings at small angles. GPS receivers either show an accuracy estimate (in meters, feet, or yards) or a dilution-of-precision number. If the estimated accuracy is a high number, the accuracy is poor. If the DOP, HDOP, or PDOP is more than 5 or 6, accuracy also is questionable. Most receivers stop giving positions when the DOP goes above 12.

Check the antenna; it should be mounted low to avoid errors as the boat rolls, and it must have a clear view of the sky. Something could be blocking the signals. When a sailboat tacks, sometimes a satellite on the new weather side gets below the antenna "mask" and becomes unavailable. It's easy to analyze this problem with a GPS receiver that shows a diagram of the satellites in use. If your receiver gives predictions of satellite availability, so much the better; you can tell when a poor situation will improve.

If a Loran-C secondary transmitter gets out of tolerance, its control system sets one of the pulses to **blink**, usually within 10 seconds (a recent improvement). Every receiver has a blink indicator, and it isn't one that you should ignore. The accuracy of that TD is degraded at the transmitter; you can't improve it at your end. You can switch to another TD or another chain if that is possible in your area. That corrects the problem by using TDs from stations that are unaffected.

Sometimes a Loran-C receiver cannot determine whether or not it is locked on to the correct cycle of the signal pulse. It will show a *cycle* alarm. Cycle problems usually occur due to interference or low signal strength; check this by the **signal-to-noise ratio (SNR)**. Different manufacturers use different SNR scales: 0–99, 0–9, A–F. Check your manual to learn what the scale means for your receiver. Some receivers have an indicator that shows which transmitters are being tracked properly, as well as the SNR.

Occasionally a Loran-C receiver will track the wrong cycle, usually at the extreme edge of the coverage area, where the signals are weak. This gives 10-microsecond errors or multiples of 10 since 100-kHz cycles recur every 10 microseconds. You can detect this at a waypoint. You also can detect the problem by plotting three TDs on a chart. One of them will be out by 10 microseconds. All of them can be high or low by 10 microseconds if the receiver is tracking the wrong cycle from the master station. In any event, there will be a big triangle.

Turning off the receiver for half a minute may correct this problem. Reacquiring the signals when you turn it back on, the receiver may track the correct cycle for all stations.

CHAPTER 6

Finding Where to Go

Having a good idea of where you are is important, but it is equally necessary to be able to find your way safely to your destination. These two steps, using similar techniques, blend together in practical navigation. Boat navigators find their way using eyesight, charts, instruments, a watch, previous information, navigation receivers, and perhaps radar.

Seaman's Eye

In harbors and in sight of land, the primary method of finding where to go is seaman's eye—visual navigation relying upon objects, angles, water color, and ranges, aided by compass, watch, and depthfinder. Seaman's eye involves looking at a chart carefully but seldom plotting positions on a chart. It can range from extremely useful to virtually worthless, depending on the skill and knowledge of the seaman (or landlubber) running the boat. Using seaman's eye, ship pilots regularly navigate the largest ships in narrow channels, with only a foot or so of water under the keel. Much of the information about finding where you are by seaman's eye in Chapter 5 is equally applicable for finding where to go.

As a boat moves, the surrounding land and visible objects change appearance. These changes give a rough fix on the boat's position. The seaman who knows the depths and the location of shoals ahead has little trouble steering clear of them. *The informed seaman has a mental picture of the way things ought to be*—not politically but navigationally. The skipper who knows he has to avoid a shoal by hugging a certain coast comes in until the appearance is right—the height of the land, the angles to points forward and aft, the depth.

The greatest assets to seaman's eye navigation are concentration and memory. The greatest enemy is inattention.

The greatest assets to seaman's eye navigation are concentration and memory. Fortunately, remembering the appearance of a scene is easier than remembering abstract things like a list of numbers. Seaman's eye aids the memory by emphasizing the appearance of the surroundings. Don't just gaze at the scenery; *concentrate* on angular relationships, ranges, heights, and colors.

It is too easy to let your attention wander when you're tired, when you're talking, or when you're operating equipment, especially in familiar waters. Last summer I qualified for the Clamcruncher's Award (bronze star in lieu of duplicate medal) by ignoring a clue that later seemed blatantly obvious. It was there all along, and had I been paying attention to what I was doing, I wouldn't have hit the sand. In rocky areas, concentration is crucial.

Seaman's eye navigation is valuable in developing routes or procedures for traveling safely from one place to another. Remembering how the land appears when you're following the safe route helps you stay in good water. In Casco Bay, Maine, a rocky shoal extends northwest from Chebeague Island nearly to Littlejohn Island. There is a buoy, but it's hard to see from a distance. Coming from either direction, local skippers steer in toward Littlejohn Island, not on any special course but toward the near end of the island, staying just outside the 20-foot contour. When they see the buoy, it is on the correct side. Many a tourist, deceived by all the open water, gets right up to the shoal and has to turn sharply to avoid it—if he does.

A good navigator operating a boat in a familiar harbor learns the visual aids-to-navigation system in detail. Anyone can look at the buoys when passing them, but knowing the numbers of the important buoys, lights, or daybeacons at the turns, and the appearance of the aids to navigation on the next leg of the course, marks a good navigator.

It is also important to know the compass course for each leg of the channel. Is that difficult? Not at all. Forget all the mumbo-jumbo about deviation and variation for a moment. Just line up in the channel and look at the compass. The course will be the same next week. This isn't strictly true in all areas; where there is a cross-channel current, you have to steer several degrees upcurrent from the slackwater course. It is useful to record the compass courses on the chart or in a booklet. Writing them down will help you to remember them, especially if they differ on ebb and flood.

You seldom steer directly toward a lateral aid to navigation; rather, you keep the boat a comfortable distance inside the channel. Lights and daybeacons don't mark the deep edge of the channel; they are built in shallow water off to the side. Going directly toward a fixed aid keeps you in shallow water, even on a straight stretch of channel. In turns, going directly from aid to aid often is impossible due to intervening shoals or land. Look at the chart to find the safe route, and watch the depthfinder.

Always search for ranges to mark the route. If you know a range marks the next leg of the channel, watching the objects line up is the best way to turn to the correct course. This is particularly true when approaching an entrance from offshore. Sometimes there are aids-to-navigation ranges, but more often you rely on natural objects that may not appear on the chart. For example, a cedar tree on shore appears in line with the gable of a blue house when you're heading along a particular leg of a channel. You turn onto the next course when the tank way off to starboard comes in line with the edge of the marsh. Specific ranges like these make piloting easy and accurate.

One summer I kept my boat in a place with a long, narrow channel with strong cross-currents. On both ebb and flood, the boat crabbed a lot. Slowing to approach the harbor and to allow the diesel to cool down required an even larger correction. I soon found that the edge of a big building and a power-line tower beyond made an excellent range, which made it easy to stay in the channel.

Figure 6-1. *You may have to carry a range open by a small angle. The tree here should be two fingers to the right of the flagpole to clear a shoal.*

You may have to carry a range "open" by a small angle to clear an obstacle. Knowing that the tree should be two fingers to the right of the flagpole, and maneuvering the boat until that angle is right, shows you where to go accurately and easily.

If there is no range, use a **leading mark** dead ahead. It is better to have something to steer toward than to use the compass alone. After all, the compass gives no indication that you are left, right, or in the middle. A leading mark's bearing changes as you move left or right.

The depthfinder gives an excellent clue that you are approaching the shallows at the side of a channel. A graph-type depthfinder is most valuable, showing the trend of the depths as well as the depth at the moment. Many depthfinders have alarms. In a 12-foot channel, you might set the alarm at 4 or 5 feet under the keel to warn you before the water stops going by.

It is important to learn the pattern of ship, ferry, and tug and barge traffic in any large harbor, including the system of piers, anchorages, and bridges. It's easier to get around when you know where the big boys go. Listen to channel 13 or another channel designated for bridge-to-bridge communication or VTS (Vessel Traffic Service), and you will hear much valuable information about ship, tug, and barge movement.

Frozen Ranges

Our 378-foot cutter was equipped with excellent navigational equipment, and several people were working to ensure that she stayed in good water. Bearing takers worked at the call, "mark." The navigator plotted fixes. A man reported the depthfinder reading. In the Combat Information Center, another team plotted fixes with radar. An officer studied the bridge radar.

But we were headed for trouble.

The executive officer and I spotted it at about the same time, before any of the complex equipment. Although the ship was on course, headed to the left of a buoy, she was moving directly toward the buoy rather than clearing it. Evidently the current was setting the ship across the channel. How had we known? We had just used one of the techniques of seaman's eye—a **frozen range.**

Deep-Draft Channels

Ship channels are typically more than 35 feet deep, wide, and well marked. Look at the chart to see if there is deep water close to the channel. A ship channel may be surrounded by wide expanses of water 15 to 30 feet deep.

Rather than contending with the ship and barge traffic, I prefer to run the boat *just outside* the right-hand edge of a major ship channel. In most cases the water is plenty deep for a boat. Large lighted buoys marking the channel draw 12 to 15 feet of water and are set in place by a ship that is deeper than a boat. Even the smaller lighted buoys often draw 5 feet of water.

> *Running outside the buoys applies to deep-draft channels only.*

Running just outside the edge of a buoyed ship channel is especially wise in foggy weather. Why stay in a channel with ships when there's 20 feet of water outside the channel edge?

Note that running outside the buoys applies to deep-draft channels only, *not* shallow channels such as the Intracoastal Waterway (12 feet deep). Get a few feet outside of a shallow channel, and the water gets thin. In addition, lights and daybeacons are usually built in shallow water, some even protected by stone riprap, either above or just under the water. In a channel marked by lights and daybeacons, stay on the channel side of these aids and give them plenty of clearance.

It is important to search for a frozen range—one with no apparent motion. When a range is frozen, the boat is traveling on that range line *regardless of heading.* When the exec and I spotted a buoy frozen against the shoreline, we knew the ship was moving directly toward that buoy.

This is a valuable way to detect that your boat is moving toward the side of the channel. If you're passing clear of a buoy, it will appear to move *aft* with respect to the shore beyond. At a long distance the apparent motion is slight, but it increases as you get closer. Learn to watch each buoy, light, or daybeacon in

Figure 6-2. *Look at buoys with respect to shoreside features. If a buoy is frozen against the shoreline, the boat is moving directly toward it.*

relation to the shore behind it. Its rate of apparent motion, or lack of it, is an excellent clue to the distance at which the boat will clear.

Steering Clear

One of the more common reasons for getting unnecessarily close to some solid object is simply not allowing enough clearance to start with. Suppose a light marks the outer point of a shoal. You head toward the light from a buoy about a mile away. (You found the distance by glancing at the chart; it was about half the space between parallels of latitude 2 minutes apart.) The light bears 035°. If the shoal is to the left of the light, what course should you steer to miss it by 200 yards?

For now, just remember that an angle of 6° will give a clearance of ⅒ the range. The range is a mile, or about 2,000 yards. A 6° angle will put the boat 200 yards away from the light. Three fingers at arm's length cover about 6°. Steer toward an object on the horizon about three fingers to the right of the light, or if there is nothing in the background, steer a compass course of 041° (035° + 006°).

Be sure to hold the course, or this tactic will start to unravel as you get closer to the light. The angle to the light should increase as you get closer. At 1,000 yards you have to steer 12° to the right of the light to be 200 yards off when it comes abeam. That's a big angle, about a hand's width. At 500 yards you have to steer 24°—about two hands' width—to the right of the light to clear it by the same 200 yards. People tend to steer at about the same angle *to the light* as they get closer to it; that technique will take you very close. Measure the angle once and pick an object on the horizon or a compass course to follow.

We found these angles by using the **rule of sixty** (see sidebar) to determine that *the angle from dead ahead to an object has the same relationship to 60° as the distance off does to a range.* In this example we planned to clear the point by one-tenth the range, so the angle is one-tenth of 60°, or 6°.

At 1,000 yards, 200 yards is one-fifth the range. One-fifth of 60° is 12°. You can see that halving the distance doubles the clearance angle. For convenience, use this table:

Clearance Fraction	Clearance Percent	Angle
1/20	5%	3°
1/10	10%	6°
1/5	20%	12°
1/4	25%	15°
1/3	33%	24°
1/2	50%	30°

Water Colors

Clear water over sand shows the water depth by changes in color. Thin water appears light, showing the color of sand beneath. Deeper water is more blue. With a little practice you can see shoals a good distance away. People who run boats in clear-water areas get remarkably good at estimating depth from water color. Using a depthfinder to compare depths with colors helps you learn this skill quickly.

Areas of weed or grass can be confusing as they appear dark (and thus deep),

Rule of Sixty

You can calculate clearance angles using trigonometry, if you're interested. The original distance to the light (the range), the course line, and the desired distance off the light at the point of closest approach form a right triangle. If you know the range and how far you want the distance off to be, you can find the clearance angle using the formula:

sine of the clearance angle = distance off ÷ range

The **rule of sixty** states that the sine of a small angle is equal to the angle (in degrees) divided by 60. This is reasonably accurate up to about 40°. So:

$$\frac{clearance\ angle}{60} = \frac{distance\ off}{range}\ (approximately)$$

or

$$clearance\ angle = \frac{distance\ off}{range} \times 60$$

but weed and grass are usually found in shallow water. Dark gray sunglasses help emphasize the colors and are especially helpful in shallow areas.

Determining the water depth by its color works best in bright sunlight. Near dusk or on overcast days, color changes are less obvious, and it's hard to judge the depths. People who operate boats in discolored water or over dark mud bottoms can't really use color to estimate depth.

Waves

Waves furnish some clues to water depth and to current. In glare or dim light they may work better than colors. First, waves break in shallow water. Shoals are easy to recognize by waves or boat wakes breaking on the sand.

Wind waves are smoother when wind and current are in the same direction, rougher when wind and current are opposed. This is particularly noticeable in a channel or an inlet, where a strong current against the wind produces steep, short waves in the channel. In shallower areas, however, the waves will be smaller—they can show you where shallows lie.

Wind waves are smoother when wind and current are in the same direction.

On the other hand, "shallow" is a relative term. You may be able to avoid the biggest waves in a deep shipping channel by running outside its limits while still staying in water deep enough for the boat. In one bay about 12 feet deep, I often avoided steep waves by running my outboard at planing speed over flats in about 2 feet of water.

A boat's wake gives a useful clue to shallow water. When a boat going slower than planing speed gets into very shallow water, the waves forming the wake at the stern get bigger; at the same time, the boat settles lower in the water. This is an excellent time to slow down and work gently toward deeper water.

There are limits to operating by seaman's eye alone. When it gets foggy, visual methods are of little help. In addition, it takes time to learn an area; go somewhere else, and you have little to go on. I talked with a lobsterboat builder a few years ago about how well the Maine lobster fishermen navigate despite adverse conditions. To earn a living, lobstermen must be able to navigate accurately whether it's clear or foggy. They know their home waters in great detail, especially the bottom contours and features. They work around dangerous rocks, in close quarters, and allow for currents and tides so naturally that it seems instinctive.

The boatbuilder said, "Don't ever tell who said this, but take 'em away from home, and they aren't that sure of themselves. Most fishermen who take delivery of a new boat have a truck take it home on a lowboy."

This is an example of depending so strongly on local knowledge that unfamiliar areas present a challenge. Few pleasure-boat skippers will learn an area as well as someone who fishes there for a living, but you can learn to navigate in familiar and unfamiliar areas by methods that are safe and practical. You can take a boat into new areas with a reasonable amount of confidence, tempered by a dash of caution.

Going to Distant Destinations

By "distant destinations," I mean places that are out of sight, or far enough away to be difficult to see, rather than across an ocean—usually within a few hours of the starting point.

Start at a departure point or a fix, and draw a line on the chart between origin and destination, as described in Chapter 2. The direction and length of the line on the chart represent the direction and distance to the destination. A custom chart has many such lines, each showing distance and direction; they're a big help aboard a boat.

To start, *take departure* from a known position, which usually just means noting the time as you clear the channel entrance buoys or depart from some other known position. If your boat has a distance log, remember either to read the mileage or to reset it to zero. Having measured the (magnetic) direction from the chart, steer that course by compass to your destination. This is the usual technique for visual navigation, vital when a navigation receiver isn't available, and it should be a part of every navigator's store of knowledge.

When there is current or leeway, you need to steer to compensate (as described later in this chapter under "Coping with Current," page 153). This requires attention; if you get off to one side, you won't know how far off you are. Your DR position is tied to your departure position, and careless steering loosens that tie.

That doesn't mean you have to steer a precise course. Going left and right of the desired course has little effect as long as you're watching what you're doing. Wandering off to one side, however, does play hob with making good the desired track. In calm weather this is usually through inattention. In a seaway it is due to wave action: a wave moves the bow of the boat in one direction, the helmsman returns to course, then another wave slaps the bow off in the same direction again. The boat begins to get off to one side of the desired course.

It is important to calculate the **estimated time en route (ETE)** to the destination, based on the cruising speed. A boat cruising at 12 knots travels a mile every 5 minutes (60 ÷ 12). If you're heading for a buoy 15 miles away, it will take 75 minutes (5 × 15) to get there. An hour and a quarter after starting, the DR position puts the boat right at the buoy. A DR should be accurate to about 10 percent of the distance. In this case the boat should be within 1.5 miles of the buoy since it is 15 miles from the starting point. A large buoy is visible from 2 or 3 miles in the daytime, so you should be all right. As you get close to the estimated arrival time, start looking carefully ahead. By the time an hour and 10 minutes have passed, the buoy should be in sight.

What if it isn't? Look off to the sides; usually you will find it off to one side or the other. Also look back—sometimes you have passed it. If another 5 minutes pass and you haven't seen it, you should be searching all around very carefully. After another 5 minutes, you would expect to be a mile past the buoy. If you still haven't seen it, it's best to stop. You still have a reasonably good DR position, and stopping gives plenty of time to look carefully.

If it still isn't in sight, you may have to start searching. If there is a shoreline or a depth reference, you may be able to get a rough line of position, but a buoy well offshore can be the dickens to find without an electronic receiver. I have used an **expanding square search** to find such a buoy when the only alternative seemed to be to go back and start over.

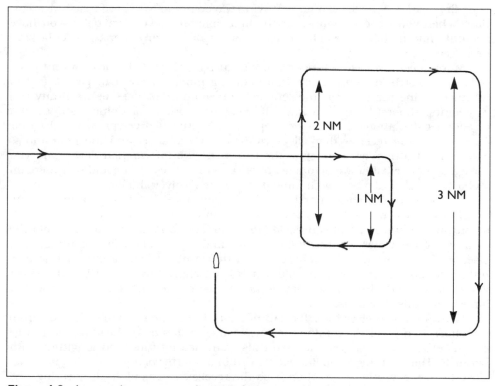

Figure 6-3. *An expanding square search pattern for locating a buoy.*

For an expanding square, turn and go a specific distance (say a mile) at right angles to your original course. That takes 5 minutes in our example. Then turn at right angles again so that you are going parallel to the original course, but in the opposite direction. Go 2 miles (10 minutes), turn at right angles again, and go 2 miles. On the next turn, go 3 miles (15 minutes), and so on. (See Figure 6-3.)

Running a search pattern to find a buoy may seem like a desperate measure, but it has the advantage of preserving the starting point of the search. Wandering aimlessly about does not. If you first go one way and then another without keeping careful track, you soon are truly confused about the boat's position. It only takes a little more time to get lost. With today's navigation receivers we seldom have to resort to such tactics, but you should know how just in case.

Electronic Navigation Systems

Electronic navigation systems come into their own for going to distant destinations. Their ability to show the distance and direction to any waypoint all the time surpasses any other navigation method. You can use a navigation receiver to find the distance and direction to a waypoint without plotting on the chart.

In most cases you are going to waypoints you have saved. The exception is your first trip, when you should be saving waypoints as you get to each destination. When you leave a channel for the first time and save a waypoint, you have accurate information for coming back. This is valuable anywhere, particularly in new areas.

Many receivers have a function to plan trips without being locked on to signals. It is worth learning to use this planning function. You can plan a trip in advance, using the receiver to calculate courses and distances between any two waypoints. Different receivers have different procedures for doing distance and direction calculations. Follow the steps to enter the two waypoint numbers or names, and the receiver then displays direction, distance, and the *from* and *to* waypoints. Do this for each leg of the trip, write the information down, and you have a complete list of waypoints, courses, and distances. You could plot them on a chart, but aboard a boat with limited space the receiver shines.

Suppose you're going north on the Intracoastal Waterway, approaching Wrightsville Beach, North Carolina. It is early in the day, the weather is fine with a southwesterly wind, and you decide to go directly to Beaufort Inlet to avoid the confines of the waterway, including bridges and a possible delay for firing exercises at Camp LeJeune. The charts reveal that a direct course is in safe water, but Masonboro Inlet at Wrightsville Beach is on chart 11539, and Beaufort Inlet is on chart 11543. How do you lay off and measure the course line? Even with a large table, this is tedious.

With a GPS receiver, find the latitude and longitude of the destination from the chart, and enter them into a new waypoint. In this case—heading for a large entrance buoy in clear weather—you also can use latitude and longitude with Loran-C. The resulting waypoint will be within a quarter of a mile, which is plenty close for clear weather navigation. Use the receiver to calculate the bearing and distance—070° magnetic, 62.3 miles.

It is important to check the data. A waypoint in memory could have been overwritten, published lists have errors, and you can make an error in taking the data from the chart or list. It is also easy to make a mistake when entering the waypoint into the receiver. If the calculated direction and distance don't seem to be approximately correct, check the data.

Knowing the distance, you can calculate the estimated time en route by dividing the distance by your estimated speed. A sportfisherman that cruises economically at 15 knots will take about 4.15 hours (62.3 ÷ 15), or 4 hours and 9 minutes, to reach the Beaufort sea buoy. If you're sailing at an estimated 7 knots, it will take about 8.9 hours to go from sea buoy to sea buoy.

If you don't have a waypoint stored at the departure entrance, store one as you depart. For one thing, it is a valuable reference. For another, it lets you do some useful calculations.

Placing waypoints. There is something of an art to choosing waypoints for a trip. Let's consider using a chart to plan a trip for clear weather. Usually you follow a route that passes a few key buoys or lights marking shoals or rocks off points of land. It's logical to follow tracks to waypoints at each turn point.

At first thought you could place a waypoint right at each buoy, getting its latitude and longitude from the *Light List* or from the chart. The *Light List* gives the position to 0.1 minute, or about 140 to 200 yards. On a coastal chart, 1:80,000, there is an error of about 60 yards or more in reading the position. And of course, the buoy swings around on its chain; three times the water depth is a typical swing radius. As already stated, GPS is usually accurate to within 50 to 150 yards of charted objects in U.S. waters, and Loran-C to within about 200 to 500 yards.

If you place the waypoint *offshore of the buoy* ¼ to ½ mile, you allow sufficient clearance for these errors while being sure you will be close enough to the buoy to see it in clear weather. A GPS waypoint should be at least a couple of hundred

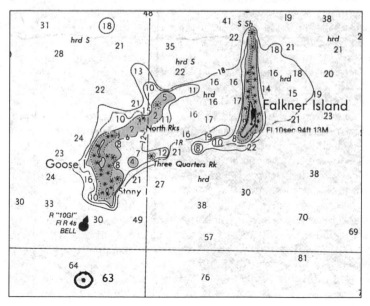

Figure 6-4. *Waypoint 63 is measured from the chart to be in deep water about 600 yards south of the buoy marking the island. This gives clearance for navigation system errors, plotting errors, steering and compass errors, and current.*

yards away from an offshore buoy, and a Loran-C waypoint at least 500 yards away. Placing the waypoint right at the buoy doesn't allow clearance for current or steering errors. I prefer to put a waypoint offshore by a comfortable amount. You should see a large lighted buoy from about 2 to 3 miles away in the daytime, and its light at about 4 to 6 miles at night, so ¼ mile is insignificant. A large lighted buoy ¼ mile away looks very close.

The same principle applies to turn points when you aren't using electronic navigation. You want to plan a track to clear a buoy, not run over it; lay off tracks to turn points that give a bit of clearance.

Another common situation involves heading for a midchannel (*safe water*) red-and-white vertically striped buoy marking the seaward end of a channel. Here it's logical to mark a waypoint a few hundred yards offshore of the buoy, in line with the channel. You want to go close to the buoy, and there is clear water all around.

Measuring waypoints from a chart. Many times we don't have premeasured waypoints available and must take them from a chart. This introduces errors due to the scale of the chart and the difficulty in making exact measurements. However, navigation is safe with waypoints measured from a chart. Be sure to allow a safety factor by placing waypoints somewhat away from hazards, as described above.

For GPS, simply measure the latitude and longitude of the desired waypoint, and enter it in your receiver. This is one of the biggest advantages of GPS: it has relatively small position errors with respect to charts and maps within the 48 states. In Alaska and Hawaii the errors are larger, and some overseas charts have large errors. For navigating U.S. waters in clear weather, waypoints measured to the nearest tenth of a minute are perfectly adequate.

With relatively new Loran-C receivers, you also can enter waypoints in latitude and longitude rather than using the charted TD lines. Most receivers have good ASF correction factors for calculating latitude and longitude. If your Loran-C receiver is a very old model that doesn't include ASF corrections, enter waypoints as TDs to avoid large errors.

Be cautious of measuring latitude and longitude from maps and charts that don't have TD lines. Loran-C ASF corrections are less accurate or are ignored entirely for inland areas. Compare the GPS or Loran-C latitude and longitude with a position on the map or chart to see how closely they agree.

If the chart has Loran-C TD lines, it's easiest to measure the TDs of a waypoint with an interpolator card, as described in Chapter 5, page 132. For clear weather it is sufficient to estimate the TDs to the nearest microsecond. While that might add a couple of hundred yards to the waypoint error, it's not worth worrying about if you're looking for a large buoy or clearing a hazard by a reasonable distance. Save new GPS or Loran-C waypoints when you go to waypoints measured from the chart or from a list. It is especially important to save waypoints at dive spots and other underwater locations.

Placing saved waypoints. As we have emphasized, waypoints measured by the receiver are more accurate than those you measure from charts. The beauty of saving waypoints lies in avoiding plotting errors, chart errors, and ASF errors. When you save a waypoint at a position, you also return to that position with the highest accuracy. Saved waypoints are thus quite useful in fog or poor visibility, and we place some of them a bit differently.

For normal turn-point waypoints at an offshore buoy or a light marking a shoal in a bay or sound, save the waypoint at least 200 or 300 yards away from it, on the deep-water side. Question: Can you tell exactly how far you are away from the buoy? Probably not. Most of the worry about accuracy involves distances the average navigator cannot measure. In practice, keep a reasonable distance off and save a waypoint. It makes little difference if you're 200 yards away from the buoy, or 300.

You can go closer using a more accurate *saved* waypoint rather than one measured from the chart, but why do that? Even in fog you don't have to see an offshore buoy. With a navigation receiver, you're no longer a slave to visual identification. It's just as valid to turn at a waypoint ¼ mile away from a buoy as one 50 yards away. You also avoid having to dodge the buoy at the last minute, a common occurrence if the waypoint is too close.

Some waypoints will be at buoys you must find and identify before going farther. This is especially so at the seaward end of a channel marked by buoys on either side; you have to see them before you go in. Be sure to save a waypoint *between the pair of entrance buoys,* or a hundred yards or so offshore of a safe-water buoy. It's also smart to save a waypoint at each channel turn, in midchannel. DGPS and WAAS are so accurate that you should save waypoints in the *right-hand side* of a major channel, each way.

If you save waypoints at each major turn of the channel and know the courses to steer, you can pick your way in poor visibility. Without the waypoints, entering the channel can be tricky indeed. Radar is a big help in poor visibility, and radar is essential for seeing other boats and ships. Good skippers use electronic navigation receivers and radar together rather than one exclusively.

One day when you're running a channel in clear weather, set the waypoints as successive destinations, and follow the navigation receiver to each waypoint to see how well you could follow them if it were foggy. You will also learn if the channel has been shifted. It's common for the Corps of Engineers and the Coast Guard to shift small entrance channels as storms and currents move the shoals around.

For underwater wrecks and rocks, or for buoys marking pots, save a waypoint right at the spot, as close to it as possible.

Organizing waypoints. You can make navigation easier by organizing GPS and Loran-C waypoints in a logical manner. Receivers store 99 to 2,500 waypoints, and many receivers allow you to enter letters as well as numbers. Consider both logical organization and ease of data entry when deciding how to organize your waypoints. Using names seems easy, but it isn't necessarily the best way. Most receivers require you to step through the letters to get the correct one, which means lots of steps to recall one waypoint. In addition, names seldom make a good sequence. Without a system, waypoints get all jumbled up in an illogical order.

In my system, the boat's home slip is waypoint 01. After I start the engine, I turn on both the GPS and Loran-C and set waypoint 01 as the destination. Usually the receivers show 0.01 to 0.03 mile to waypoint 01, in various directions. If it's off a mile or so, something's wrong.

I use waypoint 10 as the sea buoy for my home channel, and 02 through 09 for various waypoints inside the sound. Waypoints 11 through 29 are for nearby destinations—buoys, wrecks, artificial reefs, and rocks. Rather than a route, they form a star, so to speak, from the entrance buoy.

The next major channel entrance buoy is waypoint 30, and waypoints relatively near it are 31 through 49. In the other direction the next sea buoy is waypoint 50. This gives me permanent waypoints for most of my destinations within normal day-trip range.

Waypoints 60 through 79 are for trips, and I use 80 through 89 as *scratch waypoints* (described below) for finding accurate speed and course over the ground. The waypoints from 90 to 99 are for storing temporary information, such as the position of a school of fish or an updated position for an offshore buoy.

My GPS and Loran-C waypoints for the same position have identical numbers. Had I started with a receiver that could store 1,000 or more waypoints, I would have expanded the groups of numbers. I would still follow the same pattern, however: even hundreds for channel entrances, and groups of waypoints for general areas, for trips, for scratch waypoints, and for temporary information.

It is logical to use sequential waypoint numbers for a trip. For example, if you are traveling north along the Intracoastal Waterway from Beaufort, North Carolina, using waypoints for the open water stretch starting in the Neuse River, you would encounter:

Adams Creek Buoy 2 (start)

Adams Creek Light 1 AC

Neuse River Light 7 (Garbacon Shoal)

½ mile SE of Neuse River Light 4 (Piney Point)

Neuse River Junction Light

Goose Creek Light 27

This list is typical of many trips, even short ones, to many areas. Since the numbers or names of the aids to navigation at the turn points seldom follow a numerical or alphabetical sequence, I find it easier to assign waypoint numbers in order. Waypoints from 60 through 79 are my "trip" waypoints. The starting waypoint, Adams Creek Buoy 2, would be 60, and so on up to 65 for Goose Creek Light 27. It's simple to enter 61 as the first destination waypoint northbound, then 62 and so on. If the trip requires more than 20 waypoints, or for the next trip, I load new waypoints over the old ones.

Many receivers allow you to step up or down the waypoint list with the + or – key. Some receivers show the nearest waypoints on command—also easy. Either method is simpler than setting up a route.

It's not worth the bother to set up a route you plan to use only once. On the other hand, a route works well for any trip you make frequently. If you usually run in and out of a channel with several turns, it is convenient to set up a route using the home slip, the entrance buoy, and the turn points in between. When you run the channel, you can set up the route, and the receiver will go to the waypoints in sequence. Routes work in either direction and are valuable in poor visibility.

Commercial fishermen setting traps or pots save waypoints in numerical order as they work the gear. This makes it easy to go from one to the next in a round-robin sequence.

Coping with Current

In the previous discussions we have ignored two important factors: current and leeway. Current affects every boat, and leeway affects sailboats. Current carries a boat along with it, at its speed, regardless of the boat's course or speed. A 2-knot southerly current moves both a sailboat making 5 knots and a performance boat making 70 knots 2 miles to the south every hour.

If they're headed north, the sailboat makes 3 knots and the performance boat makes 68. Headed east, each will be exactly 2 miles south of a 090° line at the end of an hour. If they both head south, the 2-knot current adds to their speed: the sailboat makes 7 knots and the performance boat makes 72. We are usually interested in finding the course to steer to make good a desired track, and the correction, or **lead angle**, is quite different for boats traveling at different speeds.

Plotting

There are several ways of correcting for current. We will look first at plotting, then at a trigonometric method, then at some simpler methods. Most require that you estimate the current's direction and speed. You can learn to estimate the current at any buoy if you watch buoys in the harbor carefully and note how they appear at various current speeds. To find the current speed, first watch the "current tail" at a buoy to be sure that the current is running along the channel. Then calculate your *speed over the ground* by time and distance. Find the *speed through the water* at the same time by speed log or from rpm. The difference between speed over the ground and speed through the water is the current speed; look carefully at the buoy to learn how it appears at that speed. Some charts show the direction and speed of the average current. The *Tidal Current Tables* are also excellent sources of information for bays and sounds.

You can correct for current with a diagram on a chart, a piece of paper, or a *maneuvering board*. Suppose you plan to travel at 12 knots to make good a course of 090°M to a destination, and the current is moving south at 2 knots. It doesn't matter how far away the destination lies; the correction for current is the same everywhere along the course. First, lay off the desired track at 090°. Next, draw a line beginning at the origin going *south* (the same direction as the current) long enough to represent 2 miles. It can be 2 inches, 2 centimeters, 2 minutes of latitude on the chart, or 2 maneuvering-board circles; you'll get the same result as long as you use the same scale of units throughout.

Put a little arrow at the south end of the current line to represent the distance the current will move the boat in an hour. Set a pair of dividers to 12 units (for 12 knots) and place one leg at the point of the arrow. Swing the dividers until they touch the 090° line, and make a mark. Draw a line from the end of the arrow to the mark on the 090° line. Its direction (080° in this case) represents the course to steer to make good 090° across a 2-knot southerly current.

Try the same diagram for a boat making 6 knots. Reset the dividers to 6 units for the 6-knot speed. A line 6 units long from the point of the current arrow to the 090° line indicates a course of 070°. Halving the speed doubles the correction. Double the speed (to 24 knots) and the course is 085°. The effect of current is the same on every boat, carrying all south 2 miles in an hour, but the correction angle is less at high speed than at low speed.

The **speed made good** is equal to the distance from the origin of the plot to

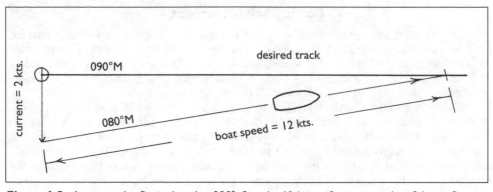

Figure 6-5. *A current plot. Desired track—090°. Speed—12 knots. Current—south at 2 knots. Draw the track. Draw an arrow from the origin, south, 2 units long (any convenient units). Set the dividers to 12 units. Put one point at the south end of the arrow and swing the other point to touch the 090° line. Draw a line connecting the end of the arrow to the mark on the 090° line. Its direction is the course to steer— 080°.*

the end of the line that touches the track. If the current isn't perpendicular to the desired track, plot the current arrow along the appropriate bearing. At times the current is nearly in line with the track, requiring small course corrections but affecting speed drastically.

The plot to find where a current will put the boat if you steer a set course is slightly different. In this case, first lay off the course and speed of the boat, and put an arrow at the end of that line. Then plot a second arrow from the point of the first one, in the direction of the current. Make its length equal to the speed of the current. At the end of one hour, the boat's estimated position will be at the end of this second arrow. The course and speed made good are represented by a line from the origin to the end of the second arrow.

Figure 6-6. *A current plot (same circum-stances) for a boat mak-ing 6 knots. The course to steer in this case is 070°. The length of the track between the origin and the end of the long arrow represents the speed made good—5.6 knots.*

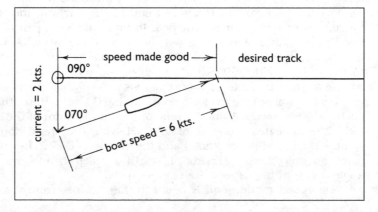

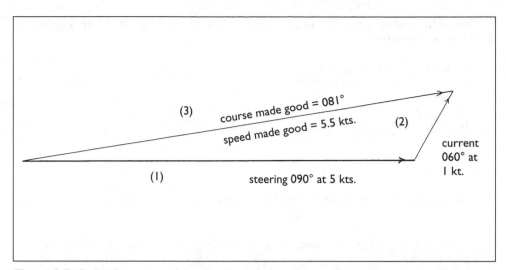

Figure 6-7. *Finding the course and speed made good when steering a set course in a current. (1) Draw an arrow in the direction you are steering, with length = boat speed. (2) Draw a second arrow from the end of the first, in the direction the current is moving, with length = current speed. (3) Connect the beginning of the first arrow with the point of the current arrow: direction = course made good; length = speed made good.*

Calculating the Lead Angle

You can also use trigonometry to find the angle you must steer upstream of the desired track to offset the effects of current. If you're so inclined, use the following formula:

$$sine\ of\ lead\ angle = \frac{current\ speed \times sine\ C}{boat\ speed}$$

C is the angle between the desired track and the current direction. If the current is at right angles to the desired track, sine *C* = 1 and can be ignored.

Shortcut Lead Angles

There is a simpler method using the **minutes-per-mile** concept of speed (pages 115–117). The number of minutes per mile (min./mi.) is found by dividing 60 by the boat speed, and it is the handiest way to calculate running time and distance. *To find the lead angle for a current at right angles to the desired track, multiply the current speed in knots by the number of minutes per mile.* For example, sailing at 6 knots (10 min./mi.) in a 1-knot cross-track current, the correction is 10°. For a 2-knot current, the lead angle is 20°. In another example, a powerboat cruising at 20 knots takes 3 minutes to go a mile. With a 3-knot current across the desired track, the lead angle is 3 × 3, or 9°.

To find the lead angle for a current at right angles to the desired track, multiply the current speed in knots by the number of minutes per mile.

I use this method more than any other. It comes from the above trigonometric formula, substituting:

$$minutes\ per\ mile = \frac{60}{boat\ speed}$$

    or

$$boat\ speed = \frac{60}{min./mi.}$$

    which yields:

$$sine\ of\ lead\ angle = \frac{current\ speed \times min./mi.}{60}$$

Since a small angle is approximately 60 times the sine of the angle, the formula becomes:

$$lead\ angle = current\ speed \times min./mi.$$

This is quite accurate for estimating the lead angle, and you don't have to plot a current diagram.

Practical Methods

There are even simpler methods of coping with current. In areas of the coast where fishermen set pots for lobsters or bottom fish, you can use the pot buoys to find the correct lead angle. This is particularly valuable aboard a sailboat, which requires relatively large course corrections for current, but it is useful for any boat in an area of tidal currents.

There may be enough pot buoys around (sometimes too many for comfort) to allow you to check the current frequently. Find a pot buoy some distance ahead, and steer slightly right or left until it is in line with the desired course. Then steer upcurrent until it ceases to change bearing. You may have to adjust a bit, but you can easily determine the course to steer to hold the buoy steady—and that's the correct course to make good the desired track. Duck downcurrent of the buoy as you approach it, then steer the new course with confidence. It will be valid until the current changes, either with time or as you go to a different area.

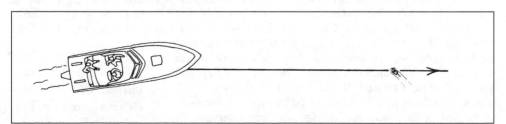

Figure 6-8. *Correcting for current using an anchored buoy. Find a pot buoy some distance ahead, and steer right or left until it is in line with the desired course. Now steer upcurrent until the buoy ceases to change bearing; the heading that holds it steady is the correct course to make good the desired track.*

When taking departure I use a similar scheme: line up the outermost buoy with some object ashore on the reciprocal bearing of the desired track. I either draw the line on the chart in advance or use a hand-bearing compass after taking departure. I steer to put the buoy and the other object in range, and adjust course to freeze the range. With no apparent motion on the range, I am steering a course that compensates for current. The current away from the inlet may be different, but at least I have a good start.

Following the Desired Track Using a Navigation Receiver

Navigation receivers provide four or five methods of keeping on track despite current, compass errors, leeway, and poor steering. The one you choose depends on the distance to the waypoint as well as on your preference. For relatively short distances, steer by the receiver-indicated bearing to the waypoint. For longer trips, learn the cross-track error function. For legs of several hours' duration, scratch waypoints have advantages. Start with the simplest method and learn more as you wish.

Bearing to Waypoint

When heading for a waypoint, most skippers check to see that the course lies in clear water, then steer the receiver-displayed bearing to the waypoint. If the bearing changes, they steer the new bearing. This is simple and perfectly adequate for distances up to a few miles in slight currents, and overcomes the problem of having to steer a consistent compass course to find a distant mark. Stray to one side when steering by compass alone, and you stay to the side, but a navigation receiver gives you a new bearing to the waypoint.

The receiver shows the new bearing quickly and accurately, with slow changes, except close to the waypoint. This makes it easy to tell whether the boat is straying to one side of the direct course to the waypoint.

Two conditions degrade the usefulness of simply steering toward the waypoint—strong currents and long distances. If there is a current from the side, steering straight at the waypoint causes the boat to follow a curved path. The bearing keeps changing, and although you keep changing course to match the new bearing, the boat is swept downcurrent. It is possible to be swept down into shoal water, discovering this problem the unpleasant way.

You can avoid this by plotting or calculating the lead angle (page 155) to counteract the current, but many people find it easier to correct the course by using the bearing to the waypoint intelligently. If the bearing to the waypoint changes from 030° to 025° over a period of time, it should be obvious that you are steering too far to the right. Try steering to the left of the new bearing, 025°, say 020°. If the bearing then changes to 026°, you've overcompensated. Steer a little more to the right, say halfway between 020° and 025°. On the other hand, if the bearing decreases to 024°, you haven't compensated enough; steer a bit more to the left. Just don't make big changes, or you'll follow a crooked track. After all, if you're an hour away from the waypoint, you don't have to solve everything in a minute or so.

This way of finding the course—keeping the bearing steady by trial and error—isn't hard to do in practice. If the waypoint is much more than 10 miles away, however, this method lacks the sensitivity to alert you that the boat is getting off to the side of the desired track since bearings are shown to the nearest degree. Twenty miles away from a waypoint, you have to stray about 700 yards to the side to change the bearing by a degree. At a mile from a waypoint, on the other hand, the bearing changes by 1° if you get 35 yards off to the side.

Cross-Track Error

All navigation receivers have a cross-track error feature. You don't have to learn it right away, but you will find uses for it after you do. The **cross-track error (XTE** or **CTE)** is best for trip legs more than a few miles long or in current. Receivers use a planned track line between the origin waypoint and the destination waypoint as a reference and show the distance left or right of that line as cross-track error. Distance is shown in yards or in fractions of a mile—0.01 mile is about 20 yards.

You can stay quite close to the desired track using the cross-track error feature, but apply it with a touch of patience. The GPS system is accurate to about 20 yards. If the receiver shows the XTE change from 0.00 to 0.01 mile left of track, wait a couple of minutes; most likely it will go back again. If it continues to increase, change course to the right a bit, say 5°. Then wait for 4 or 5 minutes to see whether the average XTE steadies, decreases, or increases.

If it steadies, your new course is fine. If it increases, you need to change course even more to the right. If it decreases, change slightly to the left. Resist the tendency to correct every error. Try to correct every cross-track error, and you'll steer a snaky course. Used patiently, the XTE feature will help you steer a course that compensates for current, leeway, or a poorly adjusted compass.

DGPS and WAAS give more accurate XTE readings, and they don't fluctuate as much as with GPS. It is easier to use the cross-track error indication to stay on course, but some patience will still be required. A boat doesn't follow a compass course exactly, not with any helmsman I have ever seen.

If you get well off to the side of the desired track and want to use the cross-track error function, reset the desired track to begin at the boat's position by redesignating the destination waypoint. That also resets the origin waypoint, and sets the cross-track error to zero, making it easier to stay on track. As always, you have to make sure the way is clear.

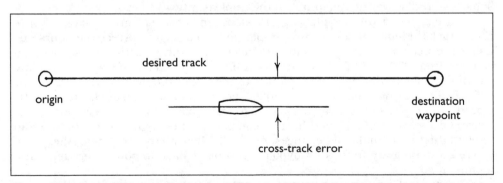

Figure 6-9. *Cross-track error is the distance left or right of the track line from the origin waypoint to the destination waypoint. If the cross-track error increases to the right, steer a little to the left of the bearing to the destination.*

Some receivers also have a pictorial indication of the cross-track error—some sort of a graph, or little boats, or arrows and imperative commands like "steer left." *How much?* you might wonder. I care little for this feature since the scale always seems to be either in odd units, or too sensitive, or too coarse. You can reset the sensitivity, but it is easier to deal with cross-track error expressed in fractions of a mile. These show minor movement quickly and never go off scale.

Receivers with plotters show cross-track error as part of the plot. The plot shows fixes at frequent intervals, which make it easy to see the normal jiggles in position and to estimate the off-track distance.

Course Made Good

Navigation receivers show **course over the ground**, called by various abbreviations, such as **COG**, **CMG**, or **Track**. They also show the speed over the ground, but the course and speed they display varies, even on a straight course. This is due to minor fluctuations in the signals and can be misleading if you think course or speed is actually varying as much as is indicated by the receiver. If the antenna is mounted high, GPS can show large variations in course and speed due to rolling and pitching. In addition, a boat's heading does vary. You may be steering 230° by compass, but the boat swings to one side, then the other. A sailboat helmsman heads up and falls off slightly with changes in wind direction and speed, especially on a beat. These swings average out to the actual course.

GPS receivers show the course every second, while Loran-C receivers show the average course over a few minutes. If you turn quickly, the Loran-C receiver continues to show the old course for a few minutes. Although the course-made-good feature is handy, it isn't particularly accurate for determining the course made good.

For best results use the setup function to make the COG *averaging period* as long as possible, and hold a steady course. Compare the course made good shown by the receiver to the course you are steering, then come left or right by the angle they differ, to follow the desired track.

Estimated Time En Route

Receivers also calculate and display the estimated time en route (ETE) based on the present speed and the distance to the waypoint—a handy feature but not very precise. These estimates suffer from the same problems as course-made-good readings; they attempt to establish the boat's speed from measurements made in a short period with systems of somewhat limited accuracy. They are useful for relatively short distances, but the method described below is superior on longer runs.

Scratch Waypoints

On a long leg of a trip, that is, a distance that requires several hours of travel, scratch waypoints are the best way to find the average course and speed over a period of time. This is the most complex way to find the course and speed, but the most accurate. While many boat operators don't go on trips long enough for this method to be useful, those who make long open-water trips will find it quite handy.

On a trip such as the one from Masonboro Inlet to Beaufort Inlet, note the time and store a waypoint as you clear the entrance. Then *store a scratch waypoint every hour.* Keep them in a certain section of waypoint numbers, say 80 to 89, and overwrite them later. Use the receiver to calculate the distance and bearing from the waypoint at the beginning of the hour to the one at the end of the hour. The bearing will be quite accurate, and the distance is obviously equal to the boat's speed over the ground.

If your receiver will only calculate course and distance from the present position to a waypoint, you can use the **look-back** method. After an hour, save a scratch waypoint, then reset the waypoint you entered at the beginning of the hour as the destination. The receiver will display the distance and direction back to the waypoint. The course made good is 180° from the direction shown by the receiver. Afterward, reset the correct destination waypoint.

If GPS scratch waypoints are 5 miles apart, the receivers can determine the distance (and speed) within about ¼ of one percent and the direction within about ⅙ of a degree. However, receivers *show* directions only to the nearest degree.

If the time between waypoints isn't exactly an hour, you can easily find the equivalent distance for 1 hour. Suppose you were at the origin at 0810 and set the scratch waypoint at 0912.5. Divide the distance covered by 62.5 minutes, then multiply by 60 to find how far the boat went in an hour.

Finding the course made good over a distance of 5 or 6 miles gives you a powerful method of adjusting course for current. You're steering 070°, heading for Beaufort Inlet, and find that for the past hour you've been making good 074° or 4° to the right of the course you steered. Reset the destination waypoint to Beaufort Inlet. Suppose it now bears 069°. If you steer 4° to the *left* of 069° (065°), you'll go directly to the waypoint. The correction takes care of compass error, current, and leeway. For long legs of a trip, this is an excellent technique.

By resetting the destination waypoint, you also reset the origin waypoint, and the cross-track error will apply from your present position. Now the cross-track error is likely to remain small. *HINT: Many receivers have two methods of resetting the destination waypoint—one doesn't change the origin waypoint, and the other resets it to the current position. It is important to learn which does what to avoid confusion. You also should check that no hazards are in the path of a reset course.*

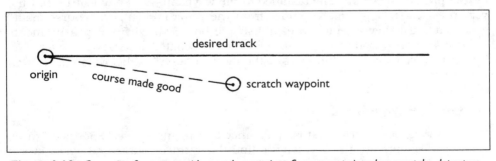

Figure 6-10. *Correcting for current with scratch waypoints. Save a waypoint when you take departure. Save a second waypoint an hour later. Use the receiver to calculate distance and direction from the first to the second scratch waypoints. Find the new bearing to the destination. Steer to the right or left of that bearing (left, in this case) by the angle between the desired track and the course made good. Save a new scratch waypoint every hour.*

Finding the Lay Line

A sailor can use Loran-C or GPS to determine the lay line to round a windward mark. Suppose you plan to round the mark on the starboard tack. Put in a scratch waypoint at the beginning of a starboard leg and another just as you tack to port. Now you can determine the course made good (over the ground) as well as the speed. You don't have to use the whole leg; two waypoints a mile or more apart usually reveal the course made good within a degree.

The lay line bearing that you determine usually is quite accurate, but three things can reduce its accuracy: The current may be different near the mark than on the leg you measured—current is often different in different parts of the waterway. Tidal currents also vary with time—a half-hour may make a noticeable difference in current velocity. A change in wind speed, even with a steady current, changes your course made good. This is a good way to determine the lay line, but it must be used with judgment.

This method provides exactly the same information as if you had plotted the two positions on the chart and measured the direction and distance between them. Using the chart, you also have to plot a line from the newest position to the destination and measure its direction and distance. You aren't skipping over anything important about navigation; you're simply using a receiver rather than a chart. Most of us find it a lot easier.

Some receivers allow you to specify a waypoint as a distance and bearing from any other waypoint. You can use this feature as an "electronic DR" by setting a DR waypoint on the bearing to the destination and at a distance equal to the boat's cruising speed in knots. At the end of an hour, set the DR waypoint as the destination to find its direction and distance from the boat's position. This information is identical to what you obtain by plotting on a chart.

Staying in Good Water

It is easy to use a GPS or Loran-C receiver to stay clear of a shoal even though you haven't entered a waypoint. For example, with my GPS receiver on, I

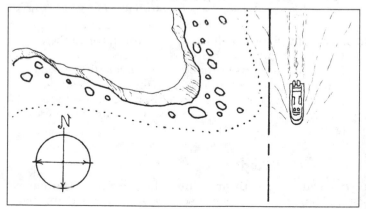

Figure 6-11. *Staying in good water is easy with a GPS receiver. Stay east of a meridian east of the shoal water by keeping the longitude a little lower than the meridian's longitude.*

was approaching a small river to anchor overnight. There was a light at the river entrance and a wide shoal area east and north of the light. I was approaching from the north. I saw on the chart that if I came south following a certain meridian until I was at the same latitude as the light, then turned west, there would be deep water all the way.

I steered a bit west of south until the GPS receiver showed the correct longitude, then turned south. When the GPS receiver showed the latitude matched the light's latitude, I turned west, steering to keep the latitude constant. This was easier than entering two waypoints, and a safe way of staying clear of the shoal.

Use the same principle with Loran-C by following one of the TD lines shown on the chart. Use more clearance when using latitude and longitude with Loran-C since it can have larger errors than those of GPS.

You can approach a waypoint along a bearing line that is in good water using a navigation receiver. Suppose there is a shoal you must avoid when going into an entrance. Draw a line well clear of the shoal extending to the entrance, and find its magnetic bearing. Set the entrance as the destination waypoint. Before you near the shoal, steer to make the receiver's bearing to waypoint agree with the line's bearing, then steer to keep the bearing constant. You will follow a clear path to the waypoint.

A bearing drawn close to a hazard can also mark a line you don't want to cross rather than one you want to follow. If the safe water is to the left of the line, just make sure the bearing to the waypoint stays larger than the bearing of the line.

These techniques work without a chart, too. Suppose you're operating in a large reservoir and have GPS but don't have a chart. Save waypoints near the ramp where you start and other places along your trip—points, coves, and places where the lake divides. Suppose you started from the launching ramp and had to steer to the left of 310° until halfway out in the lake to clear a shoal. Now it's dusk and you're headed back. Keep the bearing less than the reciprocal bearing (130°) to the waypoint at the ramp to miss the shoal.

Losing Electronic Navigation

Every system fails occasionally. Suppose you're halfway to your destination and the navigation receiver loses the signals. Its last direction and distance are more accurate than if taken from a DR. Simply continue on the same course toward the waypoint, and estimate the ETE from the distance. Since you've already come halfway, a DR from the last fix will accumulate only half the error that would come from steering by compass all the way. If you have worked out a course that corrects for current, so much the better.

On a long leg of a trip, if you have used the receiver to calculate speed and course made good, you have excellent data to continue on to the destination. If you've saved scratch waypoints every hour, plot the last scratch waypoint as a fix on the chart. You can use most receivers to make calculations even when they aren't locked on to the signals.

Radar

Radar helps you find your way with or without taking fixes. The classic range-arc fix described in Chapter 5 is seldom used aboard a boat. Using radar by comparing the PPI picture with the chart is an excellent extension of seaman's eye navigation. You can *see* your location in a harbor easily if there are enough islands, rocks, points, and piers to furnish targets. You relate the position to the angles and distances to the targets by eye, without making a plot.

Much radar navigation is simple. Two rows of paired targets on the scope, extending from an opening in the coast, mark a harbor entrance. If the cursor shows the closest pair of buoys bears 310°, they are 50° to port. Lining up the boat between the pairs of buoys makes for a straightforward harbor entry.

When set to a short-range scale, radar gives enough detail to show your location in a harbor. The picture when the boat is nearer to one side of a channel is different from when in the center. Radar is superb at showing the buoys along the next leg of a channel, buoys that can be difficult to see from a boat until you're right at the turn.

Nothing could be simpler than going between a pair of islands using radar. It is equally easy to measure the distance to the beach. When you are going from one harbor to another along a relatively straight shoreline, just set the VRM (variable range marker) to the distance you want to stay offshore, and steer to keep the beach target near the VRM circle.

The **parallel offset plot** is unique to radar. Suppose you want to pass 1 mile off a point. There's a buoy ½ mile off the point, but it's too far away to see. Move the EBL (electronic bearing line) until its origin is abeam, 2,000 yards, and align it parallel to the 000° relative bearing. This makes a line parallel to the boat, 2,000 yards off to the shore side. If you have an older radar without an EBL, you can mark a parallel line on the clear plastic cursor rotor with a grease pencil.

Figure 6-12. *Two rows of paired targets extending from an opening in the coast are the buoys at a harbor entrance. The cursor shows that the closest pair of buoys bears 310° relative—they are 50° to port. If you head for that harbor, lining the boat up between the pairs of buoys is straightforward, regardless of the visibility.*

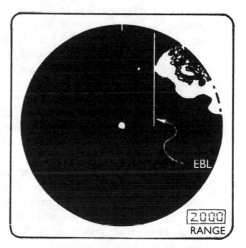

Figure 6-13. *The parallel offset plot is an easy way to stay in deep water as you pass a point. Set the EBL abeam at the desired clearance range and parallel to the course. Steer to keep the target from coming inside the EBL.*

Suppose the point's target is inside the parallel offset line at a range of 5 miles. Simply turn the boat until the point and the EBL coincide. You have turned to the course that will clear the point by 2,000 yards. Its target should slide right down the EBL. If it gets inside due to current, leeway, or compass error, you have to steer a bit more offshore. This technique requires little effort, yet it's reliable and a favorite way to stay in good water.

When you pass the point, you may not be exactly 2,000 yards away. That doesn't matter; you allowed ample clearance by planning to go ½ mile offshore of the buoy. If you adjust the VRM and see that the range to the point is actually 2,100 yards, put a mark on the chart at 2,100 yards at the approximate bearing, check the time, and you have a good fix.

Sometimes you make a course change during a parallel offset plot. Changing course rotates all targets in a bow-up radar presentation. Suppose you see a target at long range, and its plot comes vertically down the scope. With no change, you would pass it about a mile away. When it is about 2 miles away, you see that it is a buoy and decide to pass about ½ mile away from it. So you change course to put it about 15° on the starboard bow (rule of sixty—the desired distance off is ¼ the range, so the angle is ¼ of 60°). Its trace makes an arc on the scope as you turn, then follows a vertical line that eventually passes 1,000 yards to starboard.

On bold coasts radar is valuable in clear weather as well as fog. Often you can identify an island or a point by its shape on the radar PPI scope when you are still too far off to see it by eye. Having radar allows you to use several techniques that aren't available without it.

Blending Electronic and Visual Navigation

The blend of electronic receivers and visual navigation is so straightforward that you will have few problems putting the two together. Much of the information in this book blends the techniques; this section is merely a reminder. There is one important principle: *save a waypoint at every key turn point.*

Most of the time the weather is clear, and you can tell your position by eye and by depthfinder. When starting on a trip, don't just find the course to a turn point using the chart or by eye; write the course down. And when you arrive at that point, save a waypoint.

A custom chart shows the direction and distance between key positions, but a saved waypoint goes way beyond that. A receiver shows the direction and distance *to any waypoint from anywhere the boat may be*, not just from another key point. If the key points are so far apart you can't see one from another, saving a waypoint is especially valuable. Next trip, you can use the receiver to follow the desired track, allowing for current. The receiver also gives you the distance, which allows you to calculate your ETA easily.

The sun's glare can make it difficult to see an important light or buoy, or perhaps you know you have to keep close to an island to avoid a shoal. Save waypoints to mark these spots; then, the next time you approach them, even from a different direction, the waypoints will be an excellent guide. In clear weather they will point the way when you are still too far away to see the buoys or the shape of the island very well. In fog, waypoints are *the best way* to find safe passage. You have to check the chart to make sure your course is in good water—the receiver is oblivious to islands and shoals.

When running in a familiar channel, save waypoints at each key turn. Save the waypoints in succession if your receiver doesn't have a route function or if you haven't learned to use it. It's easy to shift to the next waypoint in a numerical sequence. This is an instance when the receiver's *route* function is valuable. As you pass one waypoint, the route function automatically shifts to the next one as the destination. Navigation receivers are valuable in a channel if the distances are long or if the visibility decreases. In narrow channels you need the high accuracy of DGPS or WAAS. Any of the systems help to show the distance to the next turn waypoint. In any case you must know the courses and the harbor. I once saw a gang of boats huddled around a sea buoy in fog—none of the skippers had thought of saving waypoints along the entrance channel or of remembering the courses. As we started in, they all trailed along like ducklings following mama duck.

Radar is excellent but only reaches its full potential when you supplement it with a navigation receiver, a depthfinder, a log, and traditional navigation. The navigation receiver lets you find the bearing and distance to the entrance buoys long before you see them on radar. It gives direction and distance continually to each waypoint. It gives you an estimate of the current if you compare the speed over the ground with speed by the log.

Some radar units can show electronic navigation waypoint "lollipops" on the screen, a good feature. It is often difficult to tell which buoy is which by radar alone, and easy to go past a turn or turn too early. The distance indicated by a navigation receiver guards against this nicely with little effort on your part.

In clear weather I use a navigation receiver's distance feature frequently. Running along a shore, it's convenient to know that you are 12 miles down the beach from the channel entrance. Sure, you can find this from the chart if you see a landmark or if you keep up a DR, but that requires using the chart and perhaps plotting. It's simpler to set the waypoint at the entrance as the destination and look at the distance shown by the navigation receiver.

The distance feature is excellent for calculating the speed over the bottom. Check the time for the distance to the destination waypoint to decrease by exactly one mile, and you will be able to calculate the speed quite accurately. I find this extremely useful in bays and rivers that have significant current. It's both accurate and easier than any other method used to calculate speed over the ground. Even in areas with little current, it's handy to find the boat's speed *that* day with *that* load in *that* seaway.

It is also handy to use the distance feature to two waypoints to get a good idea of the boat's location without plotting on a chart. It's like having a giant radar that gives accurate bearings and distances to any spot. This technique isn't for finding the position; rather, it is to help you visualize your boat's relationship to various places on the chart without having to plot a fix. It is particularly valuable in sailboat racing and in fishing an area with specific hotspots. For example, the destination waypoint may be 6.03 miles ahead and the point of land abeam 2 miles off. Of course, you have to have a waypoint for each spot. I put the way point numbers right on the chart.

Remember the parallel offset technique of staying a certain distance off a shoal or a point by radar? A waypoint saved in deep water off the point is just as useful—even more useful if you don't have radar. Use any of the navigation receiver techniques to stay on the desired course line.

Navigation receivers coupled to chart plotters make it easier to navigate in fog, especially with Differential GPS and WAAS. DGPS and WAAS have enough accuracy to navigate tight places, fog or no fog, using *saved* waypoints. It will take many decades before the charts match DGPS or WAAS positions exactly.

Fishermen often need to find their way back to a school of fish following a strike. It is handy to save a temporary waypoint and set it as the destination. If you're trolling or drift fishing, the receiver makes it easy to go back by displaying the distance and direction to the waypoint. It is far easier than putting a float over, and you can lose sight of a float. Seeing that it is 0.46 mile bearing 153° from the boat makes it easy to return to the spot.

Some fish stay in one spot and others move around. Fish that live near the bottom tend to stay near wrecks and reefs, but migratory fish may stay close to specific spots as well. One trip we found a school of king mackerel about 200 yards southeast of an underwater rock. Every time we trolled through that area, we got a strike. Over the rock and in other areas nearby, we had little luck. I don't know what kept them there, but it was easy to use the navigation receiver to go back through the hotspot.

Saving a waypoint and setting it as the destination is just as useful when you get a strike in a moving school. One day we started catching Spanish mackerel. The second hookup came when the temporary waypoint was 120°, 50 yards. We got the third when it was 126°, 120 yards. From then on it was simple to troll through a spot that kept moving away from the temporary waypoint.

This type of navigation with respect to a moving point is typical of nontraditional methods of electronic navigation. Navigation receivers and commonsense visual methods are also useful in waters that are difficult to find your way in by visual navigation alone. These waters are so cut up by land that you can't see where to go by prominent landmarks.

Island Chains, Marshes, and Reservoirs

Many people operate boats in areas that aren't open enough to allow straight courses from one place to another. I have been in areas with so many mangrove islands that it was easy to get confused navigating by chart and compass. I'd stand up on deck looking at the islands and the angles between them, trying to match them up with the chart. Sometimes it took a long time to find my way out, and I've even had to backtrack to find the ramp.

After getting a navigation receiver it became simple. I use trip waypoints, beginning at 60. I save a waypoint every few miles at easy-to-recognize places. Maybe I'm up to waypoint 65 when I head for home. It's comforting to know that waypoint 64 is 4.23 miles, bearing 095°. Around islands it may not be possible to go 095° in the boat, but having the bearing and the distance to the waypoint makes it easier to pick your way among them. In marshes, the same situation exists in spades.

Marshes are veined with numerous channels—some passable, some not—separated by marsh so uniform you can't distinguish one part from another. In addition to having few visible clues, marsh channels are often a high-tide-only proposition. Get caught by a falling tide near nightfall when the mosquitoes take over, and you will learn the meaning of misery. On top of that, someone may be expecting you, and it will be many hours until the tide floods.

In such places, save waypoints at key locations. Creek junctions are particularly valuable waypoints. The waypoints are a big help to keep from getting turned around, which doesn't sound quite as bad as lost, although the result is the same. It is helpful to write some notes on the chart or map, or in a booklet, and to keep track of running times and compass directions from the waypoints. If your receiver has a plotter, it's quite easy to see where you've been and to retrace your route.

A friend of mine has access to a blind on Currituck Sound. Duck hunters like to get out to the blind and get the decoys set well before legal shooting time, so they start out when it's dark. My friend got a portable navigation receiver for Christmas and had just started to learn to use it. It's far enough across the sound to make it hard to find the right marsh channel entrance in the dark. In fog it's even harder, and hard to avoid going aground.

One foggy morning he simply ran to the waypoints he had saved on clear days. No problem. He had his decoys set up in good time while hunters going to surrounding blinds couldn't even find their blinds for a couple of hours. In the marsh he couldn't go on a straight line between waypoints, but the receiver always gave the direction and distance. That was enough to follow the winding channels.

The same principles apply in reservoirs with branches and divided channels. Even though large reservoirs may be surrounded by hills to serve as landmarks, they can be confusing. Reservoirs often have many feeder streams, coves, and islands, all in an irregular patchwork. You can't go straight from one place to another on a compass course. If you forget where a certain creek is, you can spend a great deal of time searching for it by landmarks. A GPS receiver is a big help, especially when you are learning a new reservoir. A receiver with a plotter is particularly valuable.

Put a waypoint at the launching ramp. I would use 01 if this were the place I usually use the boat, or 60 if it's a trip. If the ramp or marina is on an arm of the reservoir, save a waypoint when you get to the main part of the lake. Then run down to the dam and save a waypoint there. I often set the dam waypoint as the destination even though I'm not going there. The receiver displays the distance and direction to the dam waypoint constantly, and I relate features to their *distance above the dam*.

As I travel in the reservoir, I save waypoints at places where it divides and branches. Sometimes I save a waypoint up in a narrow arm of water, particularly if it divides again. Waypoints serve as accurate, easy-to-use reference marks. They are particularly helpful in finding your way around reservoirs with undeveloped shorelines. Some reservoirs have vast areas of standing timber with relatively narrow passages. Save a waypoint at either end of these passages, and it will be easy to find them. Make note of any landmarks that are useful— power lines, buildings, even a dead tree on an island.

It is helpful to use reference waypoints to locate other areas. Suppose you enter a long arm of water from waypoint 67. Set waypoint 67 as the destination, just as you did with the dam. When you find another interesting feature, such as a feeder stream, look at the receiver. You will see, for example, that you are 0.63 mile up the arm from the waypoint. The direction shown is the direction back to the waypoint. Usually it is enough to know the general direction of the arm, the distance, and which shore. The general direction is important when several arms branch at one waypoint.

With plenty of room in the receiver, there's nothing wrong with saving additional waypoints. Fishermen will want to save extra waypoints where the under-

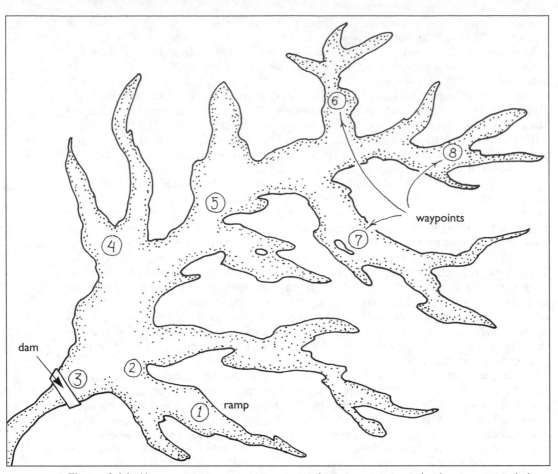

Figure 6-14. *Use a navigation receiver in a reservoir by saving waypoints in key locations, particularly where the reservoir divides and branches.*

water structure is promising. If you have a map, write the waypoint numbers on it. Copy the GPS waypoint's latitude and longitude into a notebook. This is particularly important if you plan to return later on after using the boat for other trips. Then you can reenter the waypoints for the reservoir before starting out.

The electronic navigation receiver is a wonderful supplement to traditional navigation in reservoir fishing. You can relocate shoals or other hard-to-find underwater configurations. Sometimes there is a small depth change, a foot or two, that attracts fish. You might find it almost by accident, but you can save the position with a navigation receiver. If possible, find visual ranges that cross at the spot. You usually can return to a spot within 20 to 100 yards with electronics, and within a few yards using visual ranges. There's another advantage to navigation receivers and ranges: they mark a spot invisibly. If you leave a buoy, it's bound to attract other fishermen.

River Navigation

Running a boat in a river is quite different from large lakes or coastal waters. The flood-prone bottom land beside a river tends to be a narrow strip of wilderness in the midst of civilization. You see wild animals and birds at close range. Old homes and landings dot the banks, occasionally interrupted by commercial or residential areas. River cruising is a most pleasant way to use a boat, but there are challenges.

The first challenge is due to the tendency of a free-running river to meander in a series of bends. The current cuts away at the outside of the bend, the bank turns the water, the water erodes the bank. "In the bend," as the expression goes, the current is swift and the river is deep.

Opposite the bend, "on the point," the current is slack, even eddying. Alluvial soil picked up in the current tends to settle, building a bar. The river constantly builds the points and cuts wider in the bends. Over many years, deep curves, or oxbows, develop; the river may cut through at a narrow point, leaving the old channel to silt in.

This action develops a characteristic profile of depths. The river is shallow on the points, and the depth increases across the river in the bend. There is strong current and deep water in the bends, and weak current and shallow water on the points. In straight stretches, bars tend to develop randomly. Where the water is shallow, it tends to get shallower since the current is minimum, and suspended particles settle.

Since many rivers have muddy or dark water, which keeps you from using water color as a clue to the depth, I would be uncomfortable navigating a river without a depthfinder. You can get an excellent idea of the river's bottom profile in a few hours using a depthfinder. Get one with a scale suitable for shallow water, say 15 or 20 feet at full scale, preferably with a graph display.

The next challenge is the water level in the river, which changes constantly with rain or drought, winter or summer. Watch reference marks—piers, launching ramps, or bridge clearance gauges. One year our local river went up over 8 feet in a rainy week. That wasn't a flood, just a normal rise in water level. The lower reaches of most rivers also are affected by tides.

A river's next most important characteristic is the current. It streams relentlessly downriver, except when reversed near the mouth by tidal current or when reduced in the *pool water* above a dam. As we've seen, current varies from place to place, and rain run-off or dam openings increase it dramatically. A boat skipper learns always to think about current.

Handling a boat going upstream is quite easy. You soon get the knack of turning a little later—and a little less—than in still water. Going upstream, your speed is improved if you hug the points, crossing over before approaching the next one. You have to be careful not to get too close or you'll go aground, but this technique saves distance and avoids the strongest current.

Going downstream, stay *in the bend*, or relatively close to the bank opposite the points. You're in deep water with swift current, and although you travel a greater distance over the ground, your distance through the water is shorter. The following current makes going downstream somewhat awkward. You have to turn earlier and turn farther than you would in still water.

You have to watch for driftwood. As the current undercuts the banks in the bends, trees fall into the river. Whether they hang up on the bottom or drift free,

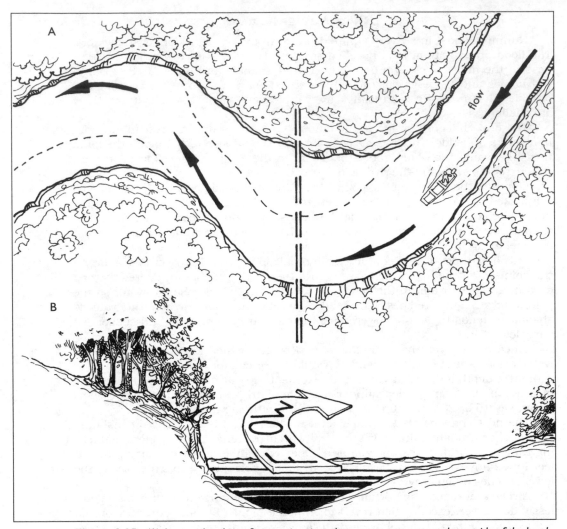

Figure 6-15. *(A) At every bend in a free-running river, the current cuts away at the outside of the bend. The current is swift (arrows) and the river is deep in the bend. Opposite the bend, on the point, the current is slack, even eddying, and the river is shallow. (B) Cross section of river at the dotted line.*

they pose a major hazard to boats. There are also pilings from old piers, and occasional wing dams that you must avoid.

Boathandling in a current poses at least as many problems as navigation. One of the worst situations involves coming downriver in the bend and spotting a log jutting out into the water. You have to turn sharply toward the point to miss the log—quite sharply, to have any effect. Slowing down, usually a good tactic, in this case makes things worse: You have less control when your speed is reduced. If your speed is slower than the speed of the current, the situation gets sticky. The current pushes you toward the log you turned to avoid. You would have to turn to starboard to go to port, since the boat is in fact backing into the current.

Navigating in a river is often complicated by the charts, or lack thereof. The U.S. Army Corps of Engineers provides maps for major rivers, and you can use topographic maps from the U.S. Geological Survey for others. Topographic maps are valuable for showing visible features but give little or no depth information.

Many rivers and associated reservoirs have aids to navigation, and there are *three* systems in use. The **coastal system** extends up many rivers and into the Great Lakes. In the Mississippi–Missouri River system, the Coast Guard uses the **Western River System** of aids to navigation (see Chapter 4). In other rivers, states use the **Uniform State Waterway Marking System (USWMS)**; the aids are similar to coastal aids in that there are red buoys that you leave to starboard and green to port going upriver. There is an important difference: A red-and-white vertically striped buoy has the opposite meaning in the two systems. The Coast Guard uses this buoy to indicate safe water, typically in midchannel. *State buoys with red and white vertical stripes indicate that it is unsafe to go between the buoy and the nearest shore.* This is confusing, and the States are shifting to a marking system that is more like the Coast Guard one.

Be careful of river buoys; at times strong current carries them completely under the surface. You may see only a swirl, or you may see nothing if the buoy is well underwater. Towboat and barge traffic often damages river buoys.

If you operate a boat on a river with barge traffic, you soon gain great respect for the towboat captains, who push awkward strings of barges along the twisting, changing river with incredible skill. They must maintain speed for control, and towboats often are moving much faster than they appear to at first sight. The helmsman usually has a blind spot extending far forward of the barges. Towboats have plenty of power, but even so, stopping a string of barges may take a mile or more. Watch for them, especially at night, and stay out of their way. Listen on channels 16, 13, or the VTS channel, and if you ever hear the danger signal of five or more short whistle blasts, head for the bushes.

The *Rules of the Road* are different for "Western Rivers." The most important distinction is that the downbound vessel actually has right of way and proposes the method of meeting. In all rivers, recognize the maneuvering difficulty of downbound vessels and give them a wide berth.

Rivers are punctuated by bridges, power lines, and buildings that provide definite but infrequent fixes. Use the old method of timing the run from a departure point to a destination, and you will know about how long it will take to get there the next time. The time returning will be quite different since the current is in the opposite direction. Time that run, too. If you calculate your speed upstream and downstream, you soon can predict reasonably accurate ETEs.

It may sound like using a sledgehammer to kill an ant, but I have found navigation receivers to be very useful on meandering rivers with few landmarks. Save a waypoint at a reference point, then use the distance to that waypoint to find where the boat is along the river. Use a map, and measure the distance directly from the reference waypoint. The distance is a line of position crossing the river, and the river is another LOP. This method is far better than guessing which bend you're approaching.

It may seem that operating in a river is all challenge, but that's only part of the story. The natural setting, the beauty, and the sights around the next bend are a constant lure. Some of my most pleasant trips have been on rivers.

Night Navigation

One of the joys of running a boat is cruising offshore on a clear night in fine weather. The sky is filled with brilliant stars, the air is cool, and the crowds of boats have gone home. It is peaceful and quiet, giving that sense of rest that only a boat can provide. While few things are visible, those that are lighted can be seen at greater distances than in the daytime.

There are some negatives. Running at planing speed in the dark is dangerous; you can't see floating logs and other hazards in time to avoid them. Visible position clues are meager, and you are likely to be more tired than in the daytime. And while operating at sea at night is easy, running a channel or entering a crowded harbor is much harder than in the daytime. Few natural features are visible at night, making it harder to see where the boat is in the channel.

Like many other things, operating a boat at night is made easier by careful preparation. Review the route, and lay out courses and distances in advance. Enter the waypoint data into your navigation receiver beforehand, and note the waypoint numbers or names on your chart.

Seeing at night also requires preparation. This is a learned technique, not a self-evident one. Our eyes are capable of seeing over a huge range of lighting intensities. In full daylight we see clearly at an illumination level up to 10,000 foot-candles. The illumination level in a typical office is between 50 and 100 foot-candles. At night we see a light easily that shows 1 sea-mile-candle, or less than a ten-millionth of a foot-candle.

Our eyes adjust to this incredible range of intensities, but they can't make the adjustment at once. Going from darkness to bright light, such as coming out of a theater into daylight, we are temporarily blinded. The same thing happens when going from light to darkness, such as going on deck from a lighted cabin.

As our eyes adjust to darkness, the pupils open to admit more light, and the cells in the retina adjust chemically to the light level. There are two types of light-sensitive cells in the retina—cones and rods. Cones are adapted to bright light and colors, rods to dim light. Neither is effective outside its range of light intensity.

We must be in total darkness for about 15 minutes to see well at night. There is additional improvement over the next 15 minutes, but any bright light interrupts the process and we have to start over. When you first step out on deck, you can see only first- and second-magnitude stars. The longer you stay out, the more stars you can see. Eventually you should be able to see sixth- or even seventh-magnitude stars, which show from $\frac{1}{250}$ to $\frac{1}{600}$ as much light as first-magnitude stars. The rods in your eyes will have adapted to the very low level of nighttime illumination.

The process of adapting to darkness begins below decks. Before you turn in, lay out all your gear where you can find it in the darkness. When you get up to go on watch, don't snap on a cabin light; it will ruin your night vision. If you have to use a light, use a penlight with a red filter, which cuts the light by four-fifths and still lets you see. When you go out on deck, your eyes will adapt quickly since they haven't been exposed to bright light.

I have heard the suggestion to close one eye to preserve its night vision. This doesn't work: flesh, eyelids included, is nearly transparent to red light. Remember sticking a flashlight in your mouth and looking into a mirror as a child? You'd need an opaque patch to keep the light out of your eye. It is better to avoid bright lights entirely. Then, when you go out on deck, you will adapt to seeing in the darkness quickly.

Even with your eyes fully adapted to darkness, you need to know *how* to see. The techniques are somewhat different from seeing in the daytime. The part of the retina that gives the most acute vision is the center, and you automatically use the central part of the retina when you look carefully at an object. The center of the retina, however, isn't as sensitive to low light levels as the area around the center. In order to see something in near-darkness, look slightly away from it. When looking for a distant light, for example, look just above or below the horizon.

Sometimes you see the object you're looking for, a pier or a boat, for example, because it is lighter than the background. At other times you look for the **absence of light**. The surface of the water usually shows many small reflections of light. When you do not detect that faint pattern, something is blocking it, and that something is often the jetty or buoy you're trying to see. This technique is particularly valuable in harbors where there are lights in the background. Jetties, groins, and log booms can be seen as a dark area in the reflected light from the water surface.

Sometimes you can use shore lights to good advantage. Coming up the Columbia River, there is a gentle turn to port near Astoria. It is hard to see ships just upriver of the turn since they are masked by the shore lights. When I was executive officer aboard a buoy tender there, I learned to watch very carefully for any dark area in the town's lights; it was a ship, "seen" by the absence of light.

You also should adapt the boat for night cruising. Install a rheostat dimmer for the compass light, and adjust it just bright enough to be seen. Turn it down more after your eyes are well adapted to the darkness. Choose your instrument lights carefully, too. Unless they are adjustable, they will be too bright. Dim red lights are good, not so much because they are red but because they are dim. Avoid "black-lighted" instruments like poison—they look snazzy but destroy night vision.

Steering stations that are suitably dark may suffer from glare from the running lights. The all-around white light of a motorboat under 12 meters (39.4 feet) is a notorious offender. The simplest solution involves fitting a flat shield under the light. Try a cardboard shield first, cutting it just large enough to block light from shining on the boat, then use that as a pattern to make a permanent shield from sheet metal.

If this isn't practical with your boat, you can shift to a 20-point masthead light forward and a 12-point stern light. The 20-point light can be mounted well forward so that it doesn't shine in your eyes. Check Rule 23 and Annex I to the *Rules* to determine the options and spacing requirements for these lights.

A radar set or a graph depthfinder must be adjusted to a low level of brightness on the screen to keep from destroying night vision. It presents a conflicting set of demands—the screen must be bright enough to see the targets but dim enough to keep from hurting night vision. Little wonder that in military ships, radar operators work in a separate compartment and are not used as lookouts. They concentrate on radar and adjust it for optimum detection.

The best night-vision wrecker aboard most boats is the searchlight. Using a searchlight will ruin your night vision until your eyes re-adjust to the darkness. The worst aspect of a searchlight is reflected light from your boat. If you must use a light, try a hand-held light, and hold it clear of the side. I have even used a light with a yellow filter to reduce the intensity (a red filter won't show green day-marks). It's better to use a small light than a large searchlight.

No discussion of night vision would be complete without mentioning binoculars. The lenses are larger than the lenses of your eyes and gather more light. The traditional "night glass" at sea is the 7 x 50, but if you're over 40, either 7 x 35 or 6 x 30 binoculars will serve just as nicely—at half the weight (see Chapter 3). Focus the binoculars on a small and faint star; a faint star is a point source of light and appears fuzzy when the binoculars are out of focus.

Binoculars are a great help in finding an unlighted object, but it takes practice. Daytime use helps. You learn not to sweep the horizon but to cover it in a series of steps. Search the binocular field carefully before moving to cover the next sector of horizon. Learn to aim the binoculars at an object quickly and accurately. When you do see something, you want to be able to find it with binoculars without extensive searching.

Night scopes are a high-tech approach to night vision. They use light amplification and a screen display to give a remarkable view in very low light levels—similar to low-light TV cameras. These devices have large lenses, expensive electronic innards, and a screen display that ruins night vision. Bright lights give them fits, which is a major limitation; nevertheless, they give a better picture of a nearly dark scene than anything else. This is a rapidly advancing technology.

In the meantime, we protect our night vision, learn the techniques of seeing, and use high-quality binoculars. These reliable and useful techniques improve night sight remarkably and have served the needs of boat operators for many years.

It is easier to see lighted aids to navigation at night than in the daytime. For example, you can see a large lighted buoy in the daytime at 2 or 3 miles, yet you can see its red or green light at 4 or 5 miles. The white light of a safe-water buoy is visible even farther.

The chart shows the **nominal range** of lights: the distance at which you can see them easily when the meteorological visibility is 10 miles, and your eyes are partly dark-adapted. It is a mistake to think you won't see a light beyond its nominal range. When the visibility is more than 10 miles and your eyes are well adapted to the dark, it isn't unusual to see a minor light or a buoy at half again its nominal range.

The distance at which you can see minor lights and buoys depends mostly on the candlepower of the light, the visibility, and your night vision. They are seldom hidden by the curvature of the earth, even from a small boat. Lighthouses are another story; their intense lights are visible until they are far enough away to be below the horizon. You can get a good idea of the maximum distance at which you can see a lighthouse by the following procedure:

1. Calculate the distance to the horizon for the light's listed height, or use the table in the *Light List*. (To calculate the distance, multiply the square root of the height in feet by 1.17.)

2. Using the height of your eyes above the water, calculate the distance from your boat to the horizon (with the same formula), or look it up in Table 5-2 (page 109).

3. Add the two distances; this is the maximum (geographic) range.

The maximum distance at which you can see the light occurs when the rays of light that skim the horizon are just at eye level at your boat. Any farther away, the light is below the horizon.

In clear weather, you may see the **loom** of a light before it shows clearly above the horizon. The loom of a city's lights is an excellent clue for the nighttime navigator.

Navigation in Fog

Navigation in fog can be either reasonably comfortable or filled with stress. It is essential to take departures, note the times of fixes, steer compass courses, and calculate running times to the next turn point. A custom chart works well, with directions and distances premeasured. A navigation receiver is invaluable in fog in open water, showing the distance and direction to any waypoint with high precision. You can use the normal techniques to stay near the desired track. In fact, other than not being able to see the destination until you are near it, electronic navigation offshore in fog is little different from navigation in clear weather. The receiver does exactly the same things, showing the way to each waypoint.

In fog I usually cut the speed to *half* the normal powerboat cruising speed. Why half? It's slow enough to allow more time to navigate and to avoid other ships or boats, and not slow enough to let current get the upper hand. Running times are twice their usual values, making it easy to think of the time to the next turn. In addition, changing to half the normal speed doubles the current lead angle. If you had to steer 094° to make good 090° at 20 knots, steer 098° at 10.

The navigation receiver also is an excellent help in fog or rain in channels if you have saved waypoints at the turns. It gives a bearing you can compare with the usual course. Unless you have DGPS or WAAS, the navigation receiver is seldom accurate enough to ensure that you stay in the channel. Steer the normal compass course, judge side-to-side positions as you pass buoys, and use the navigation receiver primarily to show the distance to the next turn. That distance is always a big question in fog. Without a waypoint, you have to find the distance to the turn point with a DR or radar.

You have little time to plot DRs and may not have radar. Either one takes time, and you are close to task-overload, if not already there. Watch the buoys as they come into sight to see how close you pass them. Adjust the course if you're too close or too far off. The navigation receiver gives instant distance information. It is accurate enough to give distances to the next turn. Knowing just when you will get close to a buoy removes the worry of going past it and not knowing how to get back. It is easy to know when you should see the buoy by watching the distance to go on the receiver.

In a dredged channel I find it useful in fog to run just to the right of the deepest portion. If the channel is 12 feet deep, run in about 10 feet. Then you will detect any drift to the right by decreasing depth, and any drift to the left by increasing depth. This lets you ride a line near the right side. Staying in the deep portion removes this advantage—if the depth begins to decrease, you don't know whether you're approaching the left or the right side of the channel.

In major harbors the advice to run just outside the right-hand limits of deep-draft channels is *especially important in fog.* You can avoid the company of big ships or tugs and barges and still have 30 feet or more of water. Check the chart to make sure there are no obstructions or rocks near the channel. Carry a good radar reflector, as well.

Radar comes into its own for fog navigation in harbors and near coasts. It gives accurate distance LOPs, using the *variable range marker (VRM)*. To determine the magnetic bearing, add the radar relative bearing from a bow-up display to the boat's heading, and apply deviation. These steps add errors to the normal radar bearing errors; distances are more accurate. In harbors, the seaman's eye method of using radar is nearly instinctive.

Radar for Collision Avoidance

As useful as radar is for navigation, perhaps its most important feature is its ability to detect boats and ships in fog. GPS and Loran-C can tell you nothing about an 800-foot container ship bearing down on you, or some idiot out running around in a boat at high speed. Radar does. But there is a problem: Navigating with radar is almost intuitive, but collision avoidance isn't. The concept of relative motion is at first hard to understand for most people.

No skipper can glance at a radar screen and tell much about a target. In clear weather you can tell at once the direction the other boat is heading and what type boat (or ship) it is. Even at night, running lights give immediate clues about size and type of vessel and the angle from the target's bow. None of this is evident from looking at radar. The target might even be a buoy rather than a boat. The lack of familiar information is the biggest drawback to using radar for collision avoidance.

A target that is on collision course stays on a constant bearing, but it takes time to see that the bearing is constant. This is particularly true on a bow-up display, which shifts the target bearing with every heading change. You have to plot a target for several minutes to tell how close it will approach, and construct a vector diagram to find its course and speed.

An untrained person using radar is a hazard. Having trained dozens of people in its use, I am well aware how much time and effort it takes to gain a full understanding of the plots. Ship's officers must attend approved training courses to gain radar certification—even though they may have prior experience. The *Rules of the Road* place stronger requirements on vessels with radar than on others. This doesn't mean radar isn't desirable; it is excellent for both navigation and collision avoidance, but there is much to learn about it. You can't just worry with it like a video game and dope out its collision avoidance capabilities. For one thing, the "You lose. Start over." sequences are far more exciting aboard a boat.

Radars aboard ships have an *automatic radar plotting aid (ARPA)* that does much of the work of a manual plot. An ARPA can find the course and speed of a target as well as the distance and direction of its closest point of approach. It can test a tentative collision avoidance maneuver in advance. An ARPA is complex and expensive, and the ship must have an accurate compass capable of sending information to it. ARPAs are just beginning to appear on large boats. In 1993, Raytheon announced an MARPA, or mini-ARPA, designed specifically for boats.

As useful as radar is for navigation, perhaps its most important feature is its ability to detect boats and ships in fog.

Few books address the subject of radar collision avoidance adequately. Most of the popular books on navigation, including *Bowditch* and *Chapman*, skip over the subject with a paragraph or two. Only *Dutton* and the *Radar Navigation Manual* (DMAHTC Publication 1310) provide a thorough treatment of the subject, but they are written for people with mathematical backgrounds. Collision avoidance is a complex subject, but it is so important that I feel a duty to present the basics.

Radar shows the range and bearing to a target, but you need to find out much more. This is possible *only* by plotting the target over a period of several minutes. The radar scope shows the boat at the center, usually bow up with 000° at the top of the scope. This is the *relative-bearing presentation,* since bearings to radar targets are relative to the boat's bow. Many large ships use the *true-bearing presentation,* in which the ship's true heading is at the appropriate bearing—to the right if going east, for example.

The motion of targets is also relative, this time to the boat's fixed position at the center of the PPI scope. This is a *relative-motion* presentation.

In the following examples, assume that we are on a trawler yacht with radar, cruising at 9 knots.

Example I. Our course is north, and another boat is to port and slightly ahead, also steering north at 9 knots. After a period of time, the radar shows the other boat's target in exactly the same spot. The *relative speed* is zero. The other boat is neither getting ahead of us nor falling behind. This is something like traveling west on I-80 at 65 miles an hour with another car alongside making exactly the same speed. Although each car is moving west at 65 MPH, their speed relative to one another is zero. Neither is gaining or losing.

This situation holds true regardless of the position of the other boat as long as it is on the same course and traveling at the same speed as our boat. Two boats proceeding north at 9 knots stay at the same distance and bearing from each other. There is no relative motion.

Example 2. We are still steering north at 9 knots. A target appears at 340°, 2 miles away. It is a buoy, anchored to the bottom. If we watch the radar target over time, it appears to move down the screen in a vertical line. *Relative to our boat* (at the center of the screen), the target is moving south. Actually, it isn't moving; we are going north at 9 knots. On the radar, however, our boat appears stationary and the target appears to move. Back to the car analogy: A sign at the side of the road moves toward the car at 65 MPH. Even though the sign is anchored in concrete, it is moving relative to the car.

Example 3. We're still steering north at 9 knots (see next page). A boat 4 miles north of us is steering south at 9 knots. Its target marches vertically down the screen toward the center. The two boats will maneuver to avoid collision when

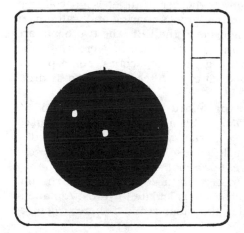

Figure 6-16. *Example 1.*

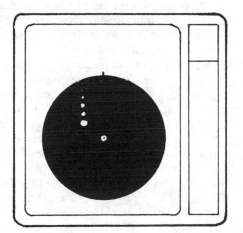

Figure 6-17. *Example 2.*

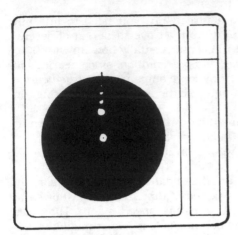

Figure 6-18. *Example 3.*

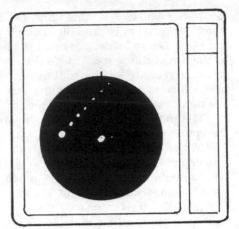

Figure 6-19. *Example 4.*

they get closer, but for now they hold course and speed. The other boat is moving south at 18 knots *relative* to our boat. In our highway analogy, this is similar to a car 2 miles ahead in the oncoming lanes, also making 65 MPH. Its speed, relative to our car, is 130 MPH.

Example 4.   Still steering north at 9 knots. We have a target 3 miles away, dead ahead. It is yet another trawler, steering west at 9 knots. As time goes on, its target moves from the top of the screen at an angle down and to the left side. Its *relative* course is southwest, even though its *actual* course is west. It passes clear of our boat by about 2 miles.

In each of these cases, we can determine the motion of the target relative to our boat by plotting successive positions over a period of time. *There is no other way to get this information.* Relative motion in itself is quite valuable. It will reveal how close the other boat will come to ours, the bearing of the **closest point of approach (CPA)**, and the time it will occur. If we wish to find the other boat's *actual* course and speed, we must remove the effect of our own course and speed from its relative motion, using another plot.

A popular shortcut method of determining whether a target is on collision course is simply turning the cursor or EBL to the target's bearing and watching it over a period of time. If the target follows right down the EBL, the two boats are headed for a collision. The bearing is constant and the range is decreasing—the classic signs of an impending collision. With large radar scopes, some people mark targets with a grease pencil, which makes it easy to see if the target is drifting left or right of its original bearing.

A plotting diagram called a **maneuvering board**, available in pads of 50 sheets from the Defense Mapping Agency (DMA Publication 5090), is widely used for radar plotting. The maneuvering board is marked with bearings and 10 distance rings for use at various scales. You might choose to let each ring represent 1,000 yards, giving a 0-to-10,000-yard range. For a plot at longer range, you may decide to let each ring represent 2,000 yards, giving a 20,000-yard maximum. You could choose to work in miles, but it's easier to calculate in yards. A maneuvering board should be mounted right beside the radar scope if there's room. A good plastic version is handy aboard a boat.

I will present one simplified method of plotting and finding the CPA and the other boat's course and speed. There are other equally valid ways to calculate speed, designate vectors, and so on. If you have learned them, in all likelihood you know how to plot, too. Don't change what you know.

To make a plot, you must hold the same course and speed. When you detect a radar target, measure its distance with the VRM and its bearing with the cursor or EBL. Take the radar bearing when steady on course; otherwise, the plot will be erratic. Put a mark on the maneuvering board at the appropriate distance and relative bearing, and mark the time. It's best to measure the distance and bearing right on the minute. *Exactly 3 minutes later*, measure the range and bearing again, and make another mark on the maneuvering board. (A 3-minute inter-

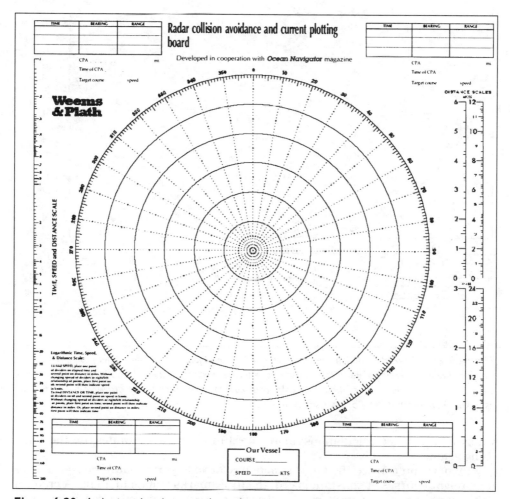

Figure 6-20. *A plastic radar plotter, similar to the maneuvering board. (Courtesy Weems & Plath)*

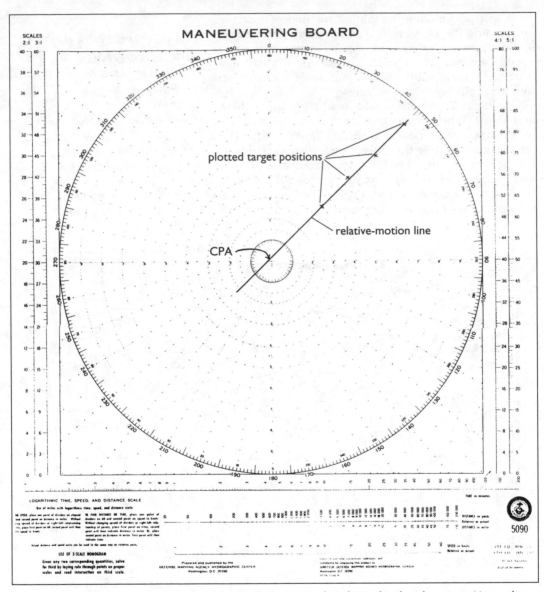

Figure 6-21. *The relative-motion line on a maneuvering board joins the plotted target positions—the range and relative bearing of the target at 3-minute intervals (each ring equals 1,000 yards). In this example, the line passes the center of the plot at only about 200 yards (marked by the arrow). This is the closest point of approach (CPA) if both vessels hold course.*

val simplifies speed calculations; more later.) In another 3 minutes, do the same thing again.

By now you can see the target's motion relative to your boat. If both boats are on straight courses at constant speed, the three marks will be in a line. A crooked line means that one of the boats has turned or changed speed. Draw a line connecting the three marks, and extend it past the center of the maneuvering board. This is the **relative-motion line**; it passes the center of the scope at the distance the boats will be apart at the closest point of approach, if both maintain course and speed.

This summarizes the most important part of radar plotting: Plot a succession of distances and bearings, note the times, and draw a line connecting them. The line passes nearest the center of the scope at the closest point of approach, or **CPA**. If this is a comfortable distance away, say 1,000 yards, you can simply continue the plot to see if the other boat changes course. A course change bends the relative-motion line and changes the CPA.

You also can determine the time of CPA. Set the dividers to a pair of marks (they're 3 minutes apart) and step down the relative-motion line in 3-minute increments from the last mark. If there are five divider steps, for example, the CPA will be in 15 minutes (5 × 3). Its range and bearing will be at the point where the relative motion line on the plot comes closest to the center. Continue plotting the target at 3-minute intervals. The additional plots give a more accurate CPA and also show if the target turns.

There is a good reason for using 3-minute time increments. Three minutes is $\frac{1}{20}$ of an hour. A nautical mile is about 2,000 yards; $\frac{1}{20}$ of a mile is 100 yards. A boat going at turtle speed of 1 knot goes $\frac{1}{20}$ of a mile in $\frac{1}{20}$ of an hour—100 yards in 3 minutes. For *any* speed, *the distance in yards covered in 3 minutes is 100 times the speed.* For example, a sailboat making 7 knots goes 700 yards in 3 minutes. We call this the **three-minute rule**.

The three-minute rule holds true for the *relative* motion on a radar plot. Let's go back to our examples. In Example 2, the buoy target moves 900 yards in 3 minutes. The relative speed is 900 ÷ 100, or 9 knots. The relative speed of the moored buoy is all due to our boat's 9-knot speed. This is always a good clue: *A target moving vertically down the scope with a relative speed equal to your boat speed is stationary.*

In Example 3, two boats, each making 9 knots, are meeting. In 3 minutes the distance decreases by 1,800 yards, so the relative speed is 18 knots (1,800 ÷ 100). This relative speed is due to the combination of our boat going north at 9 knots and the second boat going south at 9 knots.

A target moving vertically down the scope with a relative speed equal to your boat speed is stationary.

If there is risk of collision, you need another plot to deduct your own boat's motion from the target's *relative* course and speed to find its *actual* course and speed. This second plot, sometimes called the **speed triangle**, is done on the same maneuvering board used for the relative-motion plot. It is a bit complex, as you must work with *vectors*—lines that represent course and speed.

As you have seen, the relative-motion line represents the course of the target relative to your boat. The relative speed in knots is the same as the number of 100-yard increments the target moves on the plot in 3 minutes. You know your own speed. And 000° is the reference course for this second plot.

First, plot a line 000° on the maneuvering board, with a length to represent your boat's speed. This line is a vector—its length and direction are both significant. Use a speed scale different from the distance scale if it gives a better presentation. For example, you might be using one distance ring to represent 1,000 yards, but if you're plotting a fast target, you'll have to use a different scale for speed to keep the speed triangle from running off the edge. The maneuvering board has four printed scales that are handy for speed-triangle plots. Use dividers to transfer the speed from the printed scale to the 000° line representing your boat's course. Put an arrow at the top of that vector.

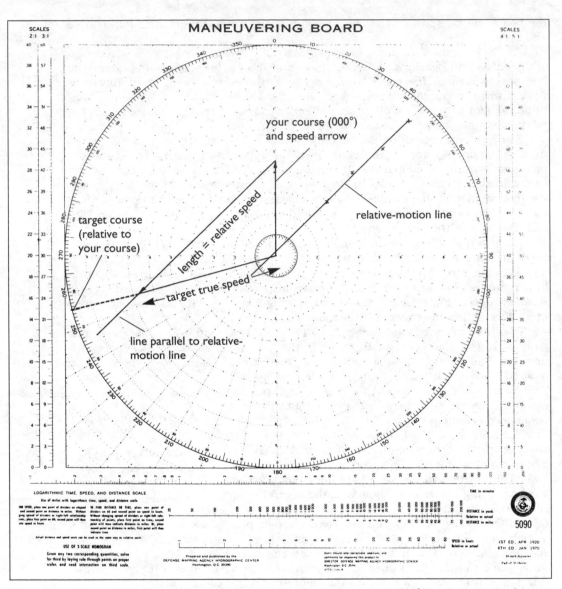

Figure 6-22. *The speed triangle for the same example. Our course is 035°M and our speed is 9 knots. We use the 2:1 scale—each ring represents 2 knots.*

1. With dividers, transfer your boat's speed from the scale to the 000° line. Draw your boat's course arrow (from the center to ring 4.5).

2. Draw a line from the tip of your course arrow parallel to the relative-motion line.

3. Calculate the relative speed (1,800 yards in 3 minutes = 18 knots), and mark the new line with an arrow at a length corresponding to 18 knots.

4. Join the center of the plot to the latest arrow point. This line represents the actual course and speed of the target—255° at 13.5 knots.

5. The target course (255°) is relative. Add it to your boat's course (035°) to find the target's magnetic course—290°.

Next, use a parallel rule to draw a line parallel to the relative-motion line, intersecting the 000° line at the top arrow. Make it long enough so that you can mark it at the correct relative speed. Remember, you find the relative speed by measuring the distance—in hundreds of yards—between marks on the relative-motion line 3 minutes apart. Reset the dividers to that speed on the appropriate printed scale, then put one divider point at the arrow end of the 000° line and the other on the parallel line you just drew. Mark the parallel line with its own arrow point at the second divider point. This arrow point is critical—it indicates the end of the relative speed vector. Now draw a third line from the center of the maneuvering board to this arrow point. This line is another vector; its direction from the center of the plot is the target's *actual* course (relative to your course) and its length represents the target's *actual* speed (measured against the same speed scale).

Collision Avoidance in Poor Visibility

Suppose by radar you detect a target on collision course in poor visibility. What do you do about it? Since you are not in sight of the other vessel, you have some freedom to maneuver under the *Rules*. Much depends on the target's bearing, course, and speed.

You have made a relative-motion plot to determine the risk of collision. It is important to make the second plot, the speed triangle, to find the target's course and speed. In this example, the target bears 032° relative at 3,500 yards and will pass about 200 yards from the center of the plot (your boat). That's much too close to allow for errors in the radar data and in the plot. In this case a turn to starboard is the best maneuver, unless there are shoals in the way.

Make a bold turn, at least 45°. It's best to turn enough to starboard to move the target *to the other side of the dead-ahead line.* That may give more than ample clearance, but in avoiding collision, more is better. This turn will swing the target sharply around the scope, but you can't relax yet. Keep up the plot, beginning with a mark as you complete the turn. Successive marks should slant more to port, leaving a larger distance at the closest point of approach.

In this example, you could also slow down. If you come to idle speed, about 3 or 4 knots, the CPA will increase.

A target approaching on the port bow, crossing from port to starboard, is more worrisome. According to Rule 19 (and common sense), you shouldn't turn to port for a target forward of the beam, unless you are overtaking it. You could slow down and let the other vessel pass ahead. If the other vessel turns moderately to starboard, however, your slowing down would decrease the CPA distance. Nevertheless, slowing down gives more time and allows the option of speeding up again. You could also turn to starboard to open up the closest point of approach, but turning to starboard and slowing down simultaneously would be unwise. One cancels the effect of the other.

Suppose a target is closing from 110° relative. Your plot shows that the target is going faster than your boat and is headed to the left of your course. Here, slowing down lets the other vessel pass clear ahead. You could also turn to port since, under Rule 19, you should avoid turning toward a vessel coming up from abaft the beam.

These general rules are no substitute for completing the plot to find the target's course and speed. You can't tell whether you are in an overtaking or a crossing situation with a target ahead unless you plot the speed triangle. For the best information, plot a second speed triangle with a proposed new course and speed

International and Inland Rules and Radar

The *Rules of the Road* contain specific requirements for vessels equipped with radar. In order to use radar for collision avoidance, you must be thoroughly familiar with Rule 6, *Safe Speed*; Rule 7, *Risk of Collision*; Rule 8, *Action to Avoid Collision*; and Rule 19, *Conduct of Vessels in Restricted Visibility*.

Rule 19, *Conduct of Vessels in Restricted Visibility*, is *radically different* from the rules that apply to vessels in sight of one another. If you attempt to apply the familiar maneuvering rules for clear weather (Rules 11–18) in restricted visibility, you will violate the *Rules*. In fog there is no such thing as a stand-on or a give-way vessel. *Both* vessels are responsible to take avoiding action if risk of collision exists. *Both* are responsible to proceed at safe speed, and to slow or stop if necessary. *Both* are cautioned to avoid turning to port for vessels forward of the beam, and to avoid turning toward a vessel abeam or abaft the beam.

We reprint Rule 7 and Rule 19 since it is so important to understand them. These two rules are identical in the *International Rules* and the *Inland Rules*. Note that Rule 7 *requires* a radar-equipped boat to plot radar targets to determine risk of collision.

Rule 7
Risk of Collision

(a) Every vessel shall use all available means appropriate to the prevailing circumstances and conditions to determine if risk of collision exists. If there is any doubt such risk shall be deemed to exist.

(b) Proper use shall be made of radar equipment if fitted and operational, including long-range scanning to obtain early warning of risk of collision and radar plotting or equivalent systematic observation of detected objects.

(c) Assumptions shall not be made on the basis of scanty information, especially scanty radar information.

(d) In determining if risk of collision exists the following considerations shall be among those taken into account:

(i) such risk shall be deemed to exist if the compass bearing of an approaching vessel does not appreciably change.

(ii) such risk may sometimes exist even when an appreciable bearing change is evident, particularly when approaching a very large vessel or a tow or when approaching a vessel at close range.

for your boat, using the target's course and speed. After you turn, the old plots are invalid; start a new relative-motion plot.

Remember, if you hear a fog signal apparently forward of the beam and you have not determined that risk of collision does not exist, you must reduce speed to bare steerageway.

VHF-FM radio is a help in avoiding collision in the fog. Ships at sea guard channel 16; in protected waters, channel 13 or the Vessel Traffic Service (VTS) channel specified for the harbor. Be sure to listen; many ships transmit their

Rule 19
Conduct of Vessels in Restricted Visibility

(a) This Rule applies to vessels not in sight of one another when navigating in or near an area of restricted visibility.

(b) Every vessel shall proceed at a safe speed adapted to the prevailing circumstances and conditions of restricted visibility. A power-driven vessel shall have her engines ready for immediate maneuver.

(c) Every vessel shall have due regard to the prevailing circumstances and conditions of restricted visibility when complying with Rules 4 through 10.

(d) A vessel which detects by radar alone the presence of another vessel shall determine if a close-quarters situation is developing or risk of collision exists. If so, she shall take avoiding action in ample time, providing that when such action consists of an alteration of course, so far as possible the following shall be avoided:

(i) an alteration of course to port for a vessel forward of the beam, other than a vessel being overtaken; and

(ii) an alteration of course toward a vessel abeam or abaft the beam.

(e) Except when it has been determined that a risk of collision does not exist, every vessel which hears apparently forward of her beam the fog signal of another vessel, or which cannot avoid a close-quarters situation with another vessel forward of her beam, shall reduce her speed to the minimum at which she can be kept on course. She shall if necessary take all way off and, in any event, navigate with extreme caution until danger of collision is over.

approximate position, course, and speed at regular intervals. When calling another vessel in the fog, be sure to give your general location, course and speed, and the distance and direction to the target you are trying to identify. Convert the relative bearing to true. Relative bearing is meaningless to another vessel unless you're both in the same narrow channel.

For boats, "close" is 100 yards or so. For ships, it is a mile or two. A ship is slow to turn and slower to stop—stopping takes well over a mile. If you're close to a ship, you must do the maneuvering; the ship can't. Do everything possible to stay away from ships.

Oh, yes. Unless you have an unshakable death wish, carry a radar reflector in foggy weather. Boats are nearly invisible on ship radar in choppy seas until they are within a couple of miles. A radar reflector allows a ship to see a boat on radar two or three times as far away.

You can't tell whether you are in an overtaking or a crossing situation with a target ahead unless you plot the speed triangle.

Try radar plotting on a trip in clear weather. That way you can gain experience plotting when there is no danger. You will learn how plots appear in various situations, and they won't be so mysterious in the fog. When practicing in clear weather, obey the *Rules of the Road* for clear weather (Rules 11–18), but think through the different action required by the rules for restricted visibility. This will build your experience quickly without the struggle of trying to learn when it's foggy.

CHAPTER 7

Special Techniques

*T*here are a number of techniques that make navigation easier or that solve unusual navigation problems. We have collected a few of the more useful ones in this chapter, along with solutions to the more common problems that occur with GPS, DGPS, WAAS, and Loran-C.

Riding a Line of Position

Ideally, you have a good idea of your boat's position at all times. Practically, you may not. At times you may know the boat's position but not have an accurate position for a destination. Perhaps you have taken its position from a chart, not having been there before. Perhaps the batteries in your portable GPS receiver have died. There are still good ways to find the destination.

Finding one good line of position and following it to your destination is a good technique. I remember looking for an entrance buoy to an unfamiliar port against a confusing clutter of buildings ashore. We got closer and closer and still couldn't see it. I saw a radio tower ashore and found it on the chart. I drew a line from the buoy to the radio tower and measured the direction. Then I took a compass bearing on the tower and found it was several degrees too low. Turning to port, I ran parallel to the coast until its bearing matched the bearing from the buoy to the tower, then I headed directly for the tower. Sure enough, the buoy eventually appeared right ahead. It had to. We were following a line of position that connected the buoy and the radio tower.

A current along the coast, in one direction or the other, can make it harder to keep a tower or other reference on the correct bearing. If its bearing decreases, you must steer more to port; if it increases, steer to starboard. This is easy in practice. It may be necessary to change course significantly to return to the right bearing and then adjust your course to hold the bearing steady.

I have used the same principle—following a single LOP—with a depthfinder. Lighted bell buoy "16" (Figure 7-1) is in about 23 feet of water. If the transducer is 2 feet below the waterline and the tide is 3 feet above MLLW, the depthfinder should indicate 24 feet at the buoy. The buoy should be relatively easy to find in low visibility by running west, keeping the depthfinder at 24 feet. Remember to check the height of the tide above MLLW to avoid confusion. Always keep the

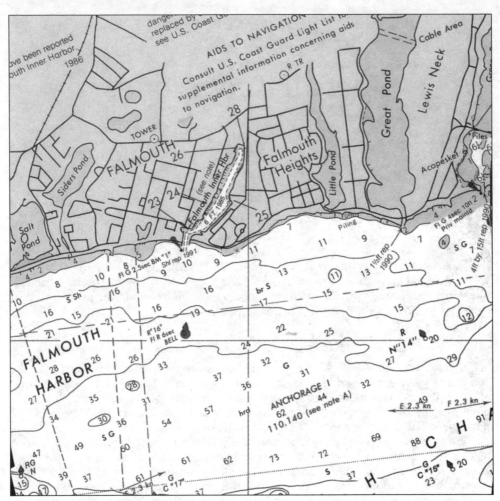

Figure 7-1. *Lighted bell buoy "16" is in 23 feet of water. The tide is 3 feet above MLLW. The transducer is 2 feet below the waterline. Going west, keep the depth reading at 24 feet (23 + 3 − 2) to find the buoy by riding a depth line of position.*

stage of the tide in mind when approaching an inlet; this is doubly important when you're using depth as a guide.

Riding a line of position is a natural for homing on a radiobeacon: Put the radiobeacon dead ahead and go—carefully if the visibility is low.

The Deliberate Miss

No, this isn't about a careful young lady. It is about a valuable technique in navigation—deliberately missing your destination. Hitting the destination on the nose usually is the essence of good navigation, but at times it is better to miss it.

I remember trying to find a small creek in Florida Bay. The creek mouth was practically covered by mangroves, difficult to see unless you were close aboard.

To add to the problem, the rest of the shoreline was the same; one area looked much like its neighbor as we approached from across an open bay. Loran-C or GPS would have made things easy, but we didn't have either then.

The logical approach would seem to be to steer directly for the creek mouth, but approaching from a wide bay, it's easy to miss a creek like this. And if you do, which way do you turn to search for it? After searching for a short distance, you remind yourself that each minute in the wrong direction means another lost minute to return to your starting point, then another minute to go in the right direction. Fishing time slips away quickly.

The cure seems illogical: Don't head right for the creek. Miss deliberately. Steer to one side of the estimated course, making sure you miss enough to *know* on which side your destination lies. Steer enough to the right, for example, to ensure that you approach the shore to the right of your target. Then simply turn left and follow the shoreline to your destination.

The deliberate miss technique worked like a charm for the creek mouth, and I have used it many other times: looking for a gap between islands, looking for an opening in a reef, looking for an inlet.

Since you usually approach the shore at an angle of less than 90°, steer toward the shore *before* you come to your destination; i.e., miss your target to the near side. This minimizes the time lost by the short dog-leg along the shore.

It is important to run parallel to the shore at a reasonable distance. If you're too far off, you may not see your destination. If you're too close, you can't see it

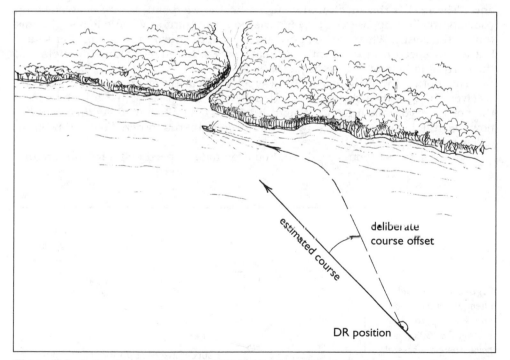

Figure 7-2. *Rather than heading directly (solid line) for the hard-to-see creek entrance, perhaps overshooting it, practice the deliberate miss. Close with the shore before the creek (dotted line) and follow the shore to the entrance.*

until you are right on top of it. Try to run close enough along shore to see the features of your destination clearly.

We have been discussing visual piloting, but the deliberate miss technique works well with precise electronic navigation, too. Suppose you are heading for a receiver-measured waypoint over a wreck. The receiver's *bearing-to-waypoint* has some delay, and it's easy to overshoot the waypoint.

The solution is simple: Miss deliberately by steering slightly off to one side, then watch the GPS latitude or longitude or the Loran-C TD readings. When one is correct, turn and follow that line of position until the other is correct. It sounds archaic but it works very well—with no calculation delay.

Although the natural inclination is to go for the direct hit, at times it's better to miss a little in a known direction than to be confused about which way to turn, whether using GPS, Loran-C, depthfinder, compass bearing, or Mark I Eyeball. Ultimately, a deliberate miss may save time.

The Electronic Navigation Hook

As you approach a waypoint using an electronic navigation receiver, its bearing often changes rapidly. You change course, the bearing changes again, and you change course again. By the time you reach the waypoint, your wake has a short curve like a fish hook. Why can't you go straight to the waypoint instead of chasing it as you get close?

There are four reasons for this, and usually two or more are happening at once. The first is the effect of any current at the waypoint as you slow down on your approach. Suppose you're going east to a waypoint and there is a slight current to the south. When you're at cruising speed, the current is setting you south, but at low speed compared with the boat's speed. If you're making 25 knots and the current is ½ knot, the set is just over 1°.

You notice the error when the waypoint's bearing given by the navigation receiver changes by a degree or so. Usually you would steer just a hair more to the north, or you might ignore it since it is such a small change. As time goes on, however, the bearing changes by another degree, then another. Now you begin to follow a curving track.

As you get close, you slow down. You drop to idle speed just a few hundredths

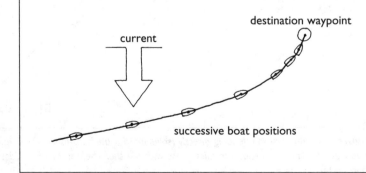

Figure 7-3. *A boat often follows a curved path when approaching a Loran-C or GPS waypoint. There are several causes: compass error, current, and small navigation system errors.*

of a mile from the waypoint. Say you're making 6 knots. Now the ½-knot current requires 5° of course correction; at 3 knots it's 10°. So you make a hook as you approach the waypoint. This will occur if everything is working perfectly.

Another more subtle cause for the hook is a misadjusted compass. Suppose there is no current. The GPS indicates that the waypoint bears 140°M at 5 miles. You steer 140°, but your compass has 4° easterly deviation. If you steer 140°, you are actually headed 144°M.

As you head for the waypoint, its bearing keeps shifting to the left since you are steering to its right. You keep correcting your course and eventually reach the waypoint, making a hook. This cause is quite common and gives rather sharp hooks near the waypoint. It is a good clue to compass errors.

The next cause of hooks is the inherent error in any electronic navigation system. Suppose it varies by only ± 20 yards. At a mile this "jitter" changes the bearing to a waypoint by less than a degree. At 200 yards it's 6°, and at 100 yards, 12°.

Another cause is the delay in calculating the distance and bearing to the waypoint. Some receivers do this very quickly after measuring each position; others take longer. The longer they take, the older their information, and the more the tendency to follow a hook as you approach the waypoint.

You can eliminate a major cause of these hooks by adjusting your boat's compass as carefully as possible. That goes without saying, but it often goes without doing, too.

There is a practical way to compensate for current or compass error. Apply a correction that is *equal to the bearing change*. Suppose you have gone about halfway to a waypoint, and its bearing has changed from 270° to 272°. You have made good about 268°. If you steer 272°, you'll only make good 270°. I would steer 274°, which should make good a course of 272°, with the same 2° set. This is a powerful technique for maintaining an accurate course.

Look Behind You

Have you ever had a problem trying to find an inlet on the way home? Ever become confused trying to thread your way back through a maze of islands? Most of us have. The problem comes from the change in the appearance of your surroundings as you reverse your direction of travel. It's easy to find your way out of a channel that may be nearly invisible on your return.

It is natural to look ahead carefully enough to become familiar with the landmarks as they appear on the way out. You notice the way the scenery unfolds and changes. You see that you must steer toward a certain point of land to stay in midchannel, or toward a small island to avoid a shoal, and you make mental notes of these leading marks and the compass courses you follow. As you approach a turn you look for clues as to when to make it. Do a pair of prominent objects come into line? Are you abeam of a buoy or a landmark? You remember that a certain buoy, hard to see at a distance, appeared a little to the right of a spit of land.

When you're new to an area, writing down the courses and making notes on the chart will make the trip easier the next time around. Problems occur, however, when you try to retrace your tracks. You may have learned your way out quite well without learning much at all about your way in. The cure for this embarrassing phenomenon is so simple that I hesitate to mention it, except for the fact that it is so frequently omitted. *Look behind you.* You will not, like Lot's wife, turn into a pillar of salt. You *will* turn into a better navigator. After all, it was best for Lot's wife to forget the place she had come from; you will be trying to remember it as well as you can. A visual image is a great memory aid.

If you're to remember, you must look back carefully and attentively. As a first step, notice the charted landmarks and aids to navigation. Buildings, clumps of trees, and other features that don't appear on the chart are useful landmarks too. Look at all of the things you see on the way out—as they would appear when coming in—by looking aft. Be particularly alert for objects that are lined up in range "over the shoulder," as pilots say.

It helps to imagine the nighttime appearance of the coast or harbor behind you as you go out in the daytime. Using the chart, check the colors and characteristics of the lights. Note how they appear in relation to each other. Notice the buildings and advertising signs that will be lighted at night.

Another trick is to keep looking back as you get farther offshore. Doing so gives you a series of mental images with which to compare the scenery on the way in. Experts in the study of memory say a mental picture is the best way to remember anything, even suggesting we devise mental images to remind ourselves of abstract ideas. I know that mental images do work in piloting, better than any other method of route finding. Take a series of looks aft on the way out, notice as many details as possible, and you will be well prepared for the return trip.

A mental image isn't foolproof and doesn't make up for sloppy navigation. You should store electronic navigation waypoints, at least at the entrance buoy. But looking back is easy to do, requires little additional time, and is a big help in piloting.

Things That Go Wrong

Electronic navigation systems are so reliable that you may have few problems even though you use a receiver regularly. Since problems are rare, you have little opportunity to learn how to diagnose what is wrong. Sometimes a skipper who has grown to rely on GPS doesn't even suspect that it might be giving unreliable information. It's also easy to become so accustomed to using a navigation receiver that you don't use the traditional navigation skills you need when the navigation system isn't doing its job.

Every navigation receiver yet invented occasionally fails to work or gets out of tolerance. The problem may be with the transmitters, with the receiver, or with interference, but the result is either no information or false information. You have to be on guard for these problems. Many times you can correct them; if not, you must know not to rely on the receiver until the problem is corrected.

Some of this information is in other parts of the book. It is repeated here to give a single source of information for detecting and solving problems with navigation receivers. It covers both electronic problems that prevent the receiver from functioning properly and problems in its operation that cause it to give incorrect information.

Many people using a receiver for the first time have trouble getting it to operate correctly. The unit expects a specific sequence of keystrokes for entering data, displaying different information, and so on. Some receivers have *Enter* keys, while others respond a few seconds after you enter the data. Some require you to enter north latitude and west longitude, while others are programmed to accept these as defaults. Some are immediately ready to accept data, while others require you to press the *Clear* key first. If you try to alter the destination waypoint, the receiver may beep back.

Many manuals emphasize complex and rare uses as much as the ordinary ones. It all gets easier as you gain experience, but it can be annoying at first (see "Beginning with an Electronic Receiver" in Chapter 5). You have to search through the manual to solve each problem. Often it is easier to call the factory or the technician who installed the receiver to learn how to correct a problem.

Signs of Trouble

Receivers indicate trouble by displaying screen messages, showing or sounding alarms, or showing blinking displays. Some of these are difficult to see, especially if you're busy with something else, but other information from the receiver can also tell you something is wrong. Watch the distance to the destination waypoint. Normally it diminishes fairly steadily. It will pause at a reading, say 12.31 miles, then go to 12.29. It might jump back to 12.30, then down to 12.29, 12.28, and so on. While the distance to go decreases in little steps and jumps, it continues to decrease. *If the distance to the destination waypoint stops decreasing, the system isn't working.*

The same thing happens to a latitude and longitude or TD display. The numbers stop changing. A "frozen" display is always a sign of trouble. You may notice it before you see "Poor Satellite Coverage," "Not Ready," or a similar message.

It is also convenient to watch the cross-track error. Problems may cause the XTE to jump ½ mile or more, and the boat can't have moved that far instantly. You may not be using the cross-track error for navigation, but keeping an eye on it gives a good indication of trouble.

Plotters are especially useful for spotting radical position jumps caused by navigation system errors.

Data Entry Errors

It is remarkably easy to hit the wrong button on a receiver or designate the wrong destination waypoint. Always check that the distance and direction to the waypoint seem to make sense with your idea of the boat's location. A custom chart marked with directions and distances between waypoints is a big help.

I also have entered waypoint data incorrectly, getting the wrong latitude and longitude. Some of these errors come from hitting the wrong number key; some are mistakes in getting data from the chart. Even some lists of waypoints contain errors. These usually show up as large errors, and comparing the waypoint with the rough distance and bearing from the chart quickly reveals the problem. Rechecking everything solves it.

Different Bearings to a Waypoint

If two receivers show radically different bearings to a common waypoint, something is wrong. Occasionally two receivers show a difference of 1° or 2° when both are working correctly. Electronic navigation receivers apply variation (the angle between true north and magnetic north) automatically to give magnetic courses and bearings. This is a good feature, but receivers don't always apply variation identically. One summer we saw three GPS receivers and a Loran-C receiver show magnetic bearings to the same waypoint that differed by 1° or 2°. One was using 8°, two 9°, and one 10° westerly variation. The chart showed 9°14'W variation in that location. (Check the compass rose on the chart to find the variation, and apply the annual change.)

Some receivers display the variation, but others don't. For these, put in a waypoint with your longitude but a degree or so north of your location. The magnetic course to that waypoint shown by the receiver indicates the variation. If it's 012°, the receiver is applying 12° westerly variation (correcting, subtract westerly).

You can set the variation manually, or you can set the receiver to use true courses. It makes little sense to set it to true unless your boat has a gyro-compass. If you set variation manually, remember to change it. In many areas, variation changes by a degree roughly every 50 miles.

Shifting Waypoints

Entering a *home-port*, *local*, *bias*, or *ASF* correction to make Loran-C latitude and longitude agree with the local chart will shift the position of every waypoint in memory. If you enter such a correction, go back and reenter each waypoint. In some cases the receiver has to be in the general vicinity of the waypoint and locked on to the signals.

A similar situation occurs if you change a Loran-C receiver's automatic ASF to manual, or vice versa. The difference between ASF *Off* or *On* can be a couple of miles.

Which One Is Wrong?

Smart skippers carry more than one radionavigation receiver, preferably one for GPS and one for Loran-C. Save a waypoint using both receivers, and set it as the destination when you want to return to it. The difference between the distance to the waypoint shown by two receivers is usually within 0.01 to 0.03 mile. Waypoints taken from charts won't be as close together as saved waypoints, but should be within a quarter of a mile. The bearings usually agree within 1° or so, except when you get close to the waypoint. Two independent systems that agree closely give an excellent check.

What if two receivers give different distances and directions to the waypoint? One is most likely correct, but which one? Erroneous data entry errors appear immediately, but other errors occur along the way. When errors appear along the way:

- Check receiver alarms. Different receivers use a variety of alarms to indicate signal problems (e.g., blinking displays, *Not Ready*, *No Fix*, *Poor Satellite Coverage*, *S*, *C*, *B*, and others). Check the receiver manual. These alarms indicate the most common signal problems and let you know that the receiver isn't giving valid information.

- Is one receiver's distance and bearing to the waypoint frozen although the boat is moving?

- Check the distance to the waypoint. Has one receiver changed significantly (jumped)? Watching the distance wind down takes little effort and gives a good reference when the receivers disagree.

- Check for a similar jump in the receiver's estimated time of arrival.

- Is there suddenly a large cross-track error with one receiver? This is an easy check.

- Check the bearing to the waypoint to see if one receiver has changed significantly.

- Check signal quality (SQ) and DOP for GPS, the DGPS beacon receiver, or signal-to-noise ratio (SNR) for Loran-C. Low SQ or SNR and high DOP indicate poor fixes.

- Turn off the Differential Beacon Receiver input to the GPS receiver and see if the position jumps. Sometimes the "corrections" have wrongly introduced large position errors.

- Check to see whether the Loran-C receiver is still using the same TDs. If it has changed from 26 and 43 to 14 and 43, for example, the position may jump a couple of miles.

- Compare the two receiver positions with a rough DR or distance-to-go. If you're sailing at 6 knots and are 10 miles from the waypoint at 0930, and at 1000 receiver A shows 5 miles to go and B shows 7, then B is probably correct.

This is sort of like detective work. If the receivers agreed when you started for the waypoint, usually one of them has lost lock on the signals and shows an alarm. This might be due to transmitter problems, or someone turning on a fluorescent light on the boat, or any number of other things. If you can't find an obvious problem, look to see which receiver has changed recently. Errors usually appear to shift both distance and direction to a waypoint, but it is possible for only one to be affected.

You can always draw a course line from the last known position and plot a DR, but often the tips listed here will reveal the problem.

Onboard Interference

Many errors come from interference in electronic equipment, particularly Loran-C. I am reminded of Pogo's famous statement: "We have met the enemy and he is us." We add a new piece of electronic gear only to find that it attacks its neighbors with Balkan intensity. To allow each to live in peace, we have to isolate the malefactors. In recent months, aboard several boats, I have experienced:

- Video depthfinders that caused navigation receiver problems
- A VHF-FM radio that interfered with a GPS receiver
- A Loran-C receiver that interfered with a VHF-FM radio
- A GPS receiver that totally wiped out Loran-C reception
- A terrorist alternator
- Power surges that damaged equipment or reset it to default settings

Add to this the "traditional" sources of interference such as bilge pumps, fluorescent lights, and television receivers, and the average boat is a hotbed of antagonistic electronic equipment.

Finding interference is fairly simple once you become suspicious of everything that uses electricity. Start with one piece of equipment operating, say, a Loran-C receiver. Watch the signal-to-noise ratio (SNR) of a distant station. (A nearby station with an SNR near the high end of the scale won't show much reduction, even in strong interference.) Suppose the SNR, which normally varies by 10 or 15 percent, is about 60. Begin turning equipment on and off, watching the SNR, and you'll soon find the culprit or culprits. To find if the alternator is causing interference, turn the receiver off, start the engine, then turn the receiver back on and check the SNR again.

Check the following and every other piece of electronic or electrical equipment:

Depthfinders

VHF-FM radios

Bilge pumps

Blowers

Windshield wipers

Fans

Fluorescent lights

Televisions

Computers

Microwave ovens

Electric refrigerators

Power windlasses

Some interference travels along the 12-volt power wires, and some travels through the air. You can install line filters at the alternator and near any piece of equipment that is causing a problem. A separate battery for your electronics is always a good idea; it isolates electronic gear from boat equipment. Run power wires away from tachometer leads and bilge-pump wiring. Ground all equipment, particularly Loran-C receivers, to the bonding system.

While you're checking for interference, run a separate ground wire from the receiver. Attach the end to a piece of copper sheet-metal and hang it overboard. If the SNR improves significantly, the boat's ground system is inadequate.

Radiated (airborne) interference is harder to cure. Try moving the two pieces of equipment farther apart. Sometimes just turning one of them on its mount helps. To test, wrap aluminum foil around equipment having a video tube, and ground the foil. One friend found that his video depthfinder was producing lots of interference, and had an aluminum box built to cover everything except the front. It reduced the interference dramatically.

Some things, like some fluorescent lights, are so nasty that they belong ashore—in a dump. Most cases of poor electronic equipment performance are due to interference aboard the boat. Any increase in outside interference then makes our equipment fail. We're as incongruous as a chain smoker carrying a *Clean Air* sign.

External Interference

GPS is succeptible to interference from solar activity, a few TV channels, and some other broadcast signals. It also is subject to deliberate jamming. Most of the jamming in this country has been from DOD jamming tests. DGPS depends on the radiobeacon system, which is degraded by lightning and other electronic "noise."

Loran-C is susceptible to interference from low-frequency broadcasts such as the Navy uses for some communications. The receivers have *notch filters* to reduce the intensity of interfering signals, but these must be set to the signals' frequency in order to work. Some receivers have methods of setting notch filters from the keyboard, but this is usually a job for a technician.

Moving the Receiver Long Distances

You can move a navigation receiver anywhere in the coverage area and it will track the signals correctly—as long as it is turned on. If you move it several hundred miles while it is turned off, however, it may have trouble locking on and giving fixes. Newer GPS receivers are nearly immune to this problem, but may take longer than usual to lock on and provide a fix. You may have to reset a DGPS beacon receiver to the closest station. A Loran-C receiver may not lock on at all. If the receiver was working previously, do a *First Start* or *Cold Start* procedure, but *don't* clear the memory. That is unnecessary and erases all the waypoints. Enter the new latitude and longitude, and time zone for GPS.

Cross-Track Error Jumps to Zero

The cross-track error shown by the electronic navigation receiver has built up to more than a mile on a long leg of a trip. You decide to check the distance and direction back to the departure waypoint, so you set it as a temporary destination waypoint. When you reset the original destination waypoint, the cross-track error is 0.0 mile. What's wrong?

Nothing. When you set a destination waypoint, the receiver resets waypoint zero, the origin, at the present position. The boat cannot be left or right of a line from the present position to the destination, so the cross-track error is zero.

Note: Some receivers have a way of changing the destination waypoint without resetting the origin waypoint. Others allow you to select any waypoint as the origin. This information is in the operator's manual.

Appendix A

How GPS Works

The Global Positioning System is designed to provide position, velocity, and time. The position is in three dimensions: latitude, longitude, and altitude. Velocity is the speed and direction of travel, and is available directly. The time is highly accurate. All are available worldwide, free of charge, to anyone with a suitable receiver. GPS uses 24 satellites in near-circular orbits 10,900 miles high. There are four satellites in each of six orbital planes, inclined to the equator by 55 degrees. The satellites orbit the earth approximately every 12 hours, giving nearly complete coverage. They transmit spread-spectrum signals continuously on 1575.42 MHz and 1227.6 MHz, allowing specialized receivers to remove some errors that come from atmospheric changes. The Department of Defense has continued to add satellites; there are now 27 in orbit.

Each satellite transmits a *pseudo-random digital code* superimposed on its signal for identification and timing. It is called a pseudo-random code due to the way it was generated and because it is repeated every $\frac{1}{1,000}$ second. If the code were random, the receiver could gain no intelligence from it. Satellites are known by their pseudo-random code numbers—for example, PRN-24. Since the code is a repetitious sequence, unique to each satellite, the receiver can identify satellites based on copies of the code in its memory. There are two codes, a *course/acquisition (C/A)* code and a *precision (P)* code. Military receivers have access to the P-code, which gives higher accuracy.

The receiver matches the satellite signal with the code in memory in a way comparable to holding two padlock keys side by side to see if they are identical. It is possible for the receiver to match the two codes correctly even though the signal from the satellite is faint and degraded by noise. The receiver measures the time difference between the code sequence in memory and the signal code sequence. It multiplies this time difference by the speed of radio waves to calculate the distance from the satellite to the receiver, known as the *pseudo-range.*

Each satellite thus gives an independent line of position, or rather *sphere of position,* based on its orbital position and the arrival time of its signals at the receiver. *Circles of position* are formed where these spheres intersect the surface of the earth. A receiver with an error-free clock could find its position using two satellites, but it can't have a clock sufficiently accurate without a means of

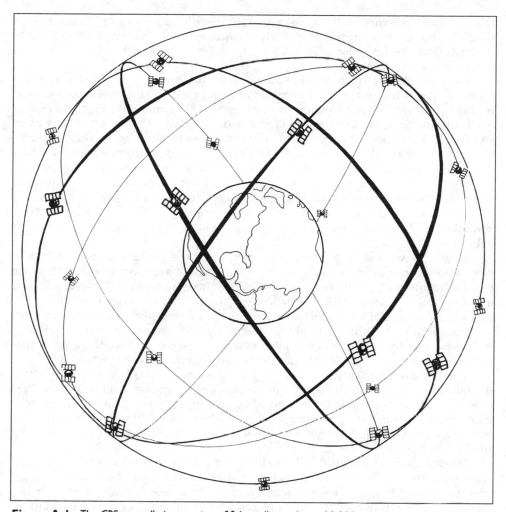

Figure A-1. *The GPS constellation consists of 24 satellites orbiting 10,900 miles high. It achieved its initial operational capability in December 1993.*

adjusting its time to the GPS system time. It compares the signals from at least three satellites to "set its clock."

The receiver obtains range measurements from three satellites. The LOPs form a triangle on the earth's surface, somewhat like visual bearing LOPs would form on a chart if there were a significant compass error. The receiver adjusts its own clock to make the LOPs coincide at a point. This sets the receiver clock to GPS system time as indicated by the three satellites.

The receiver needs three satellites for a two-dimensional (latitude and longitude) fix. Four satellites can give three-dimensional (including altitude) fixes.

Each satellite gives a range measurement that varies slightly. The range error as measured by the receiver is called *user range error*, or *URE*. Fixes always have more error than URE due to LOP crossing angles. This is known *as dilution of precision*, or *DOP*. There are several measures of dilution; DOP and HDOP (horizontal) are most common. DOP measurements are multipliers for URE; the higher the DOP, the greater the fix error. With 24 satellites in operation, DOP is usually under 2.0 in the latitudes that include the United States. If the DOP is greater than 6, fixes are unreliable.

Each satellite broadcasts information about its orbit. The receiver keeps two types of orbital information: an *almanac* to predict which satellites are above the horizon ("in view") at its location, and an *ephemeris* containing highly accurate orbital data. Some of the first receivers had one channel that processed each satellite in sequence. They were accurate but slow to produce the first fix, and these single-channel units gave reduced performance during maneuvers or when the signals were intermittent. This has little effect on boat navigation but is poor for aircraft and for use ashore, where there are many things to block the line-of-sight signals. Today's receivers are multichannel; they track several satellites at a time and can obtain orbital data without interrupting their navigation function. In addition, they give higher gain or signal amplification, an advantage for use ashore.

Most receivers select the three or four satellites giving the best fix. Some advanced receivers use all satellites above a minimum angle above the horizon for fixes; with more LOPs the DOP is less and accuracy is higher. These are known as all-in-view receivers. Other advanced receivers can use more than the minimum number of LOPs as a check—somewhat like a navigator plotting more than two visual LOPs on a chart to ensure against errors. Marine receivers generally lack these advanced capabilities. Some marine receivers can use the known altitude of a boat's antenna with three satellites to obtain the best HDOP.

The Control Segment monitors satellites from five stations and sends up-to-date orbital information to them. The Master Control Station at Fort Collins, Colorado, exerts considerable control over the satellites, to the extent of correcting many errors and maneuvering the satellites to different positions. During the Gulf War, they shut off aging satellites to conserve power until the satellites were over the Middle East.

Master Control monitors all satellites for errors and sets out-of-tolerance ones as unusable to avoid erroneous fixes. Unfortunately, it takes from 15 minutes to several hours to correct some errors. This time lag affects the system integrity, which is its ability to avoid sending erroneous position information. There are several methods of improving GPS integrity. They involve advanced receivers, additional satellites, or ground-based transmitters. Both DGPS and WAAS improve GPS integrity, as well as improving accuracy.

GPS in 2000 operates at the highest accuracy available. The Department of Defense announced that the accuracy would improve to within 20 meters (22 yards) without defining the accuracy measure, on 1 May 2000. DOD has not released the new signal specifications, and their spokesmen have also said that accuracy could be around 12 meters. Tests reveal that receivers give positions that vary by about plus or minus 10 to 20 meters (11 to 22 yards), 95 percent of the time, over short periods of time. Advanced receivers give the best results, while simpler (usually older) receivers aren't quite as good. The speed displayed by receivers seems to vary by about 0.2 to 0.3 knots. This is excellent performance, but it has not always been available. A little history is interesting.

The first satellites were Block I models, without deliberate accuracy degradation. They were replaced by Block II and Block IIR models, which have advanced error-detection features and can impose selective availability. GPS was designed to provide ±500 meters (550 yards) accuracy to civil users, but DOD decided to provide ±100 meters (110 yards) 95 percent of the time and ±300 meters (330 yards) 99.99 percent of the time. Altitude was ±156 meters (512 feet) 95 percent of the time, and system time was provided to 0.34 microsecond (but receivers may display time errors of several seconds). This is called *standard positioning service*, or *SPS*. The deliberate accuracy degradation is called *selective availability*, or *SA*. It was in effect from 1 July 1991 until 1 May 2000, when the Air Force set SA to zero, improving both accuracy and time information. There is also an *anti-spoofing (AS)* mode of operation to prevent hostile signal imitation. Anti-spoofing also degrades civil accuracy, but the term SA is used loosely to refer to all accuracy reduction.

Selective availability appeared to consist of two components: slightly erroneous orbital information in the navigation data message, and timing irregularities known as *clock dither*. Clock dither imposed short-term errors, and orbital misinformation made the fixes appear to jump when the receiver shifted satellites. Some of the jump may have been due to clock error as well. Now that SA is turned to zero, these effects do not appear in GPS positions.

The *precise positioning service* available to military users is called PPS. It uses both frequencies and the encrypted P-code to give accuracy within 21 meters horizontally and 28 meters vertically 95 percent of the time. PPS also provides high-accuracy time, and velocity accurate to 0.1 meter per second (0.2 knot) 95 percent of the time. (There was no specified SPS velocity accuracy.) Recent reports indicate that PPS is giving accuracy within about 8 meters horizontally. This is about twice as accurate as it was a few years ago.

Little of this information is needed to use GPS, and only begins to scratch the surface of this highly technical field. The GPS system has cost well over $15 billion and is expected to have an annual cost of about $1.5 billion.

For further information write or call:

U.S. Coast Guard

Navigation Center (NAVCEN)

7323 Telegraph Rd.

Alexandria VA 22310-3998

703-313-5900

The Navigation Center operates an internet Web site with up-to-date information on all Federal radionavigation systems. Its Web site is www.navcen.uscg.mil.

Appendix B

How Loran-C Works

*L*oran-C transmitters are organized in chains with a master and two to five secondary transmitting stations. The master is abbreviated "M" and the secondaries "V" through "Z." There are six chains in the continental United States, two in Alaska, three in Canada, and more worldwide. The stations are usually more than 200 miles apart and cover an area about 1,000 miles across. The transmitters range in power from 400 kilowatts to 1.6 megawatts. Each station has transmitters and duplicate timers, and many stations operate in more than one chain. Most stations have an antenna 625 to 1,350 feet high.

The stations in a chain transmit signals in pulse groups repeated at a specific interval known as the *group repetition interval*, or *GRI*. Chains repeat the groups of pulses about 5 to 10 times per second. To find the group repetition interval in seconds, divide the GRI by 100,000. Thus the U.S. West Coast Chain, 9940, repeats every 0.09940 second, or about 10 times a second. A receiver selects the chain that gives best accuracy in the area, synchronizes with its GRI, and ignores the signals at different GRIs.

All Loran-C stations worldwide operate on the same frequency—100 kHz. The signals have sidebands that extend from 90 to 110 kHz. Master stations transmit groups of nine pulses, and secondary stations transmit groups of eight pulses at 1,000-microsecond intervals. Each pulse of a group of eight (or nine) is formed of more than 20 cycles at 100 kHz, to fit a specific pulse envelope shape. Cesium-beam timers synchronize the transmitters to $\frac{1}{10}$ microsecond. The secondaries transmit their signals at a specific time interval following the master signal, in a sequence that makes them arrive at a receiver in a set order.

The W secondary signals all arrive before the X signals arrive, for example. Figure B-1 shows a typical group of Loran-C pulses. There is a system area monitor for each master-secondary pair to detect out-of-tolerance signals. A computer makes corrections within a few seconds or sets the secondaries to "blink" the eighth pulse if the error persists. The Coast Guard has installed equipment to allow most Loran-C stations to be operated remotely except for maintenance.

The receiver identifies the master pulse by its ninth pulse and the GRI. It samples the signal at a specific point for timing. This point is where the 100-kHz signal crosses zero for the third time in the pulse. The receiver must identify the correct crossing and lock on to the signals for the master and each secondary. This is typically called *signal acquisition*.

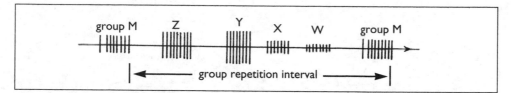

Figure B-1. *Loran-C pulses as they might appear at a receiver, moving from left to right. Each vertical line represents a pulse of about 22 cycles. Pulse heights are different at different distances from the transmitters. The receiver starts counting time at the master group of pulses, identified by its ninth pulse. The W, X, Y, and Z groups of eight pulses arrive in order, followed by the next master pulse. At any other location in the coverage area, the time differences are not the same.*

The receiver measures the time difference (TD) between the master signal and each secondary. A receiver indicates TD readings to 0.1 or 0.01 microsecond. The difference in time is a measure of the difference in distance between the two stations. Specific time delays are introduced at each secondary station to enable the receiver to calculate not only the difference in distance but which station is closer. Thus there is an unambiguous line of position for each time difference reading.

A curve that joins all points with a constant difference in distance to two points is a hyperbola. Each TD line printed on a chart represents a hyperbola on the surface of the earth. If the hyperbola passes exactly midway between the two points— the master and secondary transmitters—it is a straight line. If it passes closer to one transmitter than the other, its "tails" curve away from the farther one. The place where two time-difference hyperbolic LOPs cross marks a Loran-C fix.

The receiver (or a navigator plotting a fix using TDs) uses two secondaries that have TDs at good crossing angles. Occasionally the same two TD lines cross at two positions, but these positions are hundreds of miles apart. The ambiguity is easily resolved; you know you're out in the Gulf of Mexico, not ashore in Tennessee.

The accuracy of the TD lines of position depends on the distance between them. At the best, on the baseline joining the master and a secondary station, there are 12.36 microseconds per mile, or about 164 yards per microsecond. Away from the baseline, accuracy decreases. Within much of the coverage area, this gradient is about 200 to 500 yards per microsecond.

There is an area beyond each end of the baseline between the two stations where accuracy is extremely low. This is near the *baseline extension* (a continuation of the baseline past either station); everywhere along the extension the difference in distance is equal to the distance between the stations. Near the baseline extension, TD lines are far apart and accuracy is poor. Receivers shift automatically to another secondary or to another chain to avoid these areas of poor accuracy. If you lock a receiver to one chain and one pair of secondaries, this could cause trouble.

For example, if you start at Charleston, South Carolina, and sail offshore to Beaufort, North Carolina, the receiver should shift from 7980 to 9960 near Cape Fear. If you have it locked in to 7980 (Z), the boat will be on the M-Z baseline extension after you pass Cape Fear. Accuracy will be unacceptable. Shift to 9960, and accuracy will be excellent again. If the receiver isn't locked to 7980, it will shift automatically.

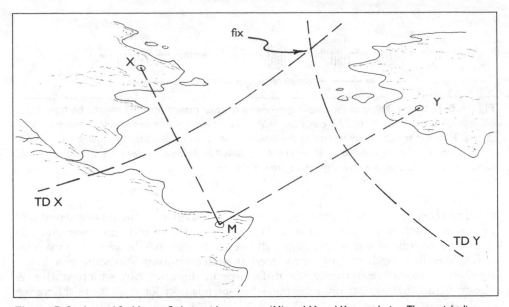

Figure B-2. *A simplified Loran-C chain with a master (M) and X and Y secondaries. The straight lines joining the master and the two secondaries are called baselines. The curved lines are hyperbolic lines of position—lines of constant time difference (TD) readings. The X and Y TD lines cross to form a fix at the receiver position.*

A few receivers use more than two TDs to determine a fix. Some aircraft receivers can maintain clock timing sufficiently accurate to measure the time of arrival of the signals rather than the time difference between the master and the secondaries. This gives circular LOPs, in some cases giving higher accuracy than hyperbolic LOPs. In addition, these advanced receivers can use a transmitter in any chain, which is another advantage.

From time to time the Coast Guard must shut down a Loran-C station, usually to install new equipment or for tower maintenance. These shutdowns affect a wide area and are announced well in advance. Most authorized off-air time is in the afternoon, for a period of about two hours. Longer off-air periods are sometimes necessary to install new equipment and occasionally occur due to tower failure. The Loran-C system in the United States costs about $17 million a year to operate.

This information is basic, but little of it is important to most navigators who use Loran-C. The Coast Guard publishes an excellent book that gives additional technical details about the Loran-C system, for those who are interested. It is the *Loran-C User Handbook 1992* (COMDTPUB P16562.6). For further information about Loran-C, write or call:

Commandant (G-NRN-1)
2100 Second St., SW
Washington, DC 20593-0001
202-267-0990

Appendix C

Good, Bad, and Ugly
Receiver Features

*R*eceivers have a large number of features; which ones are four-star and which ones are shaky?

Position: Position is the top line. Response is quick under normal conditions. There may be some "overshoot" when stopping suddenly from high speed. GPS may show position to 0.001 minute (2 yards), but positions vary by about 0.005 to 0.01 minute (10 to 20 yards). DGPS positions are reported to be accurate to about 0.005 minutes (10 yards). Loran-C positions vary by 0.1 to 0.2 microsecond or 0.02 to 0.04 minute of latitude or longitude (40 to 80 yards).

Loran-C positions usually agree with the chart within a quarter of a mile. In the U.S., GPS positions are closer to charted positions than Loran-C. Charts disagree with GPS positions in many overseas areas.

Distance to waypoint: An accurate and useful feature. Usually shown to 0.01 mile. Fast response. Distance varies by 0.01 to 0.03 mile, which seems insignificant, except when you are very close to the waypoint.

Direction to waypoint: Direction is shown to nearest degree, true or magnetic, on a *great circle* or line of sight. (Great circles are nearly identical with straight lines on Mercator charts except when the longitude differs by over 2 or 3 degrees.) Fast response. Accuracy is high except at short distances, where bearing to waypoint jumps back and forth. The boat isn't moving that quickly, but the navigation system's small errors change the bearing significantly.

Speed over the ground: SOG is often shown to 0.1 knot but is far less accurate than that. Loran-C averages speed over several minutes, so the receiver display lags changing speed. GPS gives instantaneous speed but at unspecified accuracy; a stationary GPS receiver often shows speed variations of 0.1 to 0.2 knots. When a boat is rolling, GPS shows significant speed changes. At sailing or trolling speeds, SOG variations are a high percentage of boat speed. Increasing the averaging interval will give more accurate speeds, but also introduces a lag.

Course over the ground: COG is shown to the nearest degree but seldom is that accurate. COG is similar to speed over the ground in that Loran-C lags course changes and GPS shows numerous variations. You can change the receiver averaging intervals; the slower the speed, the longer the averaging period. Short averaging intervals cause phantom changes. COG and SOG jump back and forth, even on a steady course at constant speed.

In addition, neither the boat's speed nor course over the ground is constant. Who can hold a boat exactly on course? Sea and swell affect boat speed and direction of travel. This may be obvious, as when you slam into a wave or surf down the face of a swell, or it may be subtle. A long swell moves the boat along with the swell on the peaks and in the opposite direction in the troughs; the motion is imperceptible to the navigator but not to the receiver. Instantaneous course and speed over the ground, if available, are not as useful as it might appear.

HINT: When making a long leg, put in scratch waypoints every hour, then use the receiver to calculate distance and course for the past hour. See Chapter 6.

Cross-track error: XTE (or CTE) is the distance left or right of a line between origin and destination waypoints. Due to system inaccuracies, XTE normally varies by about 0.005 to 0.03 (10 to 60 yards), with GPS being quite accurate, and DGPS and WAAS even more so. It works well on a steady course if you don't try to follow every small change.

HINT: Receivers change the origin waypoint to the present position when designating a destination waypoint. You can set XTE to zero by redesignating the destination waypoint. Some receivers have an alternate way of setting the destination that doesn't change the origin.

Velocity made good: Velocity made good indicates the speed over the ground in the direction of the destination waypoint. It is primarily useful to sailboat navigators when beating to windward. A sailboat sailing as close to the wind as possible but unable to point toward the destination may be making 6 knots through the water, but only 4 knots toward the waypoint. Unfortunately, manufacturers have two definitions of **VMG**:

1. Speed along the line from the starting waypoint to the destination waypoint (Figure C-1). This is the more useful of the two VMG definitions.

2. Speed from the current position to the destination waypoint (Figure C-2). A receiver using this definition shows VMG decreasing along a leg of the course, even though speed and heading are constant. VMG decreases to zero as a sailboat approaches the lay line, preparing to tack for the next mark.

If you use the receiver to check distance and direction to another destination and then reset the original destination, it affects the VMG calculations (see XTE HINT).

Clock and timing: Receivers have precise timing capabilities. GPS can give accurate time, but the time display is often off by a few seconds. Loran-C keeps accurate time if you set it after turning on the receiver.

Anchor watch: An anchor watch alarm sounds when you travel outside of a set circle. Seldom useful; you want to detect drag within the first few feet. False alarms are common.

Arrival alarm: An arrival alarm sounds when you get within a preset range of, or pass abeam of, a waypoint. It is a handy feature, usually automatic.

Routes: Navigation receivers can follow a route—a series of waypoints—switching to the next waypoint automatically. This feature is complex to program on many receivers but can be useful if you follow the same route regularly. Most people skip this feature; it's easy to switch manually to successive destination waypoints. Some receivers force you to put *all* waypoints into routes—an annoying feature since doing so requires extra steps to enter a waypoint as a destination.

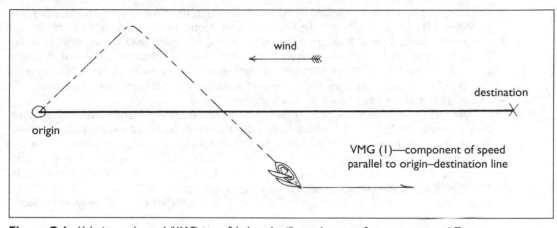

Figure C-1. *Velocity made good (VMG) is useful aboard sailboats, but manufacturers use two different definitions. The better one defines VMG as speed over the ground parallel to the line from starting waypoint to destination waypoint. A sailboat is tacking upwind in the drawing.*

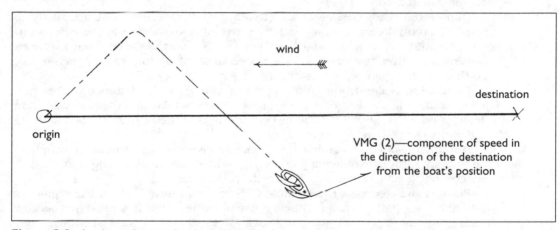

Figure C-2. *Another sailboat, in the identical situation, has a receiver made by another manufacturer. This manufacturer defines VMG as the speed made good from the present position to the destination waypoint. The two receivers show radically different values of VMG.*

Calculating distance and direction between waypoints: An excellent feature. A number of GPS receivers allow you to do these distance and direction calculations by going to the **Trip Planning** mode. Some receivers can only calculate from the present position, and if they lose the signal, they won't do any calculations. Even working normally, these receivers can't calculate distances and directions unless the destination waypoint is reset.

Setting a waypoint as a distance and direction from another waypoint: Handy for short distances and for "DR waypoints." Errors grow with distance (about 350 yards at 10 miles).

Man overboard: The MOB button stores a waypoint when pressed—useful to someone who doesn't know how to store a waypoint. It marks the general location, but a person in the water drifts with the current. Unless you find the person very quickly, go back to the man-overboard waypoint and search downcurrent.

Home-port, Local, Bias, or ASF corrections: Corrections, by several names, make latitude and longitude agree with positions of the chart. Useful but dangerous, since they *shift the position of **all** waypoints in memory*. They also prevent the receiver from changing corrections even though the boat goes hundreds of miles. This reduces accuracy in distant areas.

Accuracy indicators (EPE): Some GPS receivers state estimated accuracy in feet or yards. It is usually misleading: GPS receivers indicate estimated accuracy far better than they actually achieve. Now that SA is set to zero, receivers indicate Estimated Position Error of 3 feet or even 0 feet. The actual errors are in the range of 10 to 20 meters (33 to 65 feet). The best indication of GPS accuracy is DOP, HDOP, or PDOP, as used by various manufacturers. For Loran-C, accuracy estimates are based on LOP crossing angles and gradients, and vary with location.

GPS receivers that use Loran-C TDs: Waypoints entered in GPS receivers using Loran-C TDs are subject to the same errors as the latitude and longitude calculated by a Loran-C receiver—up to several hundred yards. *(Note: A few manufacturers combine a GPS receiver and a Loran-C receiver in one unit. These display measured Loran-C TDs.)*

Differential ready GPS receivers (DGPS):   GPS receivers that are ready to accept differential data from a special receiver offer the ability to increase accuracy dramatically, at additional cost. For DGPS use, the Coast Guard advises choosing a receiver that accepts Type 9 messages, at up to 200 bits per second, and that can be upgraded with software changes.

Distance since departure: A few receivers can show the distance you've traveled since setting the destination waypoint. This is similar to a distance log or an odometer on a car, showing distance over the ground. Reset to zero when starting a leg of the trip. A handy feature.

Automatic waypoint numbering: Some receivers assign waypoint numbers sequentially rather than giving you a choice—kind of like assigning house numbers chronologically rather than by streets. A lousy feature.

Plotters and electronic charts: Most GPS receivers have built-in track plotters that show your path of travel. This is a useful feature, and has proven especially so since it is more or less automatic. Some GPS receivers include electronic chart plotters, which show the boat's position on a screen that looks either like a simplified chart or like a conventional chart. Some chart plotters use a laptop computer with a GPS receiver input. These chart plotters are a big advance in technology, despite the more capable ones being complex and expensive. They are quite useful and are becoming popular rapidly.

As you use any electronic receiver, try to get a feel for its best features. It has powerful capabilities, some of which are confusing or difficult to learn. It often displays higher accuracy than it can measure. Concentrate on the functions that you use most often, and learn the others gradually.

Glossary

aid to navigation—"Any device external to a vessel or aircraft intended to assist a navigator to determine position or safe course, or to warn of dangers or obstructions to navigation."—33 CFR 62.3 (a). Buoys, lighthouses, Loran-C, and GPS are examples of aids to navigation. Onboard equipment such as compasses, depthfinders, and radar are not included in the definition, nor are landmarks not built specifically for navigation use.

aid-to-navigation system—One or more aids to navigation of the same type, a receiver, and equipment to display the position and the surroundings in sufficient detail for navigation.

ASF—Additional secondary phase factor, used by a Loran-C receiver to calculate latitude and longitude from TD data. ASF values vary from place to place, and different receivers use different ASF values.

beacon—A lighted aid to navigation on a fixed structure. Also called a *light*. Usually includes dayboards.

bearing—The direction to an object, measured from the boat or from another object.

chain—A group of a master and two to five secondary Loran-C stations broadcasting at the same GRI, configured to provide coverage over a broad area.

characteristic—The timing sequence of a flashing light or a foghorn.

CMG—Course made good. The direction from a beginning point to the present position. *See also* **COG**.

COG—Course over the ground. The course traveled with respect to the ground (as opposed to course through the water), measured over a short interval. Receiver manufacturers use loose definitions; some call it *course made good (CMG)*, and others call it *track*.

course—The direction in which a boat is steered, or intended to be steered.

CPA—Closest point of approach. The point at which an approaching vessel comes closest to the boat. Obtained with a relative-motion radar plot.

CTE—Cross-track error. The distance the boat lies away from a line joining the origin and destination waypoints. Also called *XTE*.

cursor—A device for measuring bearings on a radar scope. Usually a line on a clear plastic cover that can be rotated. Modern radars use an EBL.

datum—(1) Horizontal: A chart coordinate reference system. (2) Vertical: The tidal level depth reference on a chart.

daybeacon—An unlighted fixed aid to navigation.

dayboards—Flat panels on a daybeacon or light that show shape, color, numbers or letters, and retroreflective tape.

ded (dead) reckoning—*See* **DR**.

deviation—The difference, in degrees, between compass and magnetic directions. Deviation is due to magnetism aboard the boat, and is different on different headings.

direction—An angle, usually measured clockwise from north (000°) through 360°, from one point to another. Directions are *true* (T) when measured from north, *magnetic* (M) when measured from magnetic north, and *compass* (C) when measured by compass.

DOP—Dilution of precision. The distance error of a fix as compared with that of a line of position. Low DOP indicates an accurate fix. *HDOP* (horizontal dilution of precision) is used to describe latitude and longitude fixes. *GDOP* (geometric dilution of precision) and *PDOP*, similar terms, describe three-dimensional dilution.

DR—Ded (dead) reckoning. The process of navigation using the course, speed, and time since the last fix. Also refers to the position found. A strictly defined DR doesn't include the effect of current. An estimated position (EP) includes current effect and may include a line of position.

EBL—Electronic bearing line. An electronic line on a radar scope, similar to a mechanical cursor, that can be rotated to measure bearings. On some radar sets, its origin can be moved about the scope.

EP—Estimated position. "The most probable position of a craft determined from incomplete data or data of questionable accuracy."—*Bowditch.* An EP may be a DR corrected for current, a DR plot combined with one line of position, or the best estimate of position from a weak fix.

EPE—Estimated Position Error. GPS receivers display an estimate of position error, but it is often misleading. With SA set to zero and GPS giving a precision of about ± 10 to 20 meters (33 to 65 feet), some receivers show EPE of 15 feet or less, or even zero.

ephemeris—Detailed orbital information broadcast from GPS satellites to receivers to allow position calculations.

ETA—Estimated time of arrival. The time of day the navigator estimates the boat will arrive at the destination.

ETE—Estimated time en route. The estimated time interval between departure and arriving at the destination.

fix—"A relatively accurate position determined without reference to any former position."—*Bowditch.*

great circle—(1) A line of sight. (2) A straight line along the surface of the earth and the shortest distance between two points.

GRI—Group repetition interval. The interval between Loran-C pulse groups for the master and secondary stations forming a chain, expressed in 100,000ths of a second. GRI 7980 has a repetition interval of 0.0798 second. A station is identified by the GRI and a letter; e.g., 7980-X.

heading—The direction a boat is pointed *at the moment.*

lay line—The imaginary line that a sailboat beating to windward must cross to be able to clear a windward mark on the next tack. It is a bearing, representing the course made good (CMG) sailing close-hauled.

leading mark—A visible object marking the desired direction of travel.

leg—A portion of a trip. Usually a straight course from one point to the next.

light—*See* **beacon.**

log—"An instrument for measuring the speed or distance, or both, traveled by a vessel."—*Bowditch.*

LOP—Line of position. A line along which a measurement such as a bearing, depth, or distance is constant. An LOP may be a straight line, an arc, a portion of a hyperbola, or an irregular line. GPS uses spheres of position.

mile—A *nautical mile (NM)* is approximately equal to 1 minute of latitude. Often rounded to 2,000 yards, a nautical mile is 6,076.115 feet (2,025.372 yards) long, or exactly 1,852 meters. *Statute miles* used on maps and Great Lakes charts are 5,280 feet long.

navigation receiver—A loose definition of a receiver that can find the position, store waypoints, and give the direction and distance to waypoints. Usually Loran-C or GPS.

position—*See* **fix.**

PPI—Plan position indicator. A conventional radar scope. The boat is at the center and targets appear at correct relative bearings and at distances proportional to their ranges.

pseudo-random code—A specific repeating sequence that serves to identify a GPS satellite and to allow the receiver to measure the signal's time of arrival. GPS satellites are known by *pseudo-random noise (PRN)* numbers.

quadrantal spheres—Hollow iron spheres mounted on either side of a compass. Steel-hull boats often have errors on NE, SE, SW, and NW headings even though errors at N, S, E, and W are minimal. If so, it is necessary to install quadrantal spheres and move them on their brackets to remove the deviation.

range—(1) Two visible objects in line. (2) The distance to an object. (3) The average height difference between high and low tide at a tide station.

reach—(1) A straight portion of a channel; a leg of a channel. (2) To sail with the wind approximately abeam.

relative bearing—The direction to an object, measured with respect to the boat, with the bow as 000° and angles increasing clockwise.

SA—Selective availability. The deliberate degradation of Standard Positioning Service (civil) GPS signals to approximately 100 meters accuracy. Eliminated 1 May 2000.

scale—(1) The ratio of a length on a chart to the actual length. (2) A draftsman's device for measuring length. (3) The setting (one of several) on depthfinders or radar for the maximum depth or distance.

sea buoy—An informal term frequently applied to the outermost buoy marking an entrance channel. Also called an *entrance buoy*.

SMG—Speed made good. The speed from a beginning point to the present position. Receiver manufacturers often use SOG and SMG interchangeably, although in precise usage SMG refers to speed measured over a long interval. *See also* **SOG.**

SOG—Speed over the ground. The boat's speed with respect to the ground (as opposed to speed through the water), measured over a short interval. *See also* **SMG.**

TD—Time difference or time delay. The interval of time (in microseconds) from the arrival of the master series of Loran-C pulses until a secondary series of pulses arrives. The TD represents a line of position determined by the difference in distance to the two stations.

track—The path that a boat has actually followed. The *intended track*, often a line drawn on a chart, shows the preserved path of travel.

variation—The difference, in degrees, between true north and magnetic north. It is shown on charts numerically and by the inner compass rose, which is turned from the outer (true) circle by the angle of variation. Called *declination* on topographic maps.

vector—A line representing a specific distance (or speed) and direction. A line plotted on a chart for finding the distance and direction from an origin to a destination is a simple vector. Navigators use vectors when laying off DRs, plotting the effects of current and leeway, and in radar plotting.

VRM—Variable range marker. An adjustable circle on a radar PPI scope used to measure distance to targets.

waypoint—A specific location used for navigation, usually stored in memory in a navigation receiver. It is represented by latitude and longitude or by Loran-C time-difference (TD) readings.

XTE—*See* **CTE.**

Index